D1000709

The
ALTAR
of MY SOUL

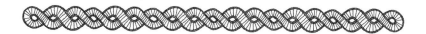

The
ALTAR
of MY SOUL

The Living Traditions of Santería

MARTA MORENO VEGA

ONE WORLD
THE BALLANTINE PUBLISHING GROUP
NEW YORK

A One World Book
Published by The Ballantine Publishing Group
Copyright © 2000 by Marta Moreno Vega
Illustrations copyright © 2000 by Manuel Vega

www.randomhouse.com/BB/

LIBRARY OF CONGRESS CATALOGING-IN-PUBLICATION DATA
Vega, Marta Moreno.
The altar of my soul : the living traditions of Santeria /
Marta Moreno Vega.—1st ed.
p.   cm.
ISBN 0-345-42137-X
1. Santeria.   I. Title.
BL2532.S3 V44   2000
299'.674—dc21
00-040339

Text design by Holly Johnson

Manufactured in the United States of America

First Edition: September 2000

10   9   8   7   6   5   4   3   2   1

Contents

Acknowledgments

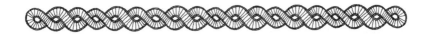

To My Guardian Angels:

There are spirits and people who have the ability to make things happen. They possess an energy force that makes the seemingly impossible a reality. Their *aché*, the ability to make things happen, flows from them like an invisible shield that encourages and nurtures. It has been my good fortune to have these guardian angels guide me throughout my growth. They have been the ones who helped me see beyond my dreams and make them real.

IN THE SPIRIT WORLD:

I praise the spirits of my parents, Flora Marcano Cruz Moreno and Clemente Moreno. To Abuela Luisa, my uncles Donato and Maximo, enlightenment. I pray for peace for the spirits of my sister Socorro Moreno and brother Alberto Moreno.

IN THE PRESENT:

I celebrate the warrior spirit of Laura Moreno, my ex-sister-in-law, who is my true sister. I ask the spirits to protect her always. She is the main source of strength and stability for our family. Like Yemayá, she is the primordial mother. To my niece Melody, who is so caring, like Ochun, may she continue to spread the honey of her kindness. I honor the creative warrior spirits that protect my sons, Sergio and Omar. I am blessed that these two spirits came through me. I am in constant admiration of how they have bloomed into principled young men. How embracing

the boundless energy and soul force of my daughter-in-law Jenna is in my life. I thank Sergio and Jenna for my granddaughter Kiya who continues to expand my heart with love and joy.

I am humbled by my spiritual blessings to have Zenaida Rodríguez and Elpidio Cárdenas as my godparents, mentors, and guides. Their wisdom is endless. Limited space does not allow me to express the love I have for all the members of my family who have been part of my growth and spiritual enlightenment. However, I must at least mention their names so they know they are in my heart: Kilani, Jovan, Eddie, Chino, Norma, Erica, Elisa, Tinesha, Yari, Kadesha, Cudjoe, Djingi, Eula, Laura P., Nyoka, Danetta. Know that you are in my heart and prayers.

TO ANGELS WHO HAVE COME INTO MY LIFE, THANK YOU:

My agent Joanna Pulcini, of the Linda Chester Literary Agency, like the calm flowing vigilance of the spirit of Yemayá, shares her knowledge selflessly and is always supportive. Joanna's nurturing spirit is encouraging and insightful. How wonderful to know that the extraordinary talents of both Joanna and Linda Chester are present in my life. To Gary Jaffe and Kelly Smith, who are always at the other end of the telephone helping solve problems, a special hug.

To the overflowing generosity of Cheryl Woodruff, vice president and associate publisher, One World Books of the Ballantine Publishing Group, how wonderful to connect to a spirit force that understands that all nature-based belief systems are inextricably linked into a global sacred circle. It is a joy to share thoughts on ways of connecting the spirits of world cultures. The drawings of Manuel Vega, an artist and Candomblé priest, creatively illustrate the sacred spirits and rites that celebrate the practices of the Lucumí/Santería belief system. A special thanks to Paulo Bispo, Brazilian Candomblé priest from Bahia, for creating the altar for Obatalá and Yemayá at the Caribbean Cultural Center that graces the back cover of the book.

To my guardian *orishas*, Obatalá Ayaguna and Yemayá, who make all things possible, *kimchamaché*. To the ultimate energy force Olodumare, the essence of *aché*, may you always protect and watch over us all.

Embracing My Sacred Inner Soul

Introduction

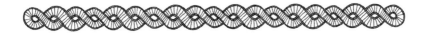

I did not know I was born into a family that practiced Espiritismo and Santería until I was grown and had children of my own. When I was growing up, my mother, father, and grandmother kept their prayers to their ancestors and the worship of their divinities behind doors that were closed to me. Still, images of Santería divinities filled our home. My mother prayed to the *orishas*, the gods and goddesses of creation, almost every day. My father called upon the powers of the spirits when my mother fell ill. And my grandmother, my *abuela*, maintained one of the most beautiful altars to an *orisha* I have ever seen.

I was not the first child to come from a family who hid their worship of African gods and goddesses and practiced their religion in secret. The Moreno family was one of thousands, all born from generations of Africans in the Americas who hid their beliefs behind the images of their captors' religion, masking their *orishas* with the faces of their enslavers' saints. And for this reason, my ancestors' religion came to be known as Santería, the Way of the Saints.

The *orishas* first came to Cuba on the ships of slaves, transported by means of the transatlantic slave trade of the early sixteenth century. On those ships were the Yoruba people, a peaceful, gentle tribe of West Africans who trace their origins back to A.D. 1000 to the sacred city of Ile Ife, today located in Nigeria. Though the enslavement of Africans was formally abolished by the Spaniards in Cuba in 1886 and in Puerto Rico in 1873, the Spanish government turned a blind eye to those who continued to smuggle African slaves into their colonies well into the late eighteen hundreds. Over a period of four centuries, more

1

than fifteen million Africans of varied ethnic groups were brought as chattel slaves to the Americas, and they would leave their imprint on the New World.

As Africans in Cuba carefully guarded their ancient religious rituals, they wisely kept their beliefs hidden from the eyes of their plantation owners. Masking their divinities, their *orishas*, behind the images of the Catholic saints of their Spanish oppressors, the devoted were able to continue practicing their Yoruba beliefs. This process of camouflage allowed the ancient *orishas*, born in the sacred city of Ile Ife, West Africa, to survive wherever Yoruba ethnic groups were taken. In Brazil, Haiti, Puerto Rico, the United States, Santo Domingo, Trinidad, and Tobago, Africans evolved similar ways of protecting the *orishas*. Throughout the Caribbean and the Americas, Africans culturally re-created their belief systems, grounding them in the traditions of their tribal heritages. In this way, ancestor worship and the age-old tales of the African divinities were preserved in the memories of their descendants, secretly passed down through more than four hundred years of enslavement.

Each geographic community fostered branches of the *orisha* tradition; the branches share many commonalities. Africans in Brazil developed Candomblé; in Trinidad and Tobago they created Shangó; in Haiti and in the southern states of the United States they created Vodun; in Jamaica, Kumina; and in Cuba, Santería.

After more than four centuries of protection by African descendants in Cuba, the Santería community now spans the globe, with millions of practitioners celebrating this religion worldwide. Historically a religion practiced only by Africans and their descendants, Santería is now practiced by people of all racial and cultural communities, all who acknowledge the contributions and struggles of our ancestors. They honor the spirits of our ancestors, and are guided by them through the practice of Espiritismo, ancestor worship. They recognize a divine connection between our secular and sacred worlds, embracing both with the power of the *orishas*. They seek to find a balance with the forces in nature, known as *aché*. They learn how to channel these forces in a way that fosters spiritual growth, good health, prosperity, and the unification of both our family and our community.

I was initiated into the Lucumí religion, popularly known as Santería, in 1981 in Havana, Cuba. In search of a religion that reflected my racial and cultural heritage, I was led to Cuba by the spirits of my ancestors. During my first visit two years earlier, I had been introduced by my friend Javier Colón to two sages who would later become my godparents and guides in learning the philosophy and practices of the Santería religion. Upon my return to Cuba, their teachings opened my mind and soul to the sacred Yoruba-based knowledge of West Africa that had been preserved in the religion of Santería. My godfather, Oluwo Elpidio Cárdenas, and his wife and my godmother, Iyalorisha Zenaida Rodríguez, are both elder initiates in Santería, who nurtured me on a path that ultimately led to my full initiation into the religion.

Through my godparents' guidance, I have connected to loved ones who reside in the spirit world. I have learned to live in balance with the forces of nature that surround me. And I have come to cherish my spiritual role as a godmother and priestess, teaching the traditions and rituals of Santería to a new generation of initiates.

In my roles of godmother, priestess, and scholar, I have occasion to address culturally diverse public forums on the subject of Santería. It is interesting to note how fascinated people are with Santería, and how much of this religion is already known through films, television, and the press. Although a glut of misinformation exists, audiences, filled with many people who are not of African descent, hold great curiosity about Santería. The history of the *orishas* in Africa, their journey to the Americas, and Santería similarities to other faiths all present intriguing questions.

I share my story with you in the desire to answer some of these questions, and with the hope that my experiences will help others who are in search of their own spirituality. I hope that the

healing rituals of Santería, which are positive influences in my life and in the lives of millions the world over, will be better understood. I have recorded my search for a religion that would answer my spiritual needs. And I share my journey so as to correct the misleading information and derogatory views about Santería that are still held by many.

In the pages that follow, you will join me on my journey from darkness into light. And along the way, you will learn that Santería espouses beliefs and practices common to all religions that honor the divine essence of nature. It is for this reason that the philosophical principles and basic practices of Santería presented in this book may seem familiar. It is my belief that each religion creates a different path toward achieving the same goals: to be embraced and healed by the divine creator, who invites us to cherish our sacred souls.

Native American religions worship every aspect of nature, and their affirmation that we live on sacred Mother Earth is similar to Santería's belief that all aspects of nature are divine. Asian religions identify the energy force, or *qi*, as well as the principle of yin-yang—our equivalent of *aché* and the positive and negative balance embodied in the *orisha* Ellegua. In Judaism, practitioners sacrifice and cleanse with animals as we do, and they also burn candles to create a spiritually charged environment during rituals. I always make these comparisons between other religions and my own, because they show we are not so different as we may appear to be.

I am often questioned about my decision to become an initiate of Santería. Because so few open forums exist to discuss our individual journeys, these discussions sometimes become sessions of soul-wrenching testimony. People who are traveling on a spiritual quest want to share their journeys; they want to feel connected to others who are on the same path. In almost every question, there is an underlying desire to know if Santería is a positive religion.

Afraid of being labeled "devil worshipers" or thought of as

members of a cult, people who are drawn to Santería often continue to hide their beliefs. Many have stopped their explorations due to the negative images portrayed in the media and the fear of being ostracized by their Christian friends and families.

I am continuously asked why I was initiated into a religion that has been misrepresented and maligned by "mainstream" religions, Hollywood, and the mass media. Friends and acquaintances of African origin still influenced by negative views of Santería approach me cautiously, out of fear of my casting a *brujo*, a spell, on them. While they admire my cultural pride in my Afro–Puerto Rican heritage and my courage in defying popular misconceptions about Santería, somewhere deep in their hearts it seems they doubt the benign beauty of their own sacred traditions.

We generally accept that there is a divine, invisible intelligence at work on our behalf. We sense it. Santería provides the means to live in the sacred moment and benefit from divine energy. Rather than viewing our premonitions, dreams, and sacred moments as extraordinary, Santería teaches us that we are protected by our guardian angels and *orishas*, who make the extraordinary seem natural. In illuminating the role of the sacred Santería divinities, my godmother, Zenaida, explained: "No one knows how water gets into the coconut. Yet we know it is there. Accept that you have an inner spirit that is the voice of the Almighty who will guide and protect you."

Santería is a way of life that reconciles the divine knowledge of the spirit world with secular knowledge. It is a coming together of the invisible and visible worlds, giving us the means for heeding our inner spirit. Like other religious systems, Santería functions through the faith of each practitioner. All I ask is that you open your mind and heart and allow your inner spirit guides to speak and blossom within you.

There are many spiritual paths that can be taken; Santería is only one of them. I have had the opportunity to participate in other belief systems. While they did not answer my needs, I have

learned that spirituality transcends all religious faiths. To respect the sacred essence we carry is to respect the divine within each of us. For me, Santería affirms that every one of us is holy, and we are all part of the sacred universe that reflects the goddesses and gods who made us in their image.

Welcome to my world.

Chapter One

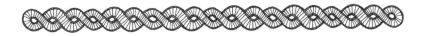

OLODUMARE

THE UNKNOWN IS THE PATH
TO KNOWLEDGE

The *orisha* Olodumare, the Supreme God, originally lived in the lower part of heaven, overlooking endless stretches of water. One day, Olodumare decided to create Earth, and sent an emissary, the *orisha* Obatalá, to perform this task. Olodumare gave Obatalá the materials he needed to create the world: a small bag of loose earth, a gold chain, and a five-toed hen.

Obatalá was instructed to use the chain to descend from heaven. When he reached the last link, he piled the loose earth on top of the water. Next, he placed the hen on the pile of earth, and ordered her to scatter the earth with her toes across the surface of the water.

When this was finished, Obatalá climbed the chain to heaven to report his success to Olodumare. Olodumare then sent his trusted assistant, the chameleon, to verify that the earth was dry. When his helper had assured him that the Earth was solid, Olodumare named Earth "Ile Ife," the sacred house.

Before he retired to the uppermost level of heaven, Olodumare decided to distribute his sacred powers—*aché*. He united Obatalá, the *orisha* of creation, and Yemayá, the *orisha* of the ocean, who gave birth to a pantheon of *orishas*, each possessing a share of Olodumare's sacred power. At last, the divine power of Olodumare was dispersed. Then one day, Olodumare called them all from Earth to heaven and gave Obatalá the sacred power to create human life. Obatalá returned to Earth and created our ancestors, endowing them with his own divine power. We are all descendants from the first people of the sacred city of Ile Ife; we are all children of Olodumare, the sacred *orisha* who created the world.

It was ten o'clock on Monday morning, August 25, 1997, when I arrived at the home of Doña Rosa, a Santería priestess of Yemayá. A short, wiry woman the color of sweet chocolate syrup, Doña Rosa was dressed in blue-and-white gingham in honor of her patron, Orisha Yemayá. She often lent her home to my godmother for initiation ceremonies, since her five-room, street-level

apartment was large, had a small inside patio, and was centrally located in Havana, Cuba.

Doña Rosa greeted me with a warm embrace and then led me into the kitchen to await instructions from my godmother, my *madrina*, Zenaida, who was in a room off the kitchen, hidden by a white curtain, finalizing preparations for the ceremony that was about to begin. My *madrina* was planning to initiate a young Puerto Rican ritual drummer, *omo añya*, Paco Fuentes, into the Santería religion. He was to receive the *aché* of his patron, Orisha Shangó. Today was the *asiento*, the ritual that would ceremoniously place the *aché* of Shangó on the head of the new initiate.

Doña Rosa asked that I sit on a high wooden stool to await the portion of the ceremony in which I would participate. She offered me a glass of water and said, "My daughter, it is only ten o'clock in the morning and the heat is already close to ninety degrees." Momentarily cooled by the water, I waited patiently for the ceremony to begin. The apartment was swarming with activity as the priestesses, the *santeras*, *iyalorishas*, prepared lunch. I tried to relax in the midst of the mounting excitement as *santeras* and *santeros*, *babalorishas*, the priests, hurried about collecting dishes, placing the sacrificial animals on the patio, and arranging the plants that would be used in the ceremony.

During Paco's ceremony, I would be an active participant undergoing the ritual, permitting me to initiate others. One of the rules of the religion is that an initiate must witness the ceremony that was performed on them. This assures that the initiate will understand all the steps that they went through in the various ceremonies for initiation. It is also a way of passing on information, learning rituals through an apprenticeship process.

The yellow walls of Doña Rosa's apartment had turned gray with age; the forties-style furniture showed signs of collapsing from the years of wear and the countless makeshift repairs. The *santeras* were busy sweeping the floors, decorating, and cooking in anticipation of the visitors who would later come to celebrate the birth of the new initiate. The humming voices of the priestesses and priests mingled with the screeching cries of the sacrificial goats and chickens that were fenced outdoors in the open courtyard between the living room and the kitchen. Recently washed red-and-white curtains were gently waving in the court-yard breeze, causing the animals to squawk louder from fright.

The kitchen felt like a steam bath. There was a hot fog billow-ing from the large aluminum pots of boiling rice, beans, chicken fricassee, and goat stew being prepared for lunch. I was nervous because for the first time I would be participating in certain por-tions of the ceremony that would prepare me to initiate others into the Santería religion.

When the *orishas* unveiled my destiny eighteen years ago, I was doubtful of all that they said lay ahead of me. As a new initiate, I was just beginning my explorations of Santería, and I thought the diviner's prediction that I would eventually become a *mad-rina* with godchildren of my own was preposterous. I should have trusted my godfather Elpidio's advice always to have faith in the *orishas*, for their word is truth.

Every fifteen days, my godchildren and I sit and conduct a *misa*, a ceremony in honor of our ancestors. Before and after these sessions, we discuss the role of the *orishas* in our lives, and the differences we are experiencing in our lives as we become one with our spirits. Our sessions, like all new experiences, began tentatively as I struggled to accept that my long years of study would prepare me to take on a greater level of responsibility.

When I at last placed the chairs for my godchildren in a circle in front of my *bóveda*, my ancestral altar table, I began to feel the spiritual energy fill my living room. The rays of the afternoon Sunday sun seemed to brighten as I set my *bóveda* in the center of the room. My hands shook as I tried to light the match for the candle to be placed before the ancestor altar. Suddenly the flame soared higher than it should have, and the room filled with the luminous energies of my spirit mothers; I knew then everything would be fine.

As a priestess and godmother, when I bring my godchildren together, I teach them the *patakís*, the teaching tales or parables of the *orishas*. The *patakís* form the heart of my religion. They are our poetry, our myths, and they bring wisdom and spiritual splendor into our lives. Through our *patakís* we come to know the powers of the *orishas*, learning lessons through the *orishas'* adventures. With my godchildren seated before me, I began: "Today, I am going to speak to you of honor, the honoring of the *orishas*, the honoring of our ancestors, and of ourselves. Because all rituals must open and close with Ellegua, the *orisha* of the crossroads, I will begin with a story of Ellegua, the trickster and the god of balance, the *orisha* of both beginnings and endings.

"A youthful, childlike *orisha*, Ellegua is an active and mischievous divinity. In this story, he is walking down a dirt road after having caused havoc in a village. Disturbed because the inhabitants of the village had not honored him, Ellegua decided to create imbalance in their lives. Everything that used to be right, he made wrong. Ellegua dried the wells and filled them with sand. He made wild animals tame. The villagers were baffled."

Ellegua's actions caused tremendous confusion in the village. The villagers could not light fires to cook their food. They had no water to drink, and their farms were barren and dry. The angry villagers went out looking for Ellegua on the same road he had taken leading out of the town. They knew he would be easy to identify because he had been seen dressed in black. In reality, though, as I told my audience, this was only partly true, for he wore his traditional ritual colors—red on one side and black on the other.

As he walked on, Ellegua had a change of heart. He decided to return to the village and give the villagers the opportunity to repent for their disrespectful behavior and to honor him properly. But when he saw that they were consumed with anger, he decided to play a trick on them to teach them a lesson. In their temper and impatience, they still had not learned from their mistakes.

One of the villagers, noticing Ellegua dressed in red, asked him if he had seen a man dressed in black. Ellegua shook his head, smiled, and said, "No, I have not seen this man." Without thinking, the villagers continued on the road looking for Ellegua, while Ellegua returned to the town, sat down, and waited. He knew that after a fruitless search, the angry villagers would return to their town with a change of heart.

And, of course, he was right. The villagers returned, tired and chastened, having recognized the error of their ways. They then set about preparing the ritual ceremonies required by Ellegua; he, in turn, set their lives in balance once again.

"Ellegua teaches us that we must look at all sides of the story in order to make an informed decision," I carefully shared with my godchildren the lesson of this tale. "He reminds us that the obvious is not always the correct answer. He shows us there is much more to gain if we stop, think, and reflect before taking an action."

Through our *patakís*, Santería teaches us the many ways of seeing the world to better understand our path in life. Santería encourages us to see and understand the sum total of the parts. To be one-dimensional in our thinking is to leave out a vast realm of possibilities, choices, and solutions. Ellegua teaches us to search actively for and to open the spiritual and secular doors to self-healing and empowerment. Other *orishas* have their own lessons, their own strands of wisdom to teach us. Woven together, their stories, energy, and power create a beautiful spiritual tapestry that is filled with portraits of pilgrims from many cultures, many faiths.

In recounting the grand pantheon of *orishas* to my students, I ask them to imagine a strong, ancient tree standing beside a beautiful, glistening ocean. The father of all *orishas*, Obatalá, is like the roots of that tree; the mother, Yemayá, is like the water that nurtures and gives life to the tree. The Supreme *Orisha*, Olodumare, could be said to be the one who planted the seed of this tree. And the *orishas*, the many gods and goddesses who represent all aspects of life and living, the children of Yemayá and Obatalá, are like the very highest branches, those closest to Olodumare in the highest reaches of heaven.

I ask my godchildren to envision, just below the highest

branches, the enlightened spirits of their ancestors. Beneath those enlightened spirits is where the spirits who need prayer would reside, and on the lowest branches are where humans would dwell. With this symbol of a tree, I teach my godchildren the sacred hierarchy of our religion.

I tell them that just as one branch on a tree has many boughs, each of the *orishas* has several roads, or *caminos*. And on each road, the *orishas* will manifest their powers, their *aché*, in a different manner. Like the *orishas*, we, too, have many *caminos*—I am a mother, grandmother, professor, godmother, and priestess; yet I do not cease to be Marta. Similarly, Yemayá, the mother of the *orishas* and the goddess of the ocean, has several *caminos*, and among them are the following: Yemayá Asesú, who moves slowly like the foam at the seashore; Yemayá Okotó, who lives in a bed of seashells and loves to be surrounded by pink and blue; and Yemayá Akuara, who lives where salt and fresh water meet and who can be both humble and haughty.

In her many manifestations, Yemayá is always the *orisha* of salt water, and her *caminos* reflect the many characteristics she possesses. Like Yemayá, each one of the *orishas* holds domain over a force of nature. Some *orishas* are guardians; others are responsible for birth, health, and community; some are *orishas* of creation; still others protect the Earth.

There are more than 401 *orishas*—the number one symbolizes the infinite range of the *orisha* pantheon. Each *orisha* represents an aspect of nature's energy, helping us to understand that we are, in fact, one with nature. Collectively, the *orishas* represent the infinite elements in nature: water, earth, wind, fire, trees, flowers, and animals. Just as the ocean is an *orisha* called Yemayá, the sweeping whirl of wind that precedes a storm is the *orisha* Oyá; thunder and lightning is the *orisha* Shangó. In ancient times Shangó was a king of the ancient sacred city of Oyó; he was then transformed by Olodumare into an *orisha* after his death. Ochun is the goddess of fresh water, and Obatalá, the creator of human beings. Ochosi is the hunter *orisha*, and Oggun is the god of truth and iron.

While these *orishas* and the elements of nature they represent are perceived as life-giving forces, they can also be destructive. In recent natural disasters, we have seen Yemayá's rage inundating Nicaragua with hurricane floodwaters, the wrath of Orisha Agayu covering the island of Martinique with volcanic lava and ashes, and the fire of Shangó devastating fields and homes in California.

The *orishas* demonstrate through natural acts that every element carries both positive, *iré*, and negative, *osogbo*, forces. And our own lives reflect the need to balance these positive and negative energy fields. If we pollute the ocean, it will cease to give us food. And the air that is essential to our lives must be kept clean if we are to survive. We are part of a divine creation. And I ask my godchildren to respect this creation, since *orun*, the spirit world, is spiritually united with *aye*, the world of the living, like two halves of a tightly fitted calabash.

Aché, the divine power of the *orishas*, is united with the secular world through Santería rituals we can trace back to our earliest ancestors. I pass on to my godchildren the traditions of Santería, just as my godparents taught me and their godparents taught them; the ceremonial rites and rituals have been passed down in this way through generations spanning centuries. And just as my godmother initiated me in the religion, I now initiate my godchildren, with the hope that I will inspire them to one day do the same. With each passing year, my spiritual family grows, new branches burgeoning from one tree.

My religious family found its roots in Cuba. It is headed by my *padrino*, Elpidio Cárdenas, and my *madrina*, Zenaida Rodríguez. Elpidio is an elder high priest, now eighty-one years old; he was trained by his godfather to interpret the complex system of divination symbols, the *odus*, used to interpret the philosophy of our religion and the accompanying *patakís*. Elpidio has initiated more than one hundred *babalawos*, priests, who are his godsons.

His wife, Zenaida Rodríguez, is my *madrina*, a priestess, or *santera*, who "crowned" me with the *orisha* who claimed me, Obatalá. She has been my mother, mentor, and friend since 1979.

Together, my *padrino* and *madrina* head an international family, with godchildren in France, Japan, Mexico, Canada, Puerto Rico, Colombia, Dominican Republic, the United States, and the former Soviet Union. But I was Zenaida's first godchild, her first *ahijada*, when I was initiated in 1981; since then, she has initiated twenty-eight others.

The initiation of an African woman ten generations ago in Ile Ife would have held much in common with the ceremony I underwent almost twenty years ago. Initiation, *asiento,* has always been conducted by the godparents who are the priests and priestesses of the religion. As a *madrina*, I now lead my students through their initiation ceremonies, guiding them to understand the wisdom of the *orishas* and the empowering presence of their ancestor spirits.

Through initiation into my religion, one is reborn. Our initiation is a conscious act of letting go of negative influences that weigh down the spirit, allowing the spirit to soar and to embark on a new beginning. The energy that naturally flows from initiation opens up inner channels, granting the initiate the ability to see, feel, smell, taste, and hear more acutely, and to be more present in the world. By combining my knowledge of the spiritual and the secular worlds, I have found a universe that unveils all of its wisdom and beauty before me. Like the great *orisha* goddess of the ocean, Yemayá, who lives both in the ocean and on Earth, we must avail ourselves of all the natural treasures of both worlds.

And so I teach my young initiates that every piece of the world possesses a divine natural power, an *aché*. According to practitioners of Santería, everyone possesses *aché* within, and we all have spiritual energies and guardian angels who watch over us. Whether we name them ancestors or *orishas*, our guardian angels all serve the same purpose. Some of us call our angels "spirits." Others refer to their presence as "intuition." They are also invoked as "powers." Whatever we choose to name them, we know they exist and are present in our daily lives.

They are the inner voice, the sixth sense, that warns us of im-

pending danger. They are the adrenaline force that makes us accomplish the impossible because they have the blessings of the highest power. My religion celebrates the *aché* in nature, and the power of our ancestor spirits, called *eguns*, and we perceive them everywhere in the world around us.

We believe our ancestors live among us and must be honored daily before our altars. These spirits can communicate with us through dreams, intuitions, visions, and metaphysical intervention. In ceremonies, *misas,* and rituals, we call down our ancestor spirits, though they surround us every day, comforting, protecting, and illuminating our spirits. The omnipresence of ancestral spirits helps guide our daily lives, allowing the ancestors to share their wisdom with us.

My loved ones who have joined the spirit world may not be with me physically, yet I know their spiritual essence continues to encircle me with their love and their power. I know them through my intuition and my spirit, through the voice that warns of imminent danger or offers a hint of great surprises. The religion of Santería provides an understanding of these special feelings and occurrences—not as extraordinary mysterious episodes, but as part of living a normal balanced life within the worlds of *aye*, heaven, and *orun*, earth.

Santería has taught me that the spiritual world is complex, composed of guardian angels who see us in different ways, and of gods and goddesses who bring different energy forces to our lives. I am initiated with the *aché* of Obatalá, the *orisha* of creation, and with the nurturing energy of Yemayá, my sacred maternal *orisha.* Among my ancestral spirit angels are the Native Indians of the Caribbean, the Moors, Kongos, and Yorubas of Africa, Gypsies and Europeans from Spain and the Caribbean.

With my godchildren encircling me before my *bóveda*, I pick up the objects on my altar one by one, offering one final lesson before we conclude our *misa.* I show my godchildren the small figurine of a Native American chief; a sculpture of a bountiful African woman draped in a red shawl; and a vibrant Gypsy adorned in yellow lace. Each one honors my ancestor spirits.

Placing the figurines back in their places, I ask my godchildren to honor also the people in their lives, their mothers and fathers, children, grandchildren, and friends.

On the occasions when I care for my seven-year-old granddaughter Kiya, she follows me as I perform my morning rituals. She acknowledges the spirit of the ancestors and the *orishas*. Playful like Ellegua, she places candies at his altars, and as I did with my grandmother, my *abuela*, she always asks for a piece of candy for herself. Sometimes, when I am rushing to get her home, I will forget to perform a ritual, but she will stop and say, "Nana, can I ring the bell to Obatalá?"

Recently, when I visited her, she took my hand and asked, "Abuela, do you want to see my altar?" My heart filled with pride as she joyfully explained each object that she had placed on her altar of toys, stones, and trinkets she loved. In the center of her altar, I noticed that my son Sergio and his soul mate, Jenna, had placed photographs of my father and other loved ones so she would know them also. In my granddaughter's glowing face, I see my *abuela*, my mother, and myself.

My granddaughter's altar is the beginning of her documenting her own life for her children, a way of remembering the life she has had with her parents and other family members. Through her, I have learned that my life is complete; there is a balance in my life like the balance between the spirit and secular worlds in Santería. My work as a professor and as a priestess, a godmother and grandmother, are not at odds; they are one. But this was not always so. There was a time when I, much like the villagers in Ellegua's tale, saw only one side of my story.

A Message from My Elders

Following the guidance of my elders, I start each morning with a hug for myself. They have taught me that if

18

I love and appreciate myself, then I will know how to appreciate and love others. The embrace is also a way of celebrating my life and blessings.

I start my mornings by looking out my living room window to the heavens, acknowledging the sacred power of Olodumare, and that of the spirits and the other *orishas*. Looking at the sky and clouds reminds me that I am part of the sacred creation and omnipresent energy force that created Earth.

To begin the day I start with the following prayer:

Olodumare, thank you for your blessings.
Spirits of my ancestors and *orishas*, protect me.
Illuminate my mind with positive thoughts.
Open the channels of positive energy so my family,
    friends, and I will always be protected from
    negative thoughts and energy.
Open the channels of positive energy that bring
    health, harmony, and unity to my family and
    community.
With the blessings of my spirit guides and *orishas*,
    I know that this will be so.

Chapter Two

YEMAYÁ

NO ONE KNOWS
WHAT TOMORROW WILL BRING

In the legends of Yoruba descendants in Cuba, Yemayá is highly honored. She is the mother of creation. Residing in the ocean, her colors are blue and white, like the rolling waves. From the depths of the sea, she possesses secret treasures known only to her. Wise and daring, she is both gentle and fierce.

It is said that Yemayá grew tried of her life in Ile Ife, and she secretly set out one day to the west in the direction of Abeokuta. She held a magic bottle filled with a mystical potion, which she intended to use only if she found herself in imminent danger. When Obatalá realized she was missing, he sent his army to find her and bring her back. But Yemayá did not want to return to Ile Ife. When she saw the approaching army, she threw the magic bottle on the ground, and it shattered into a thousand pieces. The potion began to spread far and wide, forming an enormous river that safely drew her out to sea.

Another legend tells of how Yemayá became queen of the Yoruba pantheon. According to legend, Yemayá was present when Olodumare created Earth. It was upon her home, the ocean, that Earth was formed.

It is said that Olodumare, impressed with her intelligence, appointed her queen of the Earth during a fiesta the *orishas* had planned in honor of Olodumare. Olodumare watched as the *orishas* arrived at the fiesta, ignoring his presence. He noticed that they all had forgotten to bring presents in his honor. As the fiesta came to an end, Yemayá appeared before Olodumare with a tray filled with his favorite vegetables, fruits, and meats. At the center of the tray, Yemayá placed the head of a young calf as a tribute to him. Overjoyed with Yemayá's gift, Olodumare proclaimed that she would always be the female head of the Santería religion.

Sitting in Doña Rosa's kitchen that summer day, my nervousness, together with the intense heat, began to unsettle my every attempt at calm. The white starched dress and scarf I was wearing

quickly lost their crispness. Trying to create a slight breeze, I fashioned a makeshift fan from the flaps of an old cardboard box. *Santeras* in charge of arranging the meal fluttered nervously around the kitchen, placing burning pieces of wood charcoal under the pots.

There were endless complaints about the old stove, and tidbits of gossip were exchanged about a carelessly prepared Santería ceremony the priestesses had attended the previous day. Doña Rosa, a seventy-year-old Yemayá priestess of Santería, sat next to me chopping the onions and peppers that were to season the meat for lunch. She told us, in a low whispery voice, of the importance of keeping the tradition intact by following the rules, the *Regla de Ocha*, the African elders left for us. Doña Rosa believed that the religion would be lost if the younger *santeros* and *santeras* had their way.

Carmen, a young, honey-beige, heavyset priestess in her thirties, argued that as times changed, the religion had to adapt in order to remain relevant. But not wanting to offend Doña Rosa, she quickly agreed that the ceremony of the prior evening was a display of disorganization, as well as a lack of knowledge, which she adamantly condemned.

Smiling at me, Doña Rosa asked, "Why are you so nervous? You're in one of the most respected Santería houses in Cuba. You're with your religious family and have nothing to fear. When you walk through those white curtains, you will realize the importance of following the traditional rules of the elders."

Doña Rosa's cottony white hair was in sharp contrast to her chocolate skin, and her gentle smile was warm and friendly. She placed her blue head scarf around her neck, where it hung loosely around her shoulders. Doña Rosa was present at all my godmother's ceremonies and was adored and respected because of her profound wisdom and motherly charm.

"The fear of the unknown is making me nervous," I responded, expecting her to laugh at my tentativeness.

Doña Rosa continued chopping onions as she quietly considered my reply. Then she said, "The unknown is the path to knowledge. Never fear it. We learn because we are curious to know what lies ahead. And this ritual that awaits you is only another step in understanding the unknown."

This ceremony, named *la entrega del cuarto de santo*—passing on the room of initiation—allowed me to pass on the *aché* of the divine *orishas* to my future godchildren. For the first time I would be on the other side of the white curtain and would witness each step of an initiation process that I had experienced sixteen years earlier. Afterward, I would follow the same path as generations of priestesses and priests. And just as my godmother followed in the sacred footprints of her *madrina*, I, too, would continue the tradition of sharing the divine teachings of my elders. When the white curtain parted, I would be admitted into the circle of elders who are entrusted with the passing on of *aché* to the next generation.

In that moment, as I anxiously waited to be called into the initiation room by my godmother's assistant, I could not help but think of the years of spiritual exploration that had brought me to that room. I had come a long way from my childhood home in East Harlem.

I was born Marta Moreno, the youngest of my parents' three children. My mother, Flora Cruz Marcano, was a housewife dedicated to raising her two daughters and one son. A tall, light-skinned woman, she was proud of her elegant body, which she claimed had attracted my father's roving eyes. She came to New York City in pursuit of a nursing diploma, hoping eventually to return to Puerto Rico to practice her profession. Returning home from school one day, Flora Cruz Marcano bumped into a handsome young man as she was stepping off the trolley car at 110th Street in East Harlem. She told us that she was attracted to his strong, tall body, his flirtatious smile, and his gentle romantic glance.

Every day from that day on, Clemente Moreno would wait for Flora at the trolley stop and follow her home, trying to convince

her to date him. In the mid-1920s, there were few places where Puerto Ricans could socialize. When he started courting my mother, my father would take her to Central Park or to the Spanish movie theater on 116th Street.

With a mischievous smile, revealing her sparkling gold tooth, my mother would look at us and say, "I finally took pity on him and agreed to go to the movies with your father." My father, listening to her from the kitchen table, would then chime in, "She forgot to say what a sweet-smelling, well-dressed man I was." My father, a muscular man with a dark coffee-colored complexion, was a self-taught auto mechanic. He also taught himself to read and write, after having completed a mere third-grade education in the Puerto Rican school system.

Often, at this turn in my mother's story, my father would retire to my parents' bedroom and return with a Golden Glove award in the shape of a coin, which he boasted he had won as an amateur fighter in the prime of his youth. He would smile at us, saying, "She fell in love with my body." My mother was a reserved woman, and her face showed clear embarrassment at my father's boast. Mama would continue the story, telling us how they fell in love and married. She quit school after their city hall wedding in 1929. She became pregnant four months after their marriage and was encouraged to stay home by my father. Following the Puerto Rican tradition of the time, my father did not allow her to work, because if she had, it would have implied that he was not man enough to support his woman and his family.

When my parents married, they moved to a two-bedroom apartment in a drab gray-brick tenement building at 330 East 102nd Street, paying $12 a month to the Italian owner. They would often reflect on the changes the building and neighborhood had endured over the years. When they moved in, they were the only Puerto Rican family in the building. The landlady, seeing my mother's light skin, assumed she was white. When my father showed up, with his dark complexion, the landlady tried to cancel the lease my mother had signed. After much pleading, my parents convinced her they would make excellent tenants, and they prom-

ised to tender their rent a week ahead to assure her of pay. Eventually my mother and our landlady became best friends.

My father was brought to New York City by his mother. In an attempt to start a new life away from her common-law husband, my paternal grandmother had brought my father and his older brother, Donato, to the city from Puerto Rico in the early 1920s. I remember my *abuela* telling me that she had left Puerto Rico alone to find work in the city. By working in laundries and cleaning the homes of the wealthy, she managed to bring first my uncle, and then my father from Puerto Rico.

Without mentioning the name of my grandfather, she would mutter in a low angry voice that he was a selfish, controlling man. "He had money, a fine house, a proper wife, and he thought he could keep our relationship hidden forever and continue to deny our two sons his name." When I inquired further, wanting to know his name, if he was still alive, and how he could have two wives, she snapped out of her thoughts, saying sadly I was too young to understand.

We lived in apartment number seven, and this is where my brother, sister, and I came of age. I can trace my first memories of Espiritismo and Santería to this building, my childhood home in El Barrio. I shared a bedroom with my sister, my brother slept on the living room sofa, and my parents slept in the other bedroom. The tub was in the kitchen next to the hand sink where we washed dishes. The toilet was in a small closet, also in the kitchen, with a tiny window for ventilation.

Although it was a modest apartment, my parents created a sense of privacy and space, developing a time schedule for our chores. We were taught to use the toilet when no one was eating in the kitchen, and everyone left the room after dinner in order for each of us to take our turn bathing. My parents wisely organized most of our family gatherings in the living room, allowing more privacy in the kitchen area. In spite of these inconveniences, what I remember most is the great amount of love my parents brought into our small home.

The few rooms in our apartment sparkled with the warm

colors of the tropics and the brilliant portraits of Catholic saints. My mother took care that the blue on the walls was the same color as the Puerto Rican ocean. Too poor to purchase wallpaper, our family, like many others in East Harlem, used the technique of taking the pages of a newspaper, crushing them, dipping them in silver paint and using them to imprint the clouds that covered our walls. Our curtains were plastic and had bright floral patterns in reds, oranges, and greens. The living room sofa, decorated with a rainbow of flowers, was protected with transparent plastic covers that stuck to my bare legs.

On the wall above the living room sofa, a rectangular mirror with pink flamingos completed the decor. I knew that having a mirror with beveled edges and pink flamingos was a status symbol. Often, when she looked at the mirror, my mother would say proudly, "We are poor, but not so poor."

And in the living room, above our prized television console, hung a large gold-leaf portrait of the Saint of Perpetual Help. Draped in a blue-green cloth trimmed in gold and haloed with a bejeweled crown, the saint held a child in her arms. Framed by two angels, the saint's face seemed to be looking toward someplace I could not even imagine, while the child looked at one of the angels with a slight smile. This portrait dominated the room as much as it came to dominate my imagination. I wondered if the child had lived in a home like ours, if he had had to clean his room as I did, if his mother had been warm and friendly like my mother. I finally decided that the mother and child must have had everything we had, that they must be exemplary if my mother had them prominently placed in our home.

The tenants in our building were more like family than neighbors, part of a community of Puerto Rican, African American, and Italian families that had developed a strong friendship over time. Three of the apartments in the building were rented by my family members. My aunt Moncha Cruz Marcano, my mother's sister, lived with her husband and three children in apartment number two, and my *abuela* lived in apartment number three.

My *abuela*'s apartment had a calm, peaceful feeling to it. The

walls were painted in soft shades of white. The curtains were the deep blue of the ocean. There was a tranquil quality that radiated from my grandmother as well. Luisa Correa Pérez was a slightly built woman who was born in the town of Loíza Aldea, Puerto Rico, in 1884, eleven years after the abolition of slavery. She dressed in loose-fitting white cotton dresses and kept her head covered with a white cotton kerchief, her hair fashioned in two braids that dangled to her shoulders. Peeking out from the collar of her dress were five beaded, beautifully colored necklaces that sparkled against her rich dark skin.

To me, my *abuela* seemed to be two people in one. Whenever she visited our apartment, Abuela projected an ancient, weary, quiet spirit. She was adored by my father, and her small frame seemed to shrink next to his large, muscular body. In some ways, she appeared to be the child rather than the parent in my home. But in her apartment, she filled the rooms with a presence as vast and mysterious as her shadow in the sunlight. Even her wrinkled skin seemed smoother and younger as she cleaned, cooked, and tended to her rooms.

Abuela lived alone in her warm, inviting place filled with a lingering scent of Florida water, the poignant smell of her cigars, and the smoke of burning sandalwood incense. Abuela's apartment was special to me. Each time I walked through her door, I felt as if I were entering a curious, adventurous world that resembled the fantasy of the magnificent Egyptian movie I saw serialized every Saturday at the children's matinee. Since I was only seven years old, I could not explain what I felt. Still, I knew that Abuela's apartment was a distinct and unusual place.

Every day when I returned home from public school, I would knock on Abuela's door. I would receive *la bendición*—her blessings—as she lovingly ushered me in to taste her homemade Puerto Rican candies. I looked forward to the special after-school treat she prepared for me.

Then Abuela would take me into her sacred room. Like my mother, Abuela had an image of a Catholic saint that took over the room. On the wall facing the entrance to her room rested a

large mural of Saint Michael, the archangel. Saint Michael's image was life-size and towered over me. He had flowing blond hair and large white wings, and he wore a green robe trimmed in gold. Over his shoulders fell a large shawl the color of red roses; it rippled in the breeze. In his left hand, he held the golden scale of justice over the head of an enormous black fallen angel. High over the black angel's head, Saint Michael's right hand held a razor-sharp sword. The black angel lay in fire and held his hands over his head, trying in vain to defend himself against the sword as his black wings spread out along the bottom of the mural like the lava of a raging volcano. The expressionless eyes of Saint Michael always caught my attention. I wondered why he seemed so passive, so uncaring as he prepared to slaughter the fallen angel.

The image of the fallen angel haunted me, and I would sometimes hide behind my grandmother before the sight of it. But Abuela would smile and tell me not to be frightened, saying, "There is nothing to fear. The spirits will always protect and guide you, as they have always safeguarded our family."

On those afternoons Abuela tended to the spirits at her altar, as I watched from the corner of the room. Her white cotton dress seemed to disappear into the stark white of the walls, and her dark skin appeared to be floating. Sometimes Abuela refilled the glasses of water that were placed on a long rectangular table before the mural of the archangel. Other times she would change the flowers on an altar laden with statues of Catholic saints, an Indian chief, a Gypsy woman, and African men and women.

I was intrigued by the detailed lifelike miniature features of the figurines. In the dimly lit room, they appeared to breathe and move ever so slightly as they acknowledged my presence. The Indian was a proud, bronze-skinned warrior who held a bow and arrow as he looked to the sky. His multicolored headdress fell to his waist with feathers of gold, red, green, and black. The Gypsy had olive skin, ink black hair, flirtatious dark eyes with long lashes, and sensual red lips that spoke of a joyful life. Her strong, defiant features resonated in her slim body, posed to dance an arousing flamenco in her billowing, tiered, yellow dress, with a long train trimmed in white lace curling around her feet.

Displayed in front of the Gypsy was a beautiful yellow lace fan, decorated with small red butterflies, that Abuela would sometimes let me play with. On these occasions, I danced as I imagined the gypsy danced, tossing my head from side to side and loudly stomping the heels of my shoes against the floor. Encouraging me with her laughter, my *abuela* would joyously clap her hands, imitating the fiery rhythm of the flamenco.

One African figure was a dark-skinned old man who sat quietly on a wooden chair as he smoked a cigar, steadfastly gazing at the glasses of water. His short white hair and white clothes contrasted with his ebony skin, giving him a wise air and creating a contemplative and graceful feeling. I imagined that this small image was a combination of my grandfathers, neither of whom I had ever met.

But my favorite statue was the image of an African woman. She looked stern with her hands on her ample hips. The intense colors of her clothing were what caught my fancy. The red scarf that covered her hair stood out against her deep mahogany skin. The wide white collar of her red dress seemed to pulsate against her face. Her protective eyes followed me when I walked into the room. I imagined her to be my grandmother's younger sister and called her *abuelita*, little grandmother.

I watched as Abuela lovingly arranged white flowers and lit a candle before the mural of the archangel. How carefully she refilled seven glasses with cool water, placing them on yet another table covered with an immaculate white lace cloth. The brilliant tapestry quilt of colorful flowers and statues created a gentle radiance, a comforting peace. The reflection of the candles flickered on the water glasses with a jeweled stained-glass luster. And the room was a dance of swirling, inviting colors, as the altars stood at solemn attention and vibrated with an energy I could not quite see or understand.

Many years later, while attending spiritual sessions in Cuba, I

discovered that these were Abuela's ancestor tables, her homage to our family's ancestral spirits and her religion's *orishas*. The table with the seven glasses of water was her *bóveda*—her ancestral altar table. The glasses represented her guardian angels and the spirits who continue to protect my family, while the fresh water and flowers represented the natural elements and their life-giving forces. There were seven glasses, because seven was the sacred number special to the *orisha* Yemayá, who has a close affinity to the spirit world. The *orisha* Yemayá represents the ocean itself and possesses the spiritual powers of mediumship. It is said that the spirit, *egun*, could not speak. One day *egun* stood by the ocean lamenting that lack of sound. Yemayá took pity on *egun* and created roaring waves in the ocean, and then she gave the spirit the gift of sound. In appreciation, *egun* taught Yemayá the art of mediumship.

Each glass of water on the ancestor table was dedicated to the memory of an individual spirit energy that is part of the foundation of our racial and cultural identities. One glass was filled for the Yorubas, one for the Kongos, one for the Native Americans, another for our guardian angels, one for relatives, one for loved ones, and finally, a last for unknown spirits. The *bóveda* was an offering of fresh water and flowers in their honor; my grandmother was acknowledging her devotion and gratitude for the sacred energies they shared with her.

It is believed that every altar must be maintained and cleaned so it may attract positive spiritual energy to the surroundings. Abuela's adoration of the spiritual guides created a safe environment that enveloped me with love. The figurines captured the unique individual personalities of the spirits and *orishas* that they were so valiantly protecting.

The statues disguised the images of the Yoruba spirits and *orishas*, who managed to survive the terrible journey of the Middle Passage and to enter the Americas in the souls of enslaved Africans. Our elders ingeniously hid the spirits and *orishas* behind Catholic images that carried characteristics similar to their own spirits and African gods and goddesses. The Yoruban people of Cuba used the Catholic image of La Virgen de Regla to hide the *orisha*

Yemayá. And the Yorubas in Bahia, Brazil, borrowed the Catholic image of Nossa Sra. Da Conçieçcão Da Praia to veil the universal mother *orisha* of creation, whom Bahianos call Yemanjá. In Cuba the image of Santa Bárbara hides the warrior Shangó, and Las Mercedes conceals Obatalá.

On my *abuela*'s altar, the flirtatious Gypsy dressed in yellow and the Catholic image of La Caridad del Cobre both represented the spirit of Ochun, the goddess of love and community in Africa and the Diaspora. The African woman in her red dress hid the warrior *orisha*, Shangó, as does the Catholic image of Santa Bárbara. The red and white dress and the crown and sword of Santa Bárbara were royal symbols that Shangó, the Yoruba god-king of thunder and lightning, could mask himself behind. The Indian chief was Abuela's guardian warrior spirit Orisha Ochosi, the hunter. And the childlike statue of El Niño de Atocha veiled the mischievous Ellegua. Practitioners understand that there is a sharp line demarcating the differences between *orishas* and the Catholic images that are used to camouflage them. In the Americas, Yoruba descendants have developed a creative and inclusive spiritual system that embraces all divinities in their myriad forms while understanding their distinct differences.

Abuela always called the saints by their two names. When praying to El Niño de Atocha, she would say, "Niño de Atocha protect us. Ellegua, open your roads bringing health, tranquillity, unity, and love to our family." As a child I did not understand why she used various names for one symbolic image, but today it is clear to me that for her they were different incarnations of similar energy forces.

Before leaving my *abuela*'s apartment, I would glance with curiosity at the objects she kept behind the door to the entrance of her home. She had a large triangular-shaped stone with cowry shells forming eyes, a nose, and a mouth in the center. The stone was placed on a clay plate surrounded by caramel candy and small toys. Next to the stone there was a round iron pot filled with a small set of farming tools—a hammer, shovel, anvil, and hoe. Although she often caught my roving eyes looking longingly

at these intriguing objects, Abuela never explained the meaning of these objects to me. Now I understand that these objects are symbols that represent the *orishas*. *Otanes,* stones that have undergone ceremonial rites, are the embodiment of the energy of the *orishas.* Sometimes Abuela would say, "You're a child, like Ellegua, always into everything." And she would share a piece of candy with me before placing the rest on the clay plate.

All these many years later, my *abuela's* mysterious objects and rituals have come to have meaning in my life. The spiritual objects that were an integral part of her life are equally a part of mine. Having traveled my own spiritual journey, I have come to embrace my guardian angels and the sacred energies of the *orishas.* My *abuela's* sacred space was a warm place that is always present in my thoughts. She introduced me to a tapestry of images and scents that are woven into my memory forever. The vigor I felt when entering her apartment I now understand to be the spiritual energy—the *aché*—that flowed from her sacred African divinities.

However, I often still wonder why my *abuela* didn't share more information with me about the practices of calling the ancestral spirits—Espiritismo and Santería—or about their representation as nature's energy forces. I have come to the conclusion that she continued to camouflage her African beliefs behind Catholic images in order to protect her divinities from hostile, prying eyes. My *abuela* was born during a period when practitioners of African religions were imprisoned and persecuted for their beliefs. In a tradition that could be preserved and maintained only by codes of secrecy, her own loved ones must have taught her to keep her beliefs hidden.

It saddens me to think about the abuse she must have endured to practice her religion. Court records from the late 1800s affirm how Puerto Rican women were consistently brought to trial by white men whose sexual advances they had refused. These men accused them of being *brujas*—witches and practitioners of evil magic. Women like my *abuela* lived on the margins of society, discriminated against because of their color, gender, and economic status. The suffering that Abuela and other initiates experienced must have been severe. Indeed, it was an act of pure faith and devotion for her to continue to practice her religion. In New York City, no doubt, she encountered similar restrictions and prejudices. A poor, single woman who did not speak English faced constant attacks because of her race and migrant status. In addition, the stigma of being an unmarried mother branded her as a woman of ill repute.

In her desire to pass on her sacred beliefs, Abuela took advantage of my afternoon visits to perform basic rituals, unknown to me, and these began my instruction in the religious practices she loved. Watching and following her in the altar room left imprints in my memory that appear before me now even when I perform my own rituals. The altars in my own home continue to praise the guardian angels and *orishas* that my *abuela* treasured. My *bóveda* also has the statue of the African woman in her red dress, as well as other figurines that symbolize the spirits watching over my family.

In my room dedicated to the *orishas*, sacred stones rest within their porcelain decorative bowls. Shango's sacred stones—*otanes*, symbols of his power—rest within a bowl made of wood on a wooden stand, a *pilón*. My *abuela*'s statue of the warrior Indian, with his winged arms of feathers spread to the sky, and the image of the old thoughtful African man dressed in white, carry the protective warmth and memory of my *abuela*'s apartment. Although my grandmother shared little information regarding her sacred beliefs, rituals, and ceremonies, she did inspire my search for a religion that touched my soul.

It took me more than twenty-two years of exploration to reconnect to the sacred practices of my *abuela*. Over time, I have explored faiths and attended a number of different churches, including Protestant, Catholic, and Pentecostal houses of faith as I searched for my spiritual center. But my parents offered little advice or direction as they observed my exploration. Pretending to be faithful Catholics, they never had images of the spirits or symbols of the *orishas* like Abuela did.

Although we did not attend church regularly when I was

a child, my mother considered us devoted Catholics. When we did go to services, it was for weddings and baptism ceremonies, merely to please family and friends. My only recollection of following Catholic beliefs was my mother's insistence that we not eat meat on Fridays or during Lent. My father ignored her rule, saying, "Neither God nor Jesus has done anything for me lately."

My mother would turn red with anger and lash out with stinging words, "Clemente, you'll burn in hell!" In response, my father would open a newspaper, ignoring her, winking at us while my mother's anger grew and she continued to admonish him for his lack of faith in the Almighty. My mother would then get silent, knowing that if she truly upset my father, he would hit her. Over the years she learned to take an argument to a certain point and then retreat before my father would explode in anger. Fearing these outbursts, Alberto, Socorro, and I would sit quietly, hoping that my mother would stop before my father lost control of his temper. My brother, sister, and I grew accustomed to their Friday arguments, as we dutifully ate our codfish with potatoes and onions.

My parents never connected the many scattered images of saints in our home to the images of saints in the Catholic church. In my mind, they were simply our family's special pictures and statues, which we worshiped when we had any problems.

When we caught colds, for instance, my mother prayed to the Saint of Perpetual Help to cure us. During our sicknesses, a candle would be lit before the saint's image, and my mother would say a daily prayer. She would also place a ball of camphor in a small handmade cotton bag and string it around our necks, then place fresh garlic in the four corners of the room to dispel negative energy.

If we were in need of money, my mother would light a candle, place the Bible before the Saint of Perpetual Help, and pray for assistance. Sometimes she would select the "illegal" underground horse race winning numbers—*la bolita*—which would buy food, clothes, and schoolbooks, and pay utility bills. I often wondered how a saint, through divine intervention, gave my mother the winning numbers. As soon as we all enjoyed her winnings, however, any questions I had would flee.

My sister was eleven years older than I. Overweight, light-skinned, with nappy reddish hair, she walked around with a detached air. She was named Socorro, in honor of the Saint of Perpetual Help. My brother was named Alberto after our paternal grandfather. His rich brown skin, trim figure, and wisecracking manner made him fun to have around. My brother and I would often tease Socorro because of her saintly name. When she would come after us with a broom, my brother and I would lock ourselves in the living room, shouting "Perpetuo Socorro, help us!" Inevitably we would be punished for blasphemy.

Though we grew up surrounded by religious icons in Abuela's and my own family home, my family did not provide us with formal training in any religion. Nonetheless, I did consider our family religious, as prayer was our way of solving problems. My mother was devoted to La Perpetuo Socorro and Abuela to her spirits and *orishas*. When I had an exam, a discreet hint to my mother or Abuela assured me that they would quickly put their prayers to work to help me pass my test. My mother would silently go to the bureau where the statue of La Perpetuo Socorro stood behind the Bible and then burn a candle, bowing her head to pray. Abuela would always comfort me with a warm smile and tell me that my concern "was no big thing."

I attended elementary school at P.S. 121 and junior high school at P.S. 99 in El Barrio. My community was the center of my universe, and I was happily surrounded by my family and friends who looked like me. I believed everyone lived like us and that the scenes I saw on television were mere fairy tales. In 1954, at the encouragement of my junior high school art teacher, Mrs. Siegel, I applied to and was accepted at the High School of Music and Art, for my drawing talent. Mrs. Siegel was a warm and dedicated Jewish teacher who worked hard to convince my parents that art and academic studies would eventually prepare me for a future with a good-paying job. Barely persuaded, my parents agreed to table their desires that I become a nurse or a secretary, jobs that they believed guaranteed stable incomes.

My new school opened a world of museums and art galleries.

I "discovered" the work of artists like Wilfredo Lam with his Afro-Cuban spiritual images, and Paul Gauguin, with his beautiful brown faces and tropical colors. Gaugin's work resembled images in my home and the likenesses of family and friends. These artists became my imaginary friends, as my art classes introduced me to the imposed primacy of western European art.

In high school, I was surrounded primarily by middle-class white students who lived like the actors I saw on television. I suddenly felt different about my neighborhood and myself. At home and in my neighborhood, I was social and outspoken, but I became withdrawn and shy in school. For the first time I heard my neighborhood referred to as a ghetto, my friends called spics, and my community defined as colored. Shaken by these revelations, I sought to hang out with the handful of African American and Puerto Rican students who were experiencing a shared cultural shock.

I met my first boyfriend, future husband, and father of my sons in English class. Tomás Vega looked like he had stepped out of a Gauguin painting. His silky jet black hair framed a face that looked like the East Indian movie idol Sabu. Friendly and inquisitive, he continuously irritated our pompous English teacher, who openly embarrassed the Latino and black students in class. One day she had me stand before the class and repeat the words *that* and *did* for most of the class, saying that I did not know the difference between *t* and *d*. Close to tears, I ran from the room when the bell signaled the end of the class. Tomás ran after me, offering his handkerchief to wipe away the tears that freely flowed. His caring, gentle, and mature manner belied the fact that he was only six months older than me. We became steadfast friends and were part of the small clique of students of color who hung out together in school. We created our own community.

Most of us lacked the formal art and academic training that middle-class students took for granted; we depended upon our creative, intuitive imaginations and many late hours of study to pass our classes. Drawing was my first love. I drew because I could create my own world. My art classes allowed me the oppor-

tunity to draw and paint the images that were part of my everyday life. Class assignments required that I draw still-life scenes using interesting objects in my home. Rather than use my home as the subject of my work, I chose to use objects in my *abuela*'s apartment. The colors and light in her apartment made me feel protected, as if I were surrounded by stained-glass windows.

Her sacred room—a symphony of patterns, colors, lines, and forms—was my favorite still-life scene. One of my first paintings was of my *abuela*'s *bóveda*. The crystal glasses reflected the pale yellow fire of the burning candle. The vase filled with fresh flowers on top of the white lace tablecloth possessed a serenity that I struggled to capture in my paintings. Her *bóveda* enraptured me, keeping me in the room for hours. Through my work I was able to weave the images of my home into my school environment, reducing my feeling of isolation. The spiritually charged images reflected the brown faces of my ancestry and, unbeknownst to me, my growing affinity to the *orishas*.

My *abuela* would often sit silently next to me and watch as I transformed the images of her sacred altar onto my sketch pad. Sometimes she tenderly stroked my hair and said, "Someday the drawings of my altar will hang in a museum."

I would giggle and say, "No, Abuela, I'm just a beginner," feeling proud that she thought I had talent.

"No one knows what tomorrow will bring," she would always respond. "Life is like the ocean; it is never still, and what is true today may be different tomorrow."

A Message from My Elders

My *madrina* taught me to set up a *bóveda* to my spirits on my first trip to Cuba. The *bóveda* attracts the spirit energy of loved ones to my home.

Glasses on my *bóveda* are in tribute to the Yorubas,

39

Kongos, Indians, beloved spirits, spirits that need light, guardian angels, and the unknown souls of the spirit realm. On Monday mornings I replace the water in the glasses, light a candle, and pray before my ancestor altar, calling the names of loved ones. The presence of a *bóveda* in the home spiritually charges the environment with the memory of those who are no longer on this Earth.

The *bóveda* should be placed in a quiet area in your home. Standing before the altar in a meditative state each morning, I make time to recite the names of beloved spirits. My prayer is as follows:

> With the permission of Olodumare, the Almighty, I acknowledge the presence in my life of those who have contributed to my life. Let their teachings and love guide me as I embark on a new day. Let the richness and experiences of their lives serve to help me make informed decisions.
>
> I call on the spirits of my grandmothers, María de la O, Luisa Correa, and Marta Cruz Marcano. The spirits of my grandfathers, Felipe Moreno, Alberto Moreno Sr.; my parents, Clemente Moreno and Flora Moreno; my aunt Moncha Cruz; and my sister, Socorro Moreno. I also call upon the spirits known and unknown that bring light into my life to protect and guide my family each day.

I conclude in this way: "My guardian spirits, I ask that you inspire faith, hope, and love in my life so that I can share it with my family, friends, and community."

Chapter Three

OBATALÁ

POWER RESIDES IN
COOL HEADS

One of the most valued characteristics of the Yoruba and their descendants in the Americas is the ability to remain composed, rational, and calm in all situations. To remain levelheaded allows us to critically evaluate and seek resolution for the problems we face in life. One of the many parables that describe this important quality stresses the need for patience and coolness.

One day Obatalá decided to visit his friend Shangó, the king of Oyo. Before setting out, Obatalá visited a diviner—a *babalawo*—to make certain his trip would be a safe one. The diviner told him that it was best to delay his trip, because he saw many enemies awaiting Obatalá along the way. But he was both independent and stubborn, and nevertheless insisted on visiting Shangó.

To lessen the troubles that awaited him, the *babalawo* advised Obatalá that he should take three changes of white clothing. It was most important, the *babalawo* told Obatalá, that he not lose his temper, for if he did, his life would not be spared. Heeding the advice of the diviner, Obatalá took three sets of clothing on his travels and vowed to stay calm.

Along the way, he met Ellegua, who was disguised as a poor peasant. When Ellegua asked Obatalá for help carrying a barrel filled with red palm oil, Obatalá willingly consented. Ellegua, playing his usual tricks, spilled palm oil on Obatalá's clothes. He did so three times over. Each time, Obatalá calmly went to the nearest river, washed his clothes, and changed into clean ones.

Heeding the words of the diviner, he did not lose his patience. Ellegua was unable to shake Obatalá's calm, and Obatalá was permitted to continue his journey with the knowledge that power resides in a cool head. He did not let the antics of Ellegua change his plans.

In a Cuban kitchen, many years and many miles away, the gentle hand of Doña Rosa on my shoulder woke me from my semidream

state. Doña Rosa reminded me very much of my grandmother. She dressed like my *abuela* and wore her hair in the same way, and the warm color of her skin was like my grandmother's. Both of them were much like the millions of African women who once toiled on plantations throughout the Americas. Like my grandmother, Doña Rosa was careful with her words because they carried not only *aché*, but the sacred spirit of the ancestral mothers. She selected her words as if she were choosing precious diamonds that would be handed down for generations to those who would treasure and value them forever.

As I sat waiting to be called into the initiation ceremony, Doña Rosa's words again poured over me like a waterfall of cool, sparkling water. I needed to be reminded to let go of my fear of the unknown. I settled down and let my nervousness fade away, for she had made me understand that growth is a process of discovery. It is about releasing fear, taking risks, and above all letting divine intelligence fill us with creative inspiration, flowing unhindered.

In high school, I sometimes felt that I was wasting my time pursuing an arts career. It felt as if invisible barriers were constantly placed in my way. My guidance counselor advised me against entering the field of fashion design because she felt that it was exclusionary and racist. I considered a career in commercial art and again my adviser said that doors would be closed because of the color of my skin. Then I decided that I wanted to become an arts teacher. Once again my counselor suggested I think about another career possibility. When I graduated from the High School of Music and Art in 1959, my decision was to pursue a career in art education. I would not be stopped.

Tomás and I graduated from the High School of Music and Art at the same time. Our friendship had deepened by our sophomore year in high school, and we became inseparable. With the assistance of our high school counselor, we were both

accepted by New York University's art education department in the same year, and we both enrolled against our parents' wishes.

Tom's mother, an employee in a clothing sweatshop, encouraged him to leave school to take a job in the factory. She was the sole supporter of her mother and three children and desperately needed financial assistance. Determined not to accept public assistance, Tom's mother worked fourteen-hour shifts daily. Food was so scarce in his home that Mrs. Vega placed a padlock on the refrigerator. Understanding the need to contribute financially to his family, Tom held three part-time jobs while attending school full-time. He was so anxious and exhausted that sometimes he would fall asleep in class. Nevertheless, he made the commitment to finish his education, although his mother unwittingly undermined his goals. With the help of a partial scholarship, student loans, and the money he earned, Tom continued in school.

Convinced that there was no future in the arts, my parents kept insisting that I quit school and seek a vocational education. Still, they stood by me, struggling to scrape together the money that my student loan and partial scholarship did not cover. To help meet my university expenses, I found a part-time job as a typist in a caviar factory near the college.

Tom and I provided our own motivational support network. We realized that our parents wanted the best for us, but that their vision was limited by the barriers they had faced during their own youths. Although we were confronted by racist comments in high school and at the university, it was clear to us that an education would be our path to opportunities that our families had never had.

On campus, we saw very few black or Latino students. We were the only Puerto Ricans in our department, and there was only one African American student, who eventually dropped out. Tom and I were living through our own civil rights struggle in New York City. The news reports of the civil rights fervor in the South was beginning to sweep the nation, and it empowered us, for this was our battle as well. One of our art professors was the distinguished African American artist Hale Woodruff, who

quickly became our mentor and friend. He became the adult voice of encouragement, helping us over the aesthetic and social hurdles we faced in the department.

If Tom and I considered the students at the High School of Music and Art to be rich in comparison to our economic situation, the students at New York University all seemed to be millionaires. With the other students in the art department, I felt a kind of invisible barrier. Racial, cultural, and social differences influenced their perceptions, values, and understanding. And it became increasingly apparent that most of the students in my classes had never heard of El Barrio, had never been in a tenement building, and would never have met a Puerto Rican if Tom and I had not been in their classes.

It made me laugh to see their designer sneakers hand-smudged so they wouldn't look new, while my ordinary shoes were dirty because they were truly worn. Their designer jeans were hand-torn to achieve a "hip," lived-in look, while the threads in my jeans were giving up from constant wear.

I was appalled by the arrogance and wastefulness of privilege. Many students would leave half-finished tubes of paint lying about the art studio. They would throw away almost new paint palettes and canvases in fits of artistic temperament. Since we were barely able to purchase the required art supplies for class, these pretentious acts worked to Tom's and my advantage. We waited until everyone had left, then rummaged through the garbage to salvage items we needed. Often Professor Woodruff would gather supplies left in his other art classes and save them for us.

At first, we felt uncomfortable and at the margins of the department's activities. As we made friends with some other students who were poor and white, we became part of a small group of "starving hip art students" who discussed the role of the arts as a means for social and economic revolution. We envisioned ourselves as serious artists and spent endless hours talking about how we would solve esoteric problems.

As a blossoming art student, I had begun to experience life

outside El Barrio. Tom and I would hang out in the Lower East Side or the East Village, roaming around with friends, partaking of the fringe artistic atmosphere developing in the area. I soon realized that the culture I grew up with and took for granted was not only very different from that of other students, but completely unknown to them. I was unfamiliar with the Eurocentric arts movement of downtown New York, which was as elitist as it was avant-garde, and the Caribbean images, colors, and textures that nurtured my youth were foreign to my classmates. My paintings illustrated the clashing complexity of colorful patterns that recalled the altars of my *abuela* and the vibrancy of my home.

Why paint apples and oranges, or cartoonlike images of Campbells soup, Marilyn Monroe, and Jackie Kennedy, I thought, when the Madama, the African woman, or El Kongo, the African man, surrounded by mangoes, plantains, pineapples, and other fruits my grandmother placed before the statues were ideal subjects? The colors of the objects and symbols that surrounded me daily were the images that became the focus of my paintings. The foods of the spirits placed on straw mats, the fiery defiant dance of the Gypsy swirling in reds and oranges, and many other images were my declaration that life in East Harlem also had artistic meaning. I made the conscious decision that my cultural heritage, which was ignored in my art history classes, would be the spring from which my creativity would flow.

Although my teachers were tolerant of my aesthetic vision, their puzzled faces made it clear to me that they did not really understand or appreciate my work. The instructors and students often asked for explanations of the images. I knew a mango was a tropical fruit and the Gypsy was from Spain, but when I responded to their questions about the content of my paintings, I expressed feelings of pride and demonstrated my growing knowledge of Puerto Rican history. I explained that the images of the flamenco dancer spoke to the cultural influence of the Spaniards in Puerto Rico. The Madama and old Kongo were the symbols of enslaved men and women brought to the island, and the Indian chief

represented the Taínos people, who had been decimated by Spanish conquest. Although my explanation was incomplete, it marked the beginning of my cultural studies.

By 1962, the year before our graduation from New York University, Tom and I had developed our own aesthetic cultural vision. Tom's confidence in his artistic talent was extraordinary, and he lent me the courage to express my own vision. Painting scenes in his neighborhood at the last minute between his many jobs and his school schedule, Tom was beginning to sell his work to small galleries. My images culled from my *abuela's bóveda* and my home had many echoes for him, and he convinced me that we did have an audience for our work. It did not matter that our work was often misunderstood; it was tantalizing and intriguing, and the instructors and other students often would create their own meanings. We were frequently criticized for our representative art forms, since the artistic trends supported abstract expressionist and minimalist art. After class we would laugh at the misinterpretations of our work until we finally figured out that their opinions did not matter; we were getting wonderful grades and were deepening our knowledge of our heritage.

Tom and I graduated as art education teachers in May 1963, and we started teaching in the public schools by September 1963. I taught at Manhattan's P.S. 60, a junior high school located on Twelfth Street, and Tom taught near his home in the Baruch Projects on the Lower East Side. Having accomplished our educational goals, we turned our attention to the next phase of our lives. We were sitting by the fountain in Washington Square Park, proudly examining our graduation diplomas, when Tom asked me to marry him by casually inviting me to accompany him to city hall. Knowing his work schedule, I was surprised by his request because he had to be at work in another half hour. "What about your job?" I asked. He shyly responded, "I took time off so we could go get our marriage license." In 1963, we had been together for eight years, and we believed we were finally ready to begin our lives together.

We wanted a civil ceremony at city hall since we were not

members of any formal religion, and thought it was a good way to bypass an expensive wedding. With the payment of student loans looming in the near future, we had no money to waste on what we thought was a meaningless public event. Nevertheless, my mother insisted on a Catholic church ceremony. Much loved and pampered by my mother, Tom gave little resistance to her request. Sitting at the kitchen table, I saw his resolve melt as he said, "Mom is right. We will remember our marriage day for the rest of our lives. Let's make it special." My mother wanted to make certain that the neighborhood realized her daughter was a virgin. It was important for my mother to display my "Puerto Rican señorita" virtuousness by having me wed in a white dress. Although I continued to argue against a church ceremony, my parents refused to accept my decision. They reasoned that as baptized Catholics, we must have a Catholic wedding. It was clear to me, however, that they were more concerned about our gossipy neighbors than the blessings of the religious rite.

When we went to make the arrangements, I discovered that the church insisted that I first receive my official confirmation and that I attend classes to learn the rules of the Catholic religion.

A priest in gold spectacles, dressed in a long black robe, ushered me into the church basement where I joined others for the Catechism class. His flushed pink cheeks contrasted sharply against his pale bluish skin and white collar. The sterile, cold environment was made more depressing by the image of a bleeding Christ crucified on a cross mounted on the front wall. Father Fitzpatrick's clear blue eyes, slight Irish accent, and unsmiling mouth made him appear like one of the many Catholic statues hanging in the church chapel.

In his monotonous voice, he carefully explained the precepts of the church, but once I began to learn the fundamental canon of the church, my initial interest quickly faded. I could not accept that my loved ones had been born with original sin. I did not understand why I had to confess my sins to a priest. It was difficult for me to believe that a man, or any one person, had the power to absolve me of a sin I did not commit. None of it made

sense to me. But to appease my mother, I was married in the church. To please myself, I stopped going to Sunday mass.

Finally, after six weeks, on March 29, 1964, Tom and I were married in East Harlem at St. Lucy's Church on East 104th Street. Shortly thereafter we moved to an apartment one block up from the church to be near my parents.

The first years of our marriage were wonderful. Tom and I decided to wait to have children in order to complete our graduate work at New York University. We decided to continue our studies in the field of higher education, eventually planning to become college professors. Our respective families were overjoyed at our accomplishments. They quickly forgot their opposition to our educational goals and celebrated how instrumental they had been in our achieving our professional objectives.

On reflection, I am glad I granted my mother's wish to be married in the Catholic church. She had known at the time that she was ill and her weak heart could not sustain her much longer, but she hid it from us. Six months after my marriage, my mother died. Soon after her passing, we found letters she had written to each family member.

In my letter, she explained how she had asked the spirits to let her live to see me graduate, marry, and start my professional career. "My life has been blessed by the spirits," she wrote. "They didn't take me away from my children when I experienced my first heart attack. I asked to be spared and live to see my youngest child flower into womanhood. I have been given this blessed opportunity. The time has come for me to leave you. Do not cry or mourn, because I will always be with you." And now, after many years, I do truly understand that my mother and other loved ones are, in fact, always with me.

In her letter to my father, my mother asked that he help keep the family together. She was the one who insisted the family get together for Sunday dinners. When we all left home to start our families, she would call us each day to make certain all was well. In her letter, it was clear she wanted him to take her place, but although he tried, he could not change the years of being the strong macho patriarch. Abuela had died in 1959 and my mother in 1964, leaving a large void in our family. In a short period of time we had lost two loved ones, and I was devastated. Feeling lost and in need of healing, I would get up early on Sundays to sit in church. I found sitting in the solitude of the chapel before mass spiritually comforting, and walking to church at six in the morning was so peaceful. The only people I saw walking in the shadows of dawn were elderly Italian and Puerto Rican women dressed in black on their way to church.

Those early Sunday mornings alone in the church seemed to satisfy my growing need for a connection beyond my everyday world. The altar, covered by intricately embroidered, luxurious cloths, reminded me of my *abuela's* sacred room. The brilliant colors of the statues of the saints and the scent of burning incense created a familiar feeling that was soothing to my inner being, evoking thoughts of my mother and La Perpetuo Socorro. Memories of my *abuela's* home also filled my thoughts as the flickering flames of candles and stained-glass windows reflected a rainbow of warmth.

Going to church early on Sundays became a weekly ritual. Surrounded by the echoes of silence, the solitude and privacy was like being in the bosom of my *abuela* and mother. Sometimes I was the only person in the dark, nearly empty nave. Other times, if I was joined by two or three older women who piously knelt to recite the rosary, the church felt like a tomb. In their solemn black dresses, they knelt and prayed at each of the stations of the cross, and they often wept softly. Their devotion and sacrifice expressed a deep love that was coupled with sorrow. Respecting their devotion, I felt uneasy with what appeared to be a profound sadness engulfing them. My own reasons for attending church were very different.

I looked forward to my Sunday mornings of sacred solitude with joy. Each week, however, the sacred joy that filled me on Sundays disappeared too quickly. I could never understand why this feeling did not last past the chapel's doors.

Both Tom and I continued to explore our career options after

we completed graduate school in 1966. Tom decided to teach in a private elementary school, and I decided to continue teaching in the public schools. Our worlds were suddenly different. He was in an environment that valued education and prepared students to enroll in schools like the High School of Music and Art. I was working with students who could barely stay in school because of dysfunctional homes or the need to contribute to family income. My students were no longer children; they were becoming adults, dealing with grown-up problems. Many had to baby-sit so their parents could work. Others held part-time jobs after school to help at home.

I became pregnant with our first child, Sergio, in 1968. At the time, I was teaching in Washington Irving High School, then an all-girls school. For many students I was the first Puerto Rican teacher they had ever had. I became their mentor, guidance counselor, role model, and mother. Like my junior high school art teacher had done, I spoke with parents, encouraging them to allow their daughters to pursue their artistic goals. In my position I felt that I was making a difference. There were many times when I had to defend students who were the target of discrimination by an overwhelmingly insensitive portion of the European American faculty. Since I was frequently mistaken for a student, teachers would often be extremely rude when they spoke with me. One day I was even pulled out of the teachers' lounge because one of the faculty members refused to believe that I could be a teacher.

But at home, Tom and I were elated. Together, it seemed as if we had planned our lives perfectly, and all we desired was being granted. Along with my brother's and sister's families, we purchased a three-family house in the Bronx on Olmstead Avenue. Our father contributed the down payment from his years of hard-earned savings. This was an act of love and commitment to the family, and it was my mother's wish. My father was a penny-pincher. Concerned with his retirement and lack of health insurance, he was extremely careful with his money and had refused to move from East Harlem, because he was paying only thirty-six dollars per month in rent in 1969. Although the block was now

infested with drug dealers and addicts, he chose not to move from the home he had shared with his family. The brightly lit, clean halls that had been my childhood playground were now covered with garbage and reeked from the stench of urine. Broken lights made the hallways ominous as the shadowy figures of men and women roamed aimlessly, hiding from the light of the entranceway. For my father, the act of withdrawing several thousand dollars from his savings account for a home for his children in another borough, seemingly a million miles away, was a gesture of selfless love.

Our house on Olmstead Avenue was filled with happiness and children; it spilled over with joy. We felt as if we had stepped into a television scene of the perfect American home. The new three-story redbrick house had a small front lawn and backyard. All the homes on the block looked exactly the same, but it didn't matter: 450 Olmstead Avenue was our special castle.

I felt it important to continue working with children from my community. It was clear to me that there were individual teachers who had made a critical impact on my life, and I wanted to do the same for others. In the three years before my pregnancy, through teaching and counseling, I witnessed the glorious rewards of making a difference in young people's lives.

Although giving birth to Sergio was an equally glorious event, I missed teaching. After three months of staying home trying to occupy my time with caring for Sergio, cleaning, and cooking, I was ready to go crazy. Even my paintings took on the monotones of gray that expressed my gloom. Three months later I decided to return to work. I decided that there were more important things in life than washing dishes and cooking. Motherhood did not have to mean leaving my profession. I refused to follow my mother's example and be forced to defer the dreams of a career. I didn't want to.

A friend referred me to a part-time job with a community parent group in the South Bronx, which I thought was a good solution. The mission of the project was to assist parents in improving their reading and writing skills so they could then help

their children with their schoolwork and hold their schools accountable for their children's education. I took Sergio with me and placed him in the nursery with the children of parents with whom I was working. I enjoyed my job. The parents eventually came to teach me more than I shared with them. At the time I began working with them, I was an awful cook and had no real interest in learning how to prepare anything more complicated than rice with beans and stewed chicken. They took me under their maternal wings and taught me to prepare "real" Puerto Rican and African American cuisine. I learned to make the rich brown soup *sancocho;* tasty grits with eggs and pork sausage; and my favorite dessert, *flan*—an egg caramel custard.

The Parent Center was located in the community room of the St. Ann's public-housing complex. Although the windows and doors were covered with iron bars, inside the parents had created an oasis. Each room was decorated with photographs and children's drawings illustrating heroes, heroines, and revolutionaries of the black and Latino community. The beautiful, solemn face of Puerto Rican *independentista* Lolita Lebrón; the studious, stern face of Black Power leader Malcolm X; the atomic burst of Angela Davis's Afro hairstyle, with her raised fist, ignited the room, demanding racial empowerment. The room filled with racial pride, mixing with the aromas of boiling chicken and rice; *tostones,* green plantain chips; and collard greens smothered with pork sausage, eggs, and grits. The parents enjoyed cooking and eating, so the stove was always lit. The delicious smell of food consistently greeted everyone who came to the center and always enticed me to enter the kitchen.

The parents and I shared dreams and aspirations while I conducted the reading and writing classes. Part of the Parent Center's mission was to make dreams happen. Kinshasa, one of the parents, was intent on becoming a beautician. Each day she would come to the center with a new hairstyle, new nail designs, and tight sexy outfits covering her chunky body. Each day she selected a parent on whom to test her hair designs and makeup looks. And these makeovers drew an audience for the lucky

mother who left feeling like a queen. Consuelo, the parent of four small children, was almost invisible in the crowd of fun-loving women. Painfully thin, with an almond complexion, she had dark purple circles under her dull brown eyes. Each day she seemed to wear the same clothes: worn T-shirts and jeans that seemed to be four sizes too big.

When Kinshasa selected her for a makeover session, Consuelo reluctantly accepted. Kinshasa felt challenged by Consuelo's fear and made a special effort to make her look beautiful. Disappearing into the rest room with Consuelo, Kinshasa promised us that we were in for a surprise. An hour later the door slowly opened, and Consuelo stepped out. The look of isolation and pain had left her face and body. Consuelo had a newfound feeling of self-worth and presence. We later learned that, as a result of the parent support network, she had had the courage to leave an abusive lover.

Moments of magical transformation like this seemed to happen daily. My involvement with parents who were struggling to pay their rent and untangle the maze of bureaucracy to get health care for their children and food on the table all convinced me of the importance of community. But as my commitment to community activism grew, I felt a growing uneasiness about my private life.

Tom was increasingly unhappy with my community work. He felt that it was becoming more important than my own family. He did not intervene, and even lent casual support, but he was distant and annoyed that his son was being cared for in a public nursery center. His growing involvement with the private school sector began to draw him away from what I felt were important concerns for our community. When I went to meetings, he would stay at home caring for Sergio, always remaining distant from my activism.

Responding to his growing annoyance that Sergio was in a public nursery, I asked my sister to baby-sit our son. Socorro had recently quit her job as a receptionist in a hospital to care for her twin daughters, who were entering puberty. Working in the

hospital had changed my sister. She lost weight, dyed her hair blond, and enjoyed experimenting with makeup. Her personality was also transformed. She was more charming, developed a new group of friends, and willingly volunteered to assume the motherly role left vacant by our mother's death. Sunday dinners were now in her home.

Often, Sunday dinners included the doctors and nurses she had met while working in the hospital. I noticed that our family gatherings had become an excuse for her to socialize. With a new circle of friends, she was constantly outside the house and would take Sergio with her. They often appeared late in the afternoon. She would giddily describe the wonderful day they had had visiting her former job or friends.

I soon noticed that small items were missing from my home. First I couldn't find a gold ring; then a jade bracelet and coral earrings were among the things that disappeared. I was rather disorganized, and at first I thought I had misplaced these items or left the jewelry at school. Then my graduation ring disappeared. Next my watch was missing, and then the gold brooch Tom had recently given me for our fifth anniversary. The liquor cabinet always had bottles missing or bottles that were almost empty, but Tom and I did not drink very much. It could only have been my sister, because she was the only other person with a set of keys to our apartment. Summoning my nerve, I approached my older sister with uneasiness. When I confronted Socorro, she explained that her friends had visited and she had offered them a few drinks. I believed her. But in reality I was afraid to find out what was really going on, and so I ignored her growing lies and inconsistencies.

One day my sister-in-law Laura and I arrived at the house at the same time. When we entered the apartment to greet my sister and Sergio, Socorro was lying unconscious on my sofa, and my son was sitting in his high chair, covered with vomit, crying. At first we thought she was dead. She was lying motionless on the sofa, and her skin was a shade of pale yellow. I ran to pick up my son and realized that he had been sitting in the high chair for a long time. Laura ran to help my sister and shook her. The living room reeked of liquor. Empty liquor bottles were spilled on the floor alongside bright orange plastic prescription pill bottles.

In shock, Laura and I looked at each other and began crying and shaking from fear. Laura placed a cold compress on my sister's forehead. Slowly, Socorro came to, complaining that she had an upset stomach. She was barely able to sit up. It was painfully obvious to Laura and me that she had more than a drinking problem. My thoughts suddenly jumped to the missing jewelry. How blind could I have been? After my mother's death and the purchase of our new home, I looked to Socorro as a substitute mother. My sister, a stabilizing force in our family, was out of control.

Elusive and probably afraid of the truth, Socorro refused to address the incident with Laura and me. After the incident, our relationship deteriorated. In total denial, my sister accused us of lying when we tried to discuss the problem with her husband. In turn, he accused us of jealousy and of destroying his wife's reputation, refusing to believe that my sister had a serious problem.

Our family imploded. We all lost our heads and let anger and fear control our actions. In a matter of months, our family was destroyed. My sister disappeared and abandoned her family for three months. When she resurfaced, she insisted that she would not return to the house if we were still there. In 1969, we dissolved our three-way partnership in the house.

Overwhelmed by our family problems and the task of finding a new home, Tom and I continued to ignore the fact that we were growing apart. We loved the idea of family, and neither of us had the courage to face the unhappiness in our relationship. The crisis created by my sister caused us to rally together and work toward finding a house with enough apartments to accommodate my brother's family and my father. We tried hard to repair and heal our relationship, but we didn't know how. There was something missing, yet we couldn't figure out what it was.

About the same time, I answered an ad in the employment section of *The New York Times* for a director for a school project

called El Museo del Barrio—Museum of the Community—that was located in East Harlem. The state education project dedicated to children learning about Puerto Rican history and culture sought a director. The position was tailor-made for me, and I applied. Parents and school officials were impressed by the fact that I had been born, raised, and had gone to school in El Barrio.

A week later the superintendent of District 4 called and confirmed that I had been hired. When I received the notice, I went into my room and cried. Tears kept flowing for hours. I was returning to El Barrio, my home, yet my joy was tarnished. I had lost part of my family.

The words written by my mother suddenly filled my thoughts: "Don't cry or mourn because I will always be with you." I longed to feel the touch of my mother and the caress of my *abuela*. If they were alive, everything would be fixed. We had worked so hard to escape the tragedies of miseducation, poor housing, and substance abuse that had destroyed too many families in El Barrio. I wondered what we had done wrong.

In the excitement of being interviewed for El Museo, it never occurred to me to ask to see the location of the program. I simply assumed there was a building somewhere in East Harlem that housed the emerging museum. When I reported to the superintendent's office on my first day, I was instructed to go to a school on East 123rd Street and review the material that was stored there in a classroom. It was then I realized that El Museo existed only in the dreams of the parents and school administrators and was not yet an actual institution.

I angrily emptied the material from the cardboard boxes and vowed to hand in my resignation to the superintendent at the end of the day. Then I opened a box filled with incredibly sensitive black-and-white photographs that showed the love the photographer, Hiram Maristany, had for the people and streets of El Barrio. An elderly woman's piercing eyes caught my attention. Standing before a street altar on 110th Street, she looked straight into my eyes as if she knew me. Her worn wrinkled face and hands spoke of long years of hard work. Strands of white hair peeked out from the scarf that covered her head. The white shades of her dress created an enchanting quality. Part of the altar included a table covered with a white satin cloth that fell softly to the sidewalk; the top of the altar was covered with flowers. The photograph seemed to create a feeling of illuminating whiteness. The altar on display for the world to see was her declaration that the divinities had granted her personal request. Below the woman, a strip of street was visible along the full length of the photograph, as if to say the road from El Barrio goes both ways. You can leave or return. It is your choice. I chose to return.

The four years I directed El Museo were a turning point in my life. I committed myself to making the vision of the parents of El Barrio a reality. In retrospect, I realize that my dedication grew from my devotion to my son Sergio. When he grew up, I wanted him to have a cultural organization that reflected the greatness of his heritage. I wanted him to be able to see himself in the photographs and paintings of Puerto Rican artists and to learn the history of his people. More than anything, I wanted him to understand that his parents struggled to build an educational institution that created a safe place in which he could learn and grow. Like all parents who have been on the receiving end of racial slurs, my desire was to protect my son from the debilitating wrath of racism.

The national cry for racial and cultural empowerment was the seedling from which El Museo grew. I delved into the study of Puerto Rican culture. With the dedicated assistance of my sister-in-law Laura, community parents, and many community artists, the institution flowered.

Tom contributed drawings for exhibitions and for the children's coloring books. My niece Melody and nephew Chino helped with mailings of flyers announcing programs. El Museo was like a magnet attracting marvelous people who created moments of magic. One of the exhibitions I will always remember was El Arte de la Aguja, The Art of Needlework. Parents within

the community contributed elaborate creations of crocheted doilies dipped in a sugar mixture that transformed their art pieces into airy, weblike, sculptural masterpieces.

The proud parents and their families came out in their Sunday best for the opening. Women guided their families through the exhibition, carefully explaining the history of Puerto Rico and the importance of their cultural work in maintaining our heritage. Our message was clear: The creations of our community and the homes of our people were living museums. El Museo was a mirror that reflected the beauty of our people. From a school program locked in cardboard boxes in a closet, we had developed a vibrant independent cultural institution.

I realized I was again pregnant in 1973 when my favorite blue jeans wouldn't fasten. With the demanding struggle to obtain much-needed funds for El Museo, it was impossible for me to take time off from work. The solution was simple. I worked the full nine months. Tom was furious. Not one to lose his temper, he smoldered quietly, trying to make me see how my health and commitment to our unborn child should come first. I argued that the work of El Museo would be a source of pride for our children that had been missing in our own youth.

Omar was born on August 14, 1973. Like his brother, Omar was underweight. At birth, Sergio had weighed in at five pounds and four ounces, and Omar at five pounds and eight ounces. Although they were both healthy, I felt that it was due to my negligence that they were born so small. Nevertheless, my zealousness in creating El Museo had me back to work in two months. Omar went to work with me and slept in a crib next to my desk. With the staff's help, I was able to care for him in between meetings.

A year later, Tom and I realized that our relationship was no longer working. We tried to reinvigorate our marriage by making a list of what we thought were our problems. Tom attended more meetings with me. In turn, I went with him to parties held by his friends from his job and accompanied him on camping trips. I decided to cut down on meetings outside the house. Our efforts could not save our marriage, and we decided to end it. We had

been on different paths for too long, and neither of us could turn back. But we were still very close and would remain friends forever. I had custody of our sons, and they would visit Tom on alternating weekends and during the summers. Tom tried to stay more involved, but, as in many divorces, he started another family and grew distant.

My sons were unofficial staff of El Museo. They grew up in the organization. Visitors were shocked to see Omar's crib next to my desk, but there it stayed until he outgrew it. Sergio went to the East Harlem Block Pre-School and came to El Museo after his day ended there. They traveled with me and stayed late into the night when we had an exhibition deadline.

One of the exhibitions I created for El Museo, La Esclavitud, Enslavement, reinforced my desire to better understand my African heritage. My African American friends could not understand how I could be both black and Puerto Rican. As I was growing up, my speech patterns would change when I was in the company of African Americans and then switch back to my accented Span-English when in a crowd of Puerto Ricans. The question of how to place myself in the diverse group of friends provoked unsettling and often hurtful situations.

I remember visiting a high school friend's home in West Harlem. Donna's family were African Americans from the South and had come north ten years before. A group of us were gathered in her living room because we were going to the museum to complete a class assignment. While waiting for Donna, I overheard her mother say, "Why do you include that Puerto Rican girl in the group? Don't you know spics got head lice? If you come home with head lice, I'm going to beat you upside your head." Somehow, I didn't really fit in. When I was a child, my parents had lovingly called me *negrita*, little black one, when I was growing up. I knew I was black, but I also knew I was Puerto Rican.

Curating La Esclavitud required my traveling to two black towns in Puerto Rico—Loíza Aldea and Bélgica—to gather information. Researching the archives in San Juan, I saw the grotesque iron chains and masks-of-torture used on slaves. Every

bone in my body shook from anger and sorrow. When I saw the drawings and photographs of ex-slaves, it was too much for my heart to handle. In those pictures were the faces of my *abuela*, uncles, aunts, and friends. The pictures were like a family album. They reminded me that slavery had occurred not only in the United States but in Puerto Rico as well. It was one thing to read about the dispersal of slaves in books. It was another to see the faces and hear the stories of those whose families had lived through it.

In Bélgica, I met a family of black elders. Most of them were in their late eighties and nineties when I visited in 1973, which meant that some members of their family had been born into slavery. There was a humble elegance to these soft-spoken women in their white scarves and muslin dresses that sparkled against their burnished black skin. I noticed the stoic dignity of the men, with their immaculately white starched shirts standing out against their taut, polished ebony faces. When we explained the purpose of our visit, their expressions turned joyous, welcoming the opportunity to share the untold stories of their families' oppression and struggles.

One of the most harrowing stories they told me detailed how the plantation owners punished pregnant women. They dug holes in the ground so that the stomachs were protected when the women were beaten. Doña Elsa, an old woman in her late eighties, remembered touching the lash marks on her mother's back. Constantly nodding her head ever so slightly, she swayed on the old wooden rocking chair on the front porch of her house. She explained that in this way the fetus, property of the plantation owner, would be protected.

They talked about how the plantation owners would have them work from dawn to dusk with little food and rest. Observing their quiet dignity as they shared their stories made me realize that my family must have endured the same hardships, yet they chose not to share their stories. I realized that the experiences of their families were also those of mine.

After our conversation, they decided to pull out their large wooden-barrel drums and maracas, and they played *bombas* and *plenas* for the community to enjoy. All the members of the family gathered alongside a large ceiba tree and joined in.* The oldest female member of the family was guided to the center of an imaginary circle. She gathered the lace hem of her skirt in her hands and spread it out like a half-moon. Saluting the drums with a slight bow, she slowly began moving her feet to and fro, lifting the dust off the dirt road. Her gray eyes sparkled as she danced in a circle, delicately moving her skirt up to display the edge of her decorative underskirt. Then she was joined by the other members of her family.

As my interest in understanding the African traditions of Puerto Rico grew, so did my desire to learn more about African cultures in the Americas. I decided to leave El Museo in 1974 when the idea for the Caribbean Cultural Center began to form in my mind. I applied for and was granted a Senior Rockefeller Fellowship, a six-month research grant through the Metropolitan Museum in New York. The award allowed me to travel to the Caribbean and continue my research on the Native and African cultures of the islands. The funds covered my trips to Jamaica, Trinidad and Tobago, Puerto Rico, Dominican Republic, and Haiti. The work I did for my La Esclavitud installation at El Museo was the beginning of my research into the Diaspora cultures of African descendants in the Americas.

During my fellowship, I had been invited to be part of the Caribbean Exchange Program of the Phelps Stokes Fund in New York, a program that was establishing a network of professionals in the Caribbean and the United States. My first step in developing the center was to approach the Phelps Stokes Fund, then headed by the African American ambassador Franklin H. Williams. Since he was a distinguished civil rights lawyer and former ambassador to Ghana, I believed he would understand

---

*I later learned that the ceiba tree is sacred to *orisha* worship.

the concept of uniting the cultures of the African Diaspora. As it turned out, he more than understood. Ambassador Williams immediately offered free office space in the Phelps Stokes Fund, an elegant mansion at 10 East 87th Street, for me to develop the center.

I incorporated the center in 1976, and Ambassador Williams accepted the position of chairperson of the board of directors; I became executive director. He was so impressed by the center's growth that, after three years, the Phelps Stokes Fund arranged a loan enabling the center to purchase a building, which is still the organization's location, at 408 West 58th Street in Manhattan. Although the center had no actual funds for operations, the opportunity to function from a central upscale location opened doors to foundation support.

The mission of the center grew from the recognition that there was only limited information on the Native and African cultures of the Caribbean and Latin American countries. Soon teachers, scholars, and artists were knocking on our doors, seeking to participate in the vision that would become the Caribbean Cultural Center African Diaspora Institute.

A Message from My Elders

Obatalá, the divine artist, teaches us to be creative in seeking solutions. Too often we become creatures of habit and are afraid to explore new ways of approaching situations. The legend of Obatalá teaches us to be persistent and inventive in achieving our goals.

Fostering creative energy begins with changing small things in our lives. In a recent divination session with my godfather, I learned that the symbols of the *oguele*, the divining chain, indicated that I should move. Startled, I was alarmed by the message. Gently he explained, "You

can move within your own home. Revitalize the energy in your home by moving furniture into new arrangements. Change the color scheme in your home. Introduce new colors into your life. Take another route to the train station. Approach situations in new ways." He added in his impish way, "Create change your way. Do not wait for change to befall you with your inaction. Understand the fundamental message is to reinvent yourself. Figure out different ways of surmounting the difficulties presented. Create a space that feels comfortable and allow energy to freely flow."

It made sense to me. I had been in a rut and feeling depleted. I felt a need for change and was waiting for something to happen to create it. The message shared by Obatalá's legend was that we create change. Even when obstacles are placed in our path, we can succeed in our goals with composure and a logical approach.

Just as Obatalá learned to control his temper to obtain his goals, we must use our creative thoughts to reach our goals. We must learn to take calculated risks into the unknown, seeking new knowledge without letting fear paralyze us or keep us from seeking new places and new spaces for ourselves.

Chapter Four

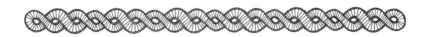

ELLEGUA

THE OBVIOUS IS NOT ALWAYS
THE CORRECT ANSWER

Ellegua is the *orisha* who opens and closes roads. He is a wise, youthful divinity, the messenger of Olodumare. According to the elders in Cuba, all ceremonies begin and end with a tribute to Ellegua to ensure that his blessings allow the ceremony to be a success. His childlike antics are a means of teaching practitioners profound lessons.

One day, the *orishas* were informed that Olodumare was very ill. He was too weak even to get out of bed. Each day his illness worsened. All of the *orishas* united their powers searching for a remedy for Olodumare. Yemayá brought medicine from the depths of the ocean for Olodumare. Her remedy did not help him. Ochosi went to the forest and brought back to Olodumare the meat of healthy animals to build up his strength. This did not heal him. Each *orisha* made a special medicine to heal Olodumare. None of them cured him. When Ellegua heard about Olodumare's illness, he begged his mother, Yemayá, to take him to see his father. He told his mother that he could prepare the medicine that would cure him. Yemayá explained to Ellegua that the more powerful *orishas* were unable to find the potion to cure Olodumare.

Ellegua begged to be taken to Olodumare. Finally, Yemayá consented as Olodumare's condition continued to worsen. Ellegua went deep into the forest and gathered herbs that he then prepared into a medicinal potion. Olodumare drank Ellegua's herbal beverage. As the liquid traveled through Olodumare's body, he began to heal. When he finished the potion, Olodumare was completely cured. In gratitude for Ellegua's medicine, Olodumare informed the elder *orishas* that from that day forward the first offering at all rituals was to be given to Ellegua. But even more, Olodumare gave Ellegua the key that would open all the roads of life.

"My child, drink some ice water to refresh you," Doña Rosa said, placing a glass in my hands. "It will make you feel better." The

adoring elder priestess of Yemayá had tender, smiling eyes that touched me with their warmth. The kitchen, a beehive of activity, was filled with the excitement of the many chattering voices of women preparing food.

Teasing me, Doña Rosa asked, "How could you fall asleep with all this noise?" Still in a dreamlike state, I responded that the heat in the room was making me drowsy. The slight breeze from the makeshift cardboard fan was of little relief. Nevertheless, I kept fanning myself. The dizzying cadence of the overlapping conversations kept me from joining in. It was enjoyable just listening to Cuban-inflected Spanish.

Dabbing my forehead with a wet towel, Doña Rosa advised me to relax, because the ceremony was delayed. "Pachuco went to pick up more large bowls for the *omiero* [a sacred herbal mixture prepared for rituals]. He will return quickly," she assured me.

I smiled, knowing that every errand in Cuba takes a long time to complete. The slow-moving cars, the obligatory pleasantries exchanged when people meet, always take longer than expected, and locating scarce objects that are in constant circulation causes long delays. At first, I had been annoyed by the long gaps of time between beginning and completing rituals in Cuba. But after eighteen years, I have grown accustomed to the fact that this is part of the process that maintains the internal network of initiates. Connecting and involving family and friends is an important part of gathering the many items needed for ceremonies. Talking and sharing information is an essential part of events in the Santería community.

Listening to the conversations, I learned that a *santera* named Iris had better roosters than Pablito and sold them at better prices. The plants used for preparing *omiero* had just come into the farmers' market in Cuatro Caminos Plaza, Four Roads Plaza. The wife of Justo, the *babalawo*, had run away with her lover and left her four children. And a fresh red palm oil used in ceremonies of Ellegua was being sold by Belen, who lived down the street. The casual chatter functioned like a daily newspaper, keeping everyone informed of current events. The joy being shared by the *santeras* and *santeros* reminded me of my child-hood, and I could not help but remember the love our family shared in our apartment in El Barrio.

My mother, a headstrong, large-boned, and imposing woman, appeared to be powerful, healthy, and self-assured. Our home re-volved around her. She prepared our favorite *sancocho* soup and kept the house meticulously clean, picked us up from school, checked our homework, disciplined us, and arranged our recre-ational trips to Pelham Bay Beach, Central Park, and Coney Island during the summer months.

Most important, she performed magic with the family's lim-ited budget. My father would turn over his paycheck to her on Fridays, and she took care of paying the bills and making his earnings stretch from week to week. When there was money missing, my mother would bravely and defiantly confront my fa-ther, asking for an accounting of the missing cash.

If he had been drinking, he would storm out of the house saying, "*Soy un hombre,* I'm a man. I don't have to account to a woman for my actions." Sober, my father would apologize, ex-plaining that he had stopped to play a few games of dominoes with friends and had a couple of beers. "Hmm," my mother would groan, sucking on her teeth and creating that unique slurping sound particular to women of the Caribbean. "We don't have enough money to pay the bills, and you're drinking beer."

My mother never went out without my father or us. She ex-changed visits with friends in the building, her children in tow, making sure that we used the bathroom and ate before we vis-ited. We understood that if we were offered food, we were to refuse, since most of our family's friends, like us, had little to spare. Wading through the dizzying aroma of rice and chicken, roasted pig, Hormel's spam with eggs and fried Vienna saugages,

we would sit quietly in the apartments of our friends, our hands crossed in our laps, making believe we were not listening to the grown-ups' conversations.

When friends visited, we went through the same ritual. Following traditional Puerto Rican customs of politeness, we were compelled to offer food even though there was barely enough for our own family. In turn, our friends adhered to the informal niceties and would dutifully decline the offer of food, saying, "We just finished eating."

The exception was when a pregnant woman passed by our door and asked for food because the aroma impelled her to do so. So as not to harm the developing baby, popular folklore demanded that, whether or not we knew the woman, she be invited to eat with us. A pregnant woman was a sign of good luck for the family, and my mother was always generous in abiding by this tradition.

When the Christmas holidays came, all of the families threw their penny-pinching budgets to the wind and splurged on goodies and toys, and everyone knew that they would suffer the consequences for their minor reckless splurges for the rest of the year. In 1949, few Puerto Ricans in East Harlem were able to find jobs that would provide adequate salaries to support their families. Our family, like others in the building, decorated with more ornate plastic curtains, crocheted doilies for the furniture, and small crystal-like figures of colorful animals for display on the living room television console, already cluttered with other figurines. Families hosted generous dinners of roast pig; rice with chicken; beans; *pasteles,* boiled plantains and seasoned meats wrapped in banana leaves; blood sauage; and *coquito,* a powerful coconut and egg drink made with 150-proof rum—our special brand of eggnog.

During Christmastime, my mother became the unofficial social coordinator of the building, scheduling gatherings to include all of the tenants. Our door was always open, welcoming the revelry of well-wishers singing Puerto Rican *aguinaldos,* Christmas songs, with their tambourines, maracas, and *güiros,* long calabashes played by rasping a wirelike comb against their surface. The building was alive; it was a Christmas tree of lights, silver trimmings, and bountiful wishes for a prosperous New Year.

Throughout the year, my mother would use her nursing skills to cure the sick. Her knowledge of bureaucracy helped tenants get welfare aid and find apartments in the area. When she needed assistance, we were volunteered to accompany newly arrived relatives and friends from Puerto Rico to the welfare office or other social service community agencies to serve as English translators.

My father would often remark that the city should pay her for her services since she was more involved in the community than in her own home. Jealous of anything that deflected attention from him, my father would complain unjustifiably that his dinner was cold and his clothing poorly ironed, or that he could not find whatever he was looking for. Feigning helplessness, my father controlled much of my mother's life.

My father may have been the power behind the throne, but my mother was a benign ruler. Nothing would happen in our home or building without her knowledge and acceptance, yet everyone seemed to admire her intelligence and her get-the-job-done, self-confident attitude. When I was little, I loved the look and feel of my mother. Mammy's black hair had a shocking streak of white that was unusually attractive, her clothing fit beautifully on her well-built body, and her strong, erect shoulders gave her a stately elegance. When we went shopping without my father, men would spontaneously say, "What a beautiful woman—*Qué mujer linda*," as she left a trail of her special perfume, Maderas de Oriente, floating in the air.

As a child, I loved to snuggle in my mother's arms as she swayed back and forth in her rocker. Sometimes when she sat in the dark, I would hear the motion of the rocking chair and crawl into her lap to drink my evening milk in a Coca-Cola glass bottle covered with a nipple that had a hole the size of a dime. As she rocked, I would feel her rubbing the left side of her chest while she softly sang a Spanish lullaby, caressing me to sleep. "*A dormir,*

a dormir, pichón del monte. A dormir, a dormir, pichón del monte. Si tú no duermes, el cuco te lleva." "Sleep, sleep, my little pigeon from the mountain. Sleep, sleep, my little pigeon from the mountain. If you do not sleep, the boogeyman will take you." In the morning, I would wake up feeling like a grown woman, with the scent of Maderas de Oriente still clinging to me.

On Saturday mornings, our building swayed to the varied rhythms of Puerto Rican music as the women opened their doors early in the morning and washed the hallway. My mother's cleaning music was the beautiful, haunting, lamenting *jíbaro* mountain songs of Ramito, which spoke of lost love, the beauty of Puerto Rico, and the need for Puerto Ricans to protect the island from American cultural and governmental control.

From other apartments, the music of Cortijo and Ismael Rivera flooded the halls with the vibrant rhythms of drums and the fast beat of the African-derived rhythms of *bombas* and *plenas*. The power of Cortijo's *bombas* placed me into another zone when the beat of his drums penetrated my body. This was island music that celebrated the beauty of being black Puerto Ricans, while the music of Machito, Graciela, and Mario Bauza swirled through the building with the song "Tanga," which united African American jazz with Afro-Cuban pulsating rhythms.

From the homes of our African American friends, "Rock Around the Clock" by the outrageous, swinging Little Richard made the halls dance, while the bittersweet pain of Billie Holiday singing "Strange Fruit," one of my favorite songs, cut through the piercing, pungent smells of ammonia, pine, and Florida water, and the sharp-as-a-guillotine scent of *rompe saragüey*, a plant used to spiritually cleanse an apartment. Nat King Cole's "Mona Lisa" intoxicated the environment with his soothing, mellow, romantic voice, and the deep, thunderous voice of vocalist Mario Lanza, singing "Be My Love," joined in from the apartments of our Italian neighbors. In our room, my sister and I would fight for our favorite radio station, switching from Tito Puente's "Hot Timbales" to my idols, Frankie Lymon and the Teenagers, singing "I Want You to Be My Girl."

From Abuela's apartment the voice of Cuba's Celina y Reutilio swelled and rumbled with the thunderous song, "Que Viva Shangó," May Shangó Live. Or I would hear the incredible voice of the Latina Patti LaBelle, Afro-Cuban vocalist Celia Cruz, singing with the orchestra of La Sonora Mantancera in the "Homenaje a Yemayá," Homage to Yemayá.

On Saturdays, when I visited Abuela's apartment, she would put away her mop and we would sing and dance to the songs of her albums, especially moved by the upbeat songs to the *orishas*. Often Abuela was so lost in the music that she forgot I was there. Her steps and hand movements changed with each song, creating visual motions of the sea, thunder, and lightning, as she moved around the kitchen like a graceful whirlwind.

Filled with the energy of the music, she would pull me into her imaginary circle, encouraging me to follow her movements. These moments of shared joy created a powerful wordless bond between us. We lived in the moment, feeling no need to speak with each other or anyone else of our delight in singing and dancing. I must admit, I used my visits to Abuela's apartment as an excuse to escape my Saturday chores, but I also looked forward to our private celebrations and the feeling of ecstasy we created with the music.

Years later, in 1981, when I found my true spiritual home in Santería, I began to recognize the mind-altering power of music in African-based religions in the New World. During ceremonies, the thunderous, rhythmic pounding of the sacred *batá* drums of the *orisha* Shangó—the double-headed hourglass-shaped drums that came from the Yoruba of West Africa—draws practitioners into the spirit world. The drums' piercing beats echo the rhythmic patterns of the heart as voices chant and escalate, causing the steps of the dancers to quicken. In this way, the powerful *orishas* are enticed to come down to Earth and take over the consciousness of the initiates.

I now understand that in traditional African belief all things are grounded in the spiritual flow of nature's patterns. Breath, movement, sight, and sound—music and song—are all deeply

entwined and are part of the daily living and sacred experience that make our spirits rise. Santería has taught me to tap into my spirituality each day, reminding me that we live in a state of holiness. Our music traces its origins to West Africa and carries sacred meaning and soul-spirit. It is a conduit that calls down and internalizes spiritual energy for divine celebration, healing, and communication with the metaphysical world.

When I was young, my mother's songs also lulled me into a dream state. She would entice me to sleep with the promise that she would dab a drop or two of her perfume on my neck. It was exciting to feel the fragrance embrace me; there was something magical in the beautiful apple-shaped bottle, adorned with a picture of a dark, olive-skinned Spanish woman with mysterious black eyes peering sensually over a yellow veil. I imagined my mother also possessed the beguiling qualities of this mysterious woman on the perfume bottle.

Since my mother had such intense spirit and warmth, it came as a terrible shock when she suddenly became ill. My life was turned upside down, and I did not understand why. I was eight years old when she suffered an almost fatal heart attack and was bedridden for six months. My father was desperate to cure her, trying every remedy he had heard of. I remember standing behind a closed door in the living room, listening to the healing prayers and songs that we all hoped would save her life. Even now, when I think of those days, I can still vividly recall the scent of Florida water that filtered through the closed door as I tried to peek into the kitchen where a group of people dressed in white were gathered. My father came to the door, admonished me not to go where I was not needed, and then shooed me away.

Without any explanation, my siblings and I were kept alone in the living room, wondering what could make our mother so sick that she was unable to get out of bed alone. My older brother and sister were as frightened as I was.

We knew it was dire when family friends came to visit and left my mother's bedroom in tears. At the sight of us, they attempted to mask their sorrow with smiles, assuring us that our mother would soon get well. But they avoided looking into our eyes, which told us they were lying. The doctor visited almost daily, always speaking to my father in a low, reserved voice to make certain we could not hear their conversation. When we asked what was wrong with our mother, the response was always, *"está descansando"*—she is resting.

When we were finally allowed to sit with our mother, we could see that she was seriously ill. She could barely speak, and it took time for her to recognize us. Her skin had turned the color of ash, and she had gotten very thin. Her strength and power had all but vanished. Looking into my mother's spiritless, skeletal face, I found a fear I had never before known. I felt she was dying, and I knew I could do nothing to save her. My brother, sister, and I grieved among ourselves, not knowing what to do to help her.

My mother lay ill in the bedroom. As we sat outside the kitchen and in the living room, we could hear the songs sung to the spirits and we could smell the wafting scents that called to them. I was transfixed by the beauty of the voices that I heard singing the enchanting songs that called upon the healing spirits.

Congo de Guinea soy.	I am a Congo from Africa.
Buenas noches, criollo,	Good evening, creoles,
Congo de Guinea soy.	I am a Congo from Africa.
Buenas noches, criollo,	Good evening, creoles,
Yo dejo mi hueso allá.	I left my bones there.
Yo vengo a	I have come to perform a
hacer caridad.	good deed.
Yo dejo mi hueso allá.	I left my bones there.
Yo vengo a	I have come to perform a
hacer caridad.	good deed.

Si la luz redentora te	If the redeeming light calls
llama, buen ser,	you, good spirit,
Y te llama con amor	And it calls you with love

a la tierra.	to Earth.
Yo quisiera ver a ese ser,	I want to see that spirit,
Cantándole gloria al	Singing gloriously to the
Divino Manuel.	divine saint Manuel.
Oye, buen ser.	Listen, good spirit.
Avanza y ven,	Hurry and come,
Que el coro te llama	The chorus is calling you
Y te dice, ven.	Asking you to come.

As I listened, I was lulled to sleep. Suddenly I was awakened by an explosive, bellowing woman's voice breaking through the prayers.

"Good evening, if it is evening. Good morning, if it is morning. Why did you call me to Earth?" she asked.

"Welcome, good spirit," the members of the group said in unison, and, gradually, sleep overtook me once again.

Three days after that evening spiritual session, my mother was up and about. There was little trace of her illness. Although she had lost a great deal of weight, her skin color was almost normal. Her hair, now with more silvery strands, shimmered, creating a crowning illumination around her gaunt, glowing face. Somehow she seemed taller, even more elegantly attractive. And she continued to project the same comforting, tranquil quality until her death in 1964.

Each time we asked about the meeting in our kitchen, our parents ignored our questions. They would say that friends had come to visit, and as children we had no business being in the middle of adult discussions. My brother, sister, and I continued to wonder about what had occurred in our kitchen to make our mother well. Eventually, though, like most children, we forgot that our mother had been so ill.

Meanwhile, my mother took great pride in having baffled the doctor, who had no explanation for her recovery. She continued to have her heart condition checked periodically, taking prescription medicines when she felt "sickness coming on." Over time, my mother's illness became a story she would tell to friends almost like a fairy tale. And she always ended with the phrase, "We must believe in the power of the spirits."

I witnessed the power of spirits again in 1957 when I was fifteen years old. My lively niece, Melody, became very ill around the time of her first birthday. After several examinations in the hospital, the doctors still could not diagnose what was wrong. As each day passed, Melody became weaker. Her chubby body became fragile. Her features were transformed. Her caramel-colored skin became pale gray. Melody's small, almond-shaped eyes were now enormous and round; she stared blankly before her without even recognizing her parents.

Although we did not openly share our fears, we knew she was dying. I could not help but compare Melody's appearance to the way my mother had looked when she was sick. Overwhelming feelings of isolation engulfed me as the panic of trying to verbalize my fears seemed to strangle me.

I later learned that my mother and sister-in-law secretly took Melody to an *espiritista.* In three days, Melody was miraculously cured. According to my mother, the *espiritista* cleansed Melody with cigar smoke and prayers. And while under the possession of her guardian spirit, the *espiritista* placed her sacred hands on my niece's body and healed her. When my mother told me the story, I was frightened, although I did not know why. Nonetheless, this experience made it clear to me that there was some obscure force that had the power to heal my loved ones.

Lurking in the recesses of my mind was always the secret desire to understand these inexplicable events. But the secrecy throughout my childhood that surrounded spirit worship had left me hesitant about probing into the unknown. Twenty-one years were to pass before I was ready to understand the presence and power of the spirits and *orishas.*

It happened in 1979 during my first trip to Cuba. I had been invited to attend the Carifesta Festival, a gala event highlighting cultural and artistic expressions of the Caribbean. During this period, I was able to learn and participate in activities that would help me to further define my racial and cultural identity. I

had experienced the blossoming of the civil rights movement and the Black Power and Latino movements of the fifties, sixties, and seventies. These ethnic actions not only revolutionized my thinking and behavior but also motivated my creation of programs for the center. Carifesta was a golden opportunity for me to attend a weeklong series of events that presented the most outstanding creative artists and scholars on African Diaspora cultures. And it allowed me to visit Cuba, an island that had been isolated and inaccessible because of its socialist government.

The main purpose of my visit was to note details of the festival's organization with the expectation of developing a similar event in New York for the Caribbean Cultural Center. Carifesta had an array of performances, art exhibits, and conferences—it was an explosion of color, music, song, and dance. Members of musical groups from Haiti, Jamaica, Barbados, and other islands, in their costumes of blazing color, resembled proud peacocks.

Visual artists painted images of the powerful African gods of Vodun, Santería, and Obeah, depicting images and symbols of the divinities that had survived the Middle Passage. The sacred iconographic paintings of the *vévés*—symbols of Haitian African divinities—were placed alongside altars to the *orishas* of Cuba. In these altars the double-headed battle-ax of Shangó called down lightning, while the nine hues of Oyá created a whirlwind of colors, expressing the artist's vivid interpretation of sacred images.

A carnival ended the weeklong festival. It was an eruption of floats and vibrant, extravagant costumes with sequins, satins, ruffles, and feathers. Music and song boomed from loudspeakers as dancers moved their undulating bodies to whatever deliriously enticing rhythm caught their fancy. The *comparsas*, the carnival bands, engaged in friendly competitions to see which could attract the largest following of dancers. Carifesta Festival wrapped the crowd in a deafening, overwhelming jubilee. It was a seemingly endless performing arts extravaganza that stretched three full miles.

Fortunately, Javier Colón, who accompanied me to Cuba, had arranged for us to ride on a float of one of the most famous composers and musicians of Cuba, Pello El Afrokan. It was a carousel that rocked with the music he created, Mozambique. I had a front-row view of the wonderful madness of the festival. Finally, I could no longer resist the beat and the frenzy. I stepped out of my shoes, clapped my hands, and danced the night away along the Malecón—an oceanfront walkway—under the midnight blue sky and jewel-like stars of Havana. Pello's orchestra seemed to have the largest following of dancers, dressed in all the colors of the rainbow, singing, shouting, and moving to the rhythms of the music.

My friend and guide Javier was planning to be initiated into the exclusively male priesthood of Ifá, the diviners, within the Santería religion. Javier had worked as a consultant to an exhibition that I curated for the center in 1978, entitled Santería and Vodun African Religions in the Caribbean. He had been raised in a recognized Santería family in Cuba, and was a vital source of information for the community of Santería initiates and scholars.

When we began working together on the exhibit, he was guarded, secretive, and unwilling to reveal too much information about the religion. Though he continued to be reserved about sharing information with me, he gradually began to open up, and eventually he became a significant contributor to the exhibition. Our friendship grew and deepened as he noted my respect for Santería and my desire to learn more about it. When the center received the invitation for representatives to attend the 1979 Carifesta, Javier decided to visit his childhood home for the first time in twenty-five years.

I was still curious to learn more about the practices of Espiritismo and Santería, so I accompanied Javier as he made preparations for his ceremony. I was invited to attend a *misa*, a spiritual session that would inform his guardian angels of his upcoming Ifá initiation ceremony. I found myself sitting in a room filled with spiritualists and initiates of the Santería religion. The apartment belonged to the spiritual medium Olga Serrano; it was located between Animas and Trocadero in Old Havana.

Olga was a long-trusted friend of Javier's family, and he had asked her to arrange the *misa*. Her home was decorated in shades of yellow—the colors of her *orisha*, Ochun. Olga's living room felt as if it were filled with sunlight and bright golden sunflowers.

Surrounded by the familiar scents of Florida water, sandalwood incense, and cigar smoke, I thought of Abuela and of my mother, who always dabbed her forehead with Florida water when she had a headache or felt pain in her chest. It had been twenty years since Abuela had died, and fifteen years since my mother had passed. Looking around the room, I noticed familiar images that also reminded me of my childhood. A portrait of Saint Michael, the archangel, was placed behind the entrance door. She had installed a small shelf. On it she placed a horseshoe alongside a glass of water and a piece of hard bread. On a small table toward the back of the room, Olga had a large statue of El Kongo, similar to the one on my *abuela*'s altar. The smell of tuberoses permeated the room and mixed with the poignant smell of sandalwood incense.

Olga's altar to Ochun was in a small room next to the living room where the *misa* was to begin. The altar, covered in yellow lace cloth, had two peacock-feather fans and a vase filled with sunflowers next to the image of La Caridad del Cobre, the Catholic image that served to hide the Yoruba goddess during enslavement and continues to be identified with the African divinity. Ochun, the *orisha* of sweet water, love, beauty, and fertility, exudes happiness and gaiety surrounded by her favorite color, yellow. High on a stool covered with satin brocade cloth was a covered yellow porcelain bowl that that held the sacred water stones of Ochun. On the floor was a small brass bell resting on a straw mat, which initiates were to ring when they asked Orisha Ochun for her blessings.

After embracing Olga, the initiates took turns gathering in the room, prostrating themselves before the altar and ringing the bell to ask Ochun for her blessings. Then they returned to the main room to greet friends and to introduce themselves to unfamiliar members of the gathering. I was struck by the congeniality

and familial feeling of this bustling group. Dressed in white, proudly wearing their beaded necklaces, old and young seemed strengthened by the ancient wisdom they possessed.

Elder men and women in their late eighties were given special attention, in honor of their long years of initiation and profound knowledge. Their cottony white hair, gray-aged eyes, and tissue-thin black skin made them appear deceptively fragile, while at the same time they seemed to glow with clarity of mind and confidence. These unassuming elders projected an aura of serenity and coolness that was reminiscent of my grandmother and my mother.

Throughout my travels I met with elders much like these in Brazil, Haiti, Trinidad and Tobago, New Orleans, Puerto Rico, Santo Domingo, and in other countries throughout the world. They have developed an inner power and strength that quietly blankets their environment with a special, magical aura of peace. This desired quality acquired over time requires that initiates set aside a period of time to meditate and acknowledge the *orisha* that resides within—the Orí—who repesents our destiny.

With tremendous pride, Javier introduced me to the Iyalorisha Mina, a longtime friend of his deceased mother. She was a thin old woman, bent with age from many years of harsh work. Ma Mina herself had been initiated by a once-enslaved African woman who taught her the ancient secrets of the African *orisha* initiation. Javier explained that she spoke Yoruba and had initiated more than fifty people into the religion.

Wearing a long white dress, her head covered with a kerchief trimmed in nine colors. Ma Mina gently held my hands. She slowly looked up, gazed intently into my eyes, and said, "The spirits of my ancestors have been good to me. Oyá, the *orisha* that claimed me, has guided me since I was ten years old. *Orisha* is love, *orisha* is health and family; do not be afraid to learn about your ancestors, because in knowing them you learn about yourself." Thanking her, I gingerly took my seat, trying to comprehend why she had directed this message to me. I wondered if she knew something I did not.

The *espiritista* Olga began the *misa* with a series of Catholic prayers from *The Collection of Selected Prayers* by Allan Kardec, a nineteenth-century French educator and philosopher well regarded in the spiritualist community. A short, husky woman with curly black hair and cashew smooth skin, Olga exuded cheer and friendship. Olga was a *santera* as well as an *espiritista*. She was initiated into the Santería religion and was a medium who could be possessed by spirits of the ancestors. She explained that Ochun saved her life when complications arose during the birth of her first child. She praised and loved her *orisha*; however, her true gift was as an *espiritista*. When she sat down in front of the group, all chatter quickly ceased. Silence fell over the room as she started the session.

Softly, the twenty-five people present began to pray with Olga and joined in the songs to attract the spirits. The room was soon filled with a thick, gray-blue haze as most participants leisurely smoked their cigars. One by one, participants went before the *bóveda*, scooped up perfumed water and flower petals from the white enamel basin on the floor, and cleansed their auras with this Florida water mixture while the others began reciting prayers. The pleasant murmuring of the prayers lulled me into a pleasant tranquillity. When everyone was seated, the songs started. Then, suddenly, my soul stood on edge as I again heard the songs calling the spirits. It was the same beautiful song that I had heard for the first time during my mother's illness.

Congo de Guinea soy.	I am a Congo from Africa.
Buenas noches, criollo,	Good evening, creoles,
Congo de Guinea soy.	I am a Congo from Africa.
Buenas noches, criollo,	Good evening, creoles,
Yo dejo mi hueso allá.	I left my bones there.
Yo vengo a	I have come to perform a
hacer caridad.	good deed.
Yo dejo mi hueso allá.	I left my bones there.
Yo vengo a	I have come to perform a
hacer caridad.	good deed.

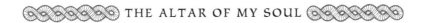

Si la luz redentora te *llama, buen ser.*	If the redeeming light calls you, good spirit.
Y te llama con amor a *la tierra.*	And it calls you with love to Earth.
Yo quisiera ver a ese ser, *Cantándole gloria al* *Divino Manuel.*	I want to see that spirit, Singing gloriously to the divine saint Manuel.
Oye, buen ser.	Listen, good spirit.
Avanza y ven,	Hurry and come,
Que el coro te llama	The chorus is calling you
Y te dice, ven.	Asking you to come.

When I looked up at Olga, she had gone into a trance, swaying gently back and forth on her chair. She tossed her head back, massaged the left side of her chest with her right hand, and started foaming at the mouth. From a low hum, she began to moan loudly.

Suddenly, her short body grew lean and tall. I was shocked. Without a word being spoken, I somehow knew my mother was present in that room. And her spirit began to speak through Olga.

"Marta, I am glad that I am finally able to speak to you. I have waited a long time for this moment. The time has come for you to assume your spiritual responsibility and open your heart to the *orishas*. My beloved family is being destroyed because I refused to follow the calling of the spirits. You must assume your spiritual calling. Open your heart and let the spirits and the *orishas* guide you. Always remember that I am by your side."

A Message from My Elders

When I started my spiritual journey into the teaching of Santería, my elders explained that the first *orishas* to be

received are Ellegua, Ochosi, Osun, and Oggun. Together they are called the warrior *orishas, guerreros.*

Ellegua is generally represented by a black triangular stone with cowry shells for eyes, nose, and mouth. He is placed by the door along with the hunter divinity Ochosi, the god of justice; Oggun, the warrior *orisha* of iron; and the *orisha* Osun, the small staff that represents the sacred head of the initiate. Each of these *orishas* possesses a particular power that helps stabilize the life of the initiate. The symbol of Ochosi is the bow and arrow, which he used to gain justice in the world. For Oggun it is iron; in ancient times in West Africa people swore on iron instead of the Bible. Osun is symbolic of the initiate's head, where the sacred *aché* is placed.

According to my elders, Ellegua is the *orisha* that brings balance into our lives. His stone talisman properly cared for—with red palm oil, candy, and toys, and annointed with rum, tobacco smoke, and candlelight every Monday—he protects the initiate by creating a sense of balance in our environment and in our lives. He uses his divine key to open avenues of opportunity for the initiate. He lives on a crossroads of life symbolized by the meeting of four converging roads.

My elder suggests that we "examine our options, carefully select what we consider the best path, and follow it without fear. Our inner spirit will guide us." Elpidio offers a simple way of actualizing this advice by doing the following: "When you are undecided of what path to follow, try standing in a space that leads in four directions. Think about your choices and decide on one. You can follow only one path."

Chapter Five

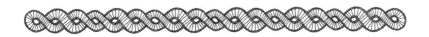

OCHUN

THE GODDESS
OF HONEY

My godmother Zenaida explained that there are many *patakís* in Santería that address the resiliency and power of women to struggle and thrive against all odds. Ochun is one of the powerful female *orishas*. She holds others accountable when they disrespect her. According to Yoruba legend in Africa and the Americas, the *orisha* Ochun lives in sweet water. Gold, copper, fertility, and love are all her domain.

It is said that when the male *orishas* came to Earth, they held a secret meeting. When Ochun heard that they were meeting, she attempted to attend but was turned away. She became so angry that she made all women barren and turned the affairs of the world into chaos. Frightened, the *orishas* turned to Olodumare for help. The world was in disorder, and no one but Olodumare knew why.

Olodumare called the male *orishas* before him and asked if they had invited Ochun to their meeting. When they answered no, Olodumare became enraged and told them to hold another meeting and to invite Ochun. He explained that without women and children, the world could not function. Without Ochun, the world would always be in a state of confusion.

When the *orishas* returned to Earth, they followed Olodumare's orders. However, Ochun was angry and refused to attend the meeting. The *orishas* went to her home with gifts of gold and copper, hoping to change her mind. But it was not until the *orishas* brought her an offering of honey that Ochun finally decided to forgive them. At last, she made women fertile again and brought order back to the world. Ochun teaches us that the world will be in disorder as long as women and children are neglected, disrespected, and abused.

In the comfort of her kitchen, Doña Rosa, in her gentle way, enjoyed passing on information to younger initiates. When she heard the kitchen chatter settle down to a low hum, she said, "My children, we need a little gaiety in the room." She walked to the

cupboard and pulled out a jar of honey. With a coquettish twinkle in her eyes, she placed the jar on her head and started dancing and singing to Ochun, and then said, "Let us remember that when the *orishas* rushed to Earth and failed to invite Ochun to their meeting, the world went into chaos. Ochun reminds us to put care and love into everything we do." Quickly, everyone in the room livened up and joined Doña Rosa in song. A joyfulness embraced them as Doña Rosa ceremoniously lifted the jar from her head and gave each of us women and men a spoonful of honey, saying, "May the spirit of Ochun bless you."

When the spirit of my mother spoke to me in Olga's home, my soul released a sea of tears that had been stored within me for more than twenty years. The room seemed to disappear into the distance, and I was watching Olga and the other participants as if from afar. Mama's spirit remained close and touched me, sending a warm, arching wave that overwhelmed and cleansed my soul. Gradually, my body surfaced—light as a feather, motionless, and numb. My mother and I became one; her thoughts were also mine. I felt the sensation of two worlds, the spiritual and secular, harmoniously joining. I could see, feel, and comprehend more than ever before. A soothing yellow wave of tranquillity covered my body and cradled me in its cresting foam.

My mother's arms reached within me; her hands held the pain of our family's separation and transformed it into a golden amber liquid nestled in her palms. Her body was surrounded by the intense yellow-white glowing light of Ochun. She calmly shared her thoughts, placing messages in my mind as I sat silent and motionless, treasuring her presence inside me.

Mama cautioned me to let go of the anger toward my sister's wrongdoings, which had caused our family to break apart like shattered glass. She said it was more important to concentrate my energy on healing and uniting the healthy pieces of our family, rather than continuously trying to figure out what had gone wrong. It was time to look toward the future.

I asked her how I could look to the future when I knew that my brother's marriage to Laura was ending. Laura was angered by his womanizing and had decided it was time for them to divorce. She had struggled to hold the marriage together for the sake of their children; however, my brother continued to disrespect his family and obligations. Again I felt helpless in not knowing how to protect my family.

My mother admitted that she had pampered us for too long; she claimed she was blinded by her misguided maternal love. In her desire to be surrounded by a loving family like the one she left in Puerto Rico, she was lenient in disciplining my brother, sister, and me. She assuaged her lonely youth in New York with the strong desire to have a family and find happiness in bringing children into the world. Imploringly, she asked, "How could I punish the children who brought me the desire to live?" Then my mother continued her story.

The spirits had claimed her at an early age in Puerto Rico. During a spirtual session in her hometown, Caguas, the *espiritista*, became possessed by my mother's guardian angel, in the form of a Spanish flamenco dancer dressed in yellow. The *espiritista* described the dancer as having an olive complexion with deep jet black hair; with sensual, captivating eyes, she was as sweet as Ochun's honey. The spirit of the dancer laid claim to my mother, saying she would eventually become a medium as a young girl. But my mother had no interest in becoming a medium. When she was a little girl, her father had died of a heart attack while eating dinner with the family. His early death was attributed to his refusal to become a spiritualist. From that day forward, she shunned the spirits; she refused to have anything to do with these elusive beings who she thought had killed her father.

My mother told herself that Espiritismo was the religion of superstitious old people, and she ran away to New York, fleeing her destiny. She left behind her mother, sister, and brother.

Under the pretense of pursuing a career, she enrolled in a training program that was available only in the city.

Now the guardian angels she had tried so hard to keep at bay were causing confusion and destruction in our family. These spirits were at the lowest tier of spiritual enlightment, having not received prayers to elevate them to the upper level of the spiritual realm; they were in a state of bewilderment. My mother felt that, due to her neglect, these disoriented spirits had attached themselves to my brother and sister, causing Alberto's womanizing and Socorro's drug and alcohol abuse. She explained that when our souls are weak, we can be easily overwhelmed by negative thoughts and temptations.

My mother understood that Laura was tired of Alberto's philandering and drinking; she had no choice but to divorce him. My brother had lost all sense of decency. Women were calling the house letting Laura know of their affairs with my brother. My sister's alcohol addiction, coupled with her lying and stealing, finally caused my father, Laura, and me to sever our ties with her. One day Socorro shouted out the window to her twin thirteen-year-old daughters, "Don't you dare look at or speak to your grandfather." After this incident my father broke down crying. It was the first time I had ever seen my father cry.

My father, Laura, my husband, and I decided that the damage done by my siblings' destructive behavior justified our decision to separate them from our lives. We understood that our children would lose contact with immediate members of the family, and because we were close it was very painful to realize that my sons would never get to know their aunt, uncle, and cousins. The family that we thought invincible was actually fragile and finally shattered. With a tremendous load of grief, anger, and guilt, we disassociated ourselves. Several years passed before we heard through friends that my brother had moved to Venezuela in pursuit of a much younger woman he planned to marry, and my sister had died somewhere in Florida—we assumed of an overdose or alcoholism. To this day, we do not know the circumstances of Socorro's death or where her burial site is located.

Before departing, my mother's spirit focused on me and said, "I know you have been hurt and you are trying to protect yourself from further pain; however, you must stop trying to be the judge and jury in all situations. If people or situations don't act according to your ethics, you are too willing to dismiss them from your life. You were the youngest in the family, and your father and I let you have your way. Life is a balance; it is a give and take. Learn to adjust, be flexible. Life is like a tree; learn to sway with the wind. Learn to listen to your head and your soul."

My mother accepted the choices we had made and left instructions as to how we should prepare for the future unification of our family. She explained that, as a family, we had to develop a relationship with the spirit world, and that opportunities for reconnecting the family would eventually occur. She said it was necessary for me to begin my spiritual journey and then others in our family would follow.

Years later my sister's spirit appeared in a *misa* in Cuba, asking for forgiveness. Every day, I pray for the elevation of her spirit and find that now when she appears in the *misas*, her confusion and grief have diminished. As the pain lifts and I continue to heal, the fragments of our family are all gradually coming together. Daily prayer is dissolving the confusion of the spirits in turmoil, and their enlightenment is helping the members of our family find resolution to problems.

My mother understood that, in 1970, we were unprepared to deal with these confused spirits. For reasons of her own, she had not taught us how to defend ourselves from the turmoil released by the perplexed spirits. I felt defenseless when my brother and sister turned against the rest of the family. And the hurt and resentment my father felt caused him to talk incessantly of his children's betrayal. I, too, felt the inexplicable family guilt entangle me, for we had turned our backs on our own flesh and blood.

Sitting in the *misa* in 1979, nine years after the dissolution of my family, I was exchanging spiritual thoughts with my mother. Our conversation opened an inner door. I possessed tremendous love for my mother, and I realized that she had been trapped

93

in the traditions of her time. She struggled to build a loving family in spite of my father's domination and physical abuse; she tried to carve a safe space for her children to succeed within the boundaries she understood. But her sense of tradition presented certain contradictions about the roles of men versus those of women.

My brother was taught that, as a man, he would be the bread-winner and supporter of his family. This gave him power. It gave him the sense that he had the right to philander outside the home as long as he met the responsibility of financially support-ing his family. The fact that Laura helped finance his education as an X-ray technician and worked outside the home as hard as he did mattered little. He carried the assumption that a "real man" did not need to answer to his wife or family, as long as he brought home the paycheck. My sister was trained to be a house-wife. Although she started college, she did not receive the same moral or financial support given my brother. My parents' atti-tude was that my sister and I would quit school as soon as we de-cided to marry. School was just a way of occupying our time until the right man came along. We were instructed to keep our legs "tightly shut" until we married, protecting the virginity that Latino men desire in their women. Against her will, Socorro ful-filled their prophecy, quitting school and marrying as a way of escaping the contradictory rules of the house that had worked against her.

The conversation with my mother made me aware that I had to view my role as a black Puerto Rican woman differently. My sons would be exposed to more liberated ways of thinking, so they would behave as equal partners in the family and in their fu-ture relationships. My thoughts were understood and encour-aged by my mother. She let me know that following my spiritual path would open more choices that would help restructure the lives of the children.

My mother was the glue that held our family together. Now I understand that her misguided love created a false sense of family unity. She often told "white lies" to our father to protect us from his harsh discipline. If my brother failed a class in school or arrived home after his curfew, she would tell my father that Alberto was obedient and doing fine. Even when my father found out that he had been lied to, he was actually proud of my brother for acting like a "man."

However, when my sister was more than fifteen minutes late from school or received a poor grade, my parents' reaction was very different. She would be punished and scolded because, according to my parents, "she was trying to act like a man." One of my father's favorite phrases was, "Women are supposed to be at home, not in the streets." I know my parents treated my sister unfairly in the name of love. Believing that they were preparing her for motherhood and my brother for manhood, my parents bestowed privilege and punishment with an uneven hand. As the girls, my sister and I accepted the fact that my brother had privileges that applied only to him. We learned that part of being a woman required that we quietly accept being less favored.

Our parents ignored my brother's and sister's growing problems. They pretended that my brother's inability to hold a job was not his fault. According to my father, my sister's increasing moodiness was an "attitude problem" that could be straightened out with a good slap. To protect my mother from dealing with problems that could affect her heart condition, my father would use his domineering behavior to block questions or discussion on these issues. When my sister asked my mother for permission to register for college, she was directed to my father. My father's response was, "What a waste of money." When my sister responded that my brother was going to college, my father angrily said, "He is a man; he needs an education." Finally, relenting to my mother's pleading, my father allowed my sister to register, while he openly bemoaned the waste of her time and his hard-earned money.

As our thoughts mingled during the *misa*, my mother assured me that love required a healthy, forgiving, healing environment to grow. In order for resolution to flourish, she said, my desire for vengeance had to be left behind. Gently, she implored me to

allow my spirituality to grow and my emotional recuperation to start. My presence in the *misa* was a beginning step, and her warmth melted away my hurt. The glow in her hands became a brilliant yellow beam that she spread over my body, cleansing my aura. She looked into my eyes, read my thoughts, and said, "I brought you here. Let your spiritual guides lead you now. Don't be afraid; you have found a spiritual home."

My mother's image then began to disappear, slowly fading into the glow that outlined her body. Mama's final words lifted the resentful feelings I held toward my brother and sister, creating a space to be filled by the warmth she radiated over and within me. I learned not to nurture pain, but to find a way of actively healing by seeking spiritual health.

The *misa* began my spiritual journey into the teaching of the spirits and Santería. My memory of the first encounter with my mother's spirit deepened with time, and the lessons she shared became clearer as I learned more about the power of the spirit world. I have learned, for example, that spiritual energy can be inherited; therefore, it is important that we learn as much as possible about our ancestral history. I also learned not to dwell in the past. In order to heal, it was necessary to accept and leave the pain behind me. The deep love I held for my childhood family was to be cherished forever; however, I had to accept that it no longer existed in the same form. It was necessary for me to help re-create a new, healthy family that would assist in healing and nurturing the future generations that would be born into our family.

The need to move on, to re-create and transform our reality, does not disrespect our past but rather honors it. Too many of our people have suffered and withstood pain so we could inherit their spiritual guidance and create a better world for our children. Every time we allow negative energy to interrupt us or distract us from a positive path, we dishonor our ancestors and the sacred powers. To grow spiritually, we must work with our guardian angels to build positive, functional lives. Part of the process is understanding the dynamic and ever-changing forces in our lives. Change is a symbolic form of dying; it is the elimination of the dysfunctional parts of our lives through acceptance. Acceptance spawns invigorating ideas that encourage new behavioral patterns, creating an environment of spiritual renewal. Renewal requires letting go of unnecessary grief so that space is free for nurturing new, exhilarating thoughts.

Mother's spirit helped me to understand that sometimes we must experience physical pain to appreciate better and make full use of the limited gift of life we have on Earth. She explained it is through identifying our guardian angels that we learn to better comprehend our behavior.

Before I was initiated into Santería, my godmother, Zenaida, held a *misa* to identify my spirit guides. When I asked why this was necessary, my godmother explained, "We all have spirits who protect and guide us. They present themselves to the living in many forms. Sometimes you hear an invisible inner voice guiding you; other times an intuitive feeling protects you from harm. There are times when you are alone in a room and feel that someone is there. In spiritual sessions, *misas,* the spirits have the opportunity to speak through a medium and give direct advice to the living. Spirits that are enlightened led a healthy life on Earth. These are spirits that are honored by the family and friends and through prayers and rituals; these spirits gain enlightenment and are in turn helpful to the living. Those spirits who have led unhealthy lives often have family and friends who ignore them in their prayers and do not place candles in their honor. These spirits are confused and afflicted in the afterlife. They bring chaos into the lives of the living.

"Each of your guardian angels, *cuadro espiritual,* is made known to you in a special *misa.* If one of your spirits was a professor in life, in the afterlife that spirit will help you with your studies. It could be that one of your spirits was initiated into the Santería religion. That spirit will encourage and help initiate you into the religion and share the knowledge that it possesses with

you. Perhaps one of your guardian angels was an artist, and now the spirit is sharing this talent with you. We will determine this in the *misa*."

My godmother urged me to do my part to create a positive spiritual future for my family by nurturing my guardian angels while on Earth. She told me that we must all live actively, fulfilling our earthly and spiritual obligations, because this is what prepares us for our afterlife. Like the spirits, we have many roads that we travel simultaneously, and these paths eventually converge into the totality of our complex identities.

Back in Olga's sacred space in Havana, I gradually began to feel part of the *misa*, surrounded by the initiates praying and singing the songs that call the spirits. During the *misa*, Javier's spirits came forward and blessed his plans for initiation into the Ifá priesthood. No longer was I simply an observer; my newfound spiritual connection made me feel part of the group. My mother's visit had changed me. A destructive emotional weight had been lifted, and I felt embraced within a healing warmth. It was on July 18, 1979—when the spirit of my mother spoke to me—that my journey into the religion of Santería actually began.

The other participants remained focused on the *misa*. They seemed unaware of what had just happened to me. I had been completely unprepared for the revelations of the *misa* and found myself pleasantly shocked, confused, and filled with a myriad of questions. Glancing at my watch, I realized only a few minutes had passed, although it seemed as if I had spent hours with my mother. As I sat in perplexed wonder, I made eye contact with Zenaida, and her gentle smile assured me that everything was all right. When the *misa* ended, the participants again filled the room with chatter. As they left the apartment, everyone enthusiastically assured Javier that they would attend the celebration of his initiation the following week.

Seated at the far end of the room next to Javier, the revered elder, Ma Mina, shared her wise thoughts with the *santeras* and *santeros*, who respectfully asked for her blessing before they left. With a gentle yet firm glance, she addressed the gathering: "Open your hearts; remember that the world needs kindness. If not, we will destroy ourselves. In Cuba, we may lack many things, but we have each other. Bring a little honey into your life," she advised. "Remember that you can attract more bees with honey than with vinegar. Be more flexible, less rigid in your ways. A tree that doesn't bend with the wind cannot survive." Her message was comforting as I continued to rejoice in the advice from my mother's spirit.

To Javier, she said, "You needed to come home to initiate. The *aché* of your ancestors is in the earth here in Cuba. Here is where the *orishas* of your mother were born and remained awaiting your return."

Ma Mina's wise, aging eyes guided me silently to her side. Embracing me with delicate arms, she whispered in my ear, "Don't be afraid; your spirits will protect and guide you. You are home. I know the spirit of your mother spoke with you. In your heart, you know it was she. Trust your inner spirit." Pointing to my head, she said, "There is where your wisdom lives. Trust it." Warm tears of happiness filled my eyes and trickled down my face, and Ma Mina, with her slender fingers, tried to wipe them away.

Zenaida soon joined us, indicating that our car was waiting and that it was time to leave. Zenaida's joyous expression complemented her bouncy, abundant body. She had large, flirtatious eyes and mahogany-colored skin. Her short Afro was covered with a creatively wrapped white scarf that danced on her head, adding inches to her tall frame. About thirty-five years old, she projected a youthful essence that rubbed off on all around her. Yet Zenaida also had a commanding, no-nonsense quality that made people follow her directions without hesitation. Together, Ma Mina and Zenaida created a beautiful portrait of the inheritance of African spirituality across generations.

In later years I would recall this moment, while witnessing

the respect granted to elders in Brazil, where the priestesses and priests are highly honored and protected by the younger members of the community. Throughout the Brazilian community, elders sit in regal magnificence, on thrones in the ritual houses. They are clothed in exquisitely handcrafted dresses with delicate layers of lace and satin petticoats. Their heads, covered in carefully wrapped cloth, create indescribable visions of goddesslike dignity. The younger initiates approach them with respect and love, prostrating themselves in honor of the *orisha*'s *aché* that the priestesses possess, and wait for a blessing. The attention to detail and proper conduct reflects the importance placed upon passing tradition down through the ages. Practitioners learn through a system of mentorship, since the rituals, dances, chants, and music are not generally written down.

The sisterhood and brotherhood societies—the *irmandades*—are examples of the protective systems developed to pass on African beliefs and to re-create a sense of family and community. Within these communities elders hold a privileged position, in acknowledgment of their wisdom and age. The noble spiritual strengths of these women radiate an empowering energy field that touches everyone around them.

The elders are like guardian angels living on Earth. They are teachers, mothers, fathers, friends, and doctors. Like the *orishas*, they possess many skills to protect their children. They take great pride in their roles as sages, exercising extreme caution in sharing information. The high level of spiritual knowledge they have acquired through the years has cultivated their divine essence, making their very breath a medium for *aché*. Elders speak only when necessary. The moments when individuals like Ma Mina choose to give advice are seen as wondrous gifts that must be cherished.

Elders like Ma Mina are protected and cared for by both their families and religious godchildren. On the night that my mother spoke to me, Zenaida assumed the responsibility for making certain that Ma Mina returned safely to her apartment. She gently helped Ma Mina to her feet with tremendous adoration and respect, honoring the ancient *aché* she possessed.

Before leaving, we thanked Olga for conducting the *misa*. Smiling shyly, she asked whether the session had accomplished its mission: to inform Javier's spirits of his initiation.

It was at that moment I fully understood that, as a trance medium, Olga did not remember what occurred during the times when various spirits claimed her body. Olga asked for a detailed explanation of what had occurred during the session. The exchange between Ma Mina, Zenaida, and Olga held my rapt attention. They talked about the spirits who had manifested during the session as if they were talking about old friends they held in common.

Zenaida, swinging her head from side to side as if she were preparing to testify before a congregation, raised her hands to the sky and then dramatically placed her hands on her broad hips. Her eyes conveyed an abounding enthusiasm for the splendid *misa* she had just witnessed. She complimented Olga upon having the spiritual authority to call on the spirit of my mother.

"You started foaming at the mouth and rubbing the left side of your chest, calling out Marta's name," Zenaida explained.

"When she did this, I knew it was my mother," I added.

Then Olga asked me to confirm the accuracy of the information the spirit of my mother communicated. When I did so, their excitement was overwhelming. Ma Mina and Zenaida agreed that Olga had an extraordinary gift, as verified by her ability to be the conduit for my mother's spirit. Olga modestly responded that my mother's spirit had been eagerly awaiting the opportunity to communicate with me. Beaming with pride, Olga simply stated, "It is my duty to heed the call of the spirits." Suddenly she appeared exhausted; she raised both hands to the heavens and candidly thanked her guardian angels for giving her the powers to work on their behalf.

Like many other gifted *espiritistas*, Olga had at first attempted to avoid the responsibility of mediumship. However, the spirits

eventually have their way. Olga explained that before she accepted the call, she was continuously ill and often disoriented, because the spirits would possess her in public places. "Imagine going to the grocery store and waking up by a lake. The nearest lake is a two-hour bus ride. The *orisha* Ochun kept taking me to the lake, her home, asking me to initiate for health reasons." Zenaida, understanding that I needed an explanation, added, "Often the *orishas* claim you as their child because they want to give you health. To gain their protection, you are crowned with their *aché*. In these cases, the *orisha* is in your home to safeguard your well-being. The *orisha* understands that your gift is in the spiritual realm of mediumship."

Laughing to herself, Ma Mina mused, "The ancestors, the *eguns*, are all-knowing; they understand what their children need. The ancestor spirits and the *orishas* work together; they are all members of the same family. Like the branches of a tree, they are separate, yet they belong to the same trunk. There is little difference between the *orishas* and ancestors. The *orishas* once lived on the Earth, and now they are ancestors as well."

Their intriguing conversation was so inviting that I was quickly drawn into the fascinating world of spirits—the very same world I had shunned and refused to acknowledge as a younger woman.

During the *misa*, five different spirits had possessed Olga's body. Javier's guardian angels each appeared, giving their consent and showing their support for his initiation rites. Javier was especially delighted when the spirit of his mother—a renowned *santera* who had been initiated as a child by a Yoruba ex-slave woman—also possessed Olga's body. Her spirit tenderly expressed her satisfaction that he had returned home to meet his spiritual obligations. The appearance of this spirit confirmed that the initiation ceremony would proceed smoothly and with her blessings. The spirit of Javier's mother gathered the skirt of her dress and cleansed her son from head to foot, and then lit a cigar and cleansed him with puffs of smoke that covered his body. Finally, she sprayed him with three mouthfuls of strong rum.

After her spirit left, a succession of other spirits came through Olga's body. Each time a different spirit manifested, they gave their names, greeted the gathering, acknowledged Olga's guardian angels, and thanked her for allowing them to materialize through her body.

One of Javier's spirits stormed through Olga's body, making her eyes open wide and bulge as if they were going to spring out of her head. The spirit then picked up a bottle of rum and drank generously, gulping down the liquor as if it were water. Then the spirit lit a cigar and leisurely puffed away for several minutes. Complaining that he was not a woman, the spirit gathered Olga's wide skirt from back to front, creating a trouserlike effect. He flirted with some of the women and competitively challenged the men present, prancing around the room like a proud stallion. The spirit then turned to Javier, covered his head with the smoke of his cigar, and said, "My son, I am your father, the *orisha* Shangó. You are strong and brave like me. You have nothing to fear as long as you respect me." Embracing Javier tightly, the spirit then sat at the table, took another thirsty mouthful of rum, and left Olga's body.

Javier had been initiated with his patron, Orisha Shangó, in New York. When I asked Zenaida how Shangó had claimed him, she smiled and said, "Unlike the spirits, we identify the *orisha* through the process of divination with palm nuts. It is a priest of Ifá, *babalawo*, who, through his consultation with the oracle *orisha*, Orula, identifies the *orisha*. The purpose of today's *misa* is to inform Javier's guardian angels of his initiation as a priest of Ifá."

I was fortunate that my mother made her appearance in the body of someone so skilled, someone who could sustain the energy drain without causing any harm to herself. Olga gave each of us a heartfelt hug as we said our good-byes. The feeling of pride and satisfaction was evident in her face as she closed the door behind us.

A Message from My Elders

My *madrina*, Zenaida, always reminds me of the importance of attracting the energy of the *orisha* Ochun. As she is the divinity of love, harmony, and community, Ochun's delicate symbols generate and attract sweetness and happiness. To enhance the energy of Ochun, Zenaida suggested that I take five consecutive baths—with perfume, shredded sunflowers, a little honey, and cascarilla (powdered eggshell).

Ochun's color and symbols are shades of golden yellow, the perfect color to activate a joyful environment. Surround yourself with yellow, wear her colors, place sunflowers around the house to remind you of the power of sweetness. Her energy is present wherever there is sweet water; lakes are the home of Ochun. Zenaida advises that to fill yourself with Ochun's energy, you should take a moment to sit by a lake and meditate. If you can, she recommends that you settle into the water and enjoy the cool gentle spray of Ochun's sweet water.

Chapter Six

OYÁ

IN ORDER TO LIVE
YOU MUST DIE

It is said in Cuban Yoruba legends that the *orisha* Oyá is the guardian of the cemetery gateway. She protects the spirit of those who have died, so that we may live. According to the elders, when a novice is to be initiated with the *orisha* Oyá, he or she must be taken to a cemetery for nine consecutive days before the initiation. Oyá represents air, one of the five elements of life.

In drumming ceremonies for the *eguns*, it is a child of Oyá who dances. Oyá is gracious when happy, but when angered she is as strong as Oggun and Shangó. She is a female warrior who manifests herself in the whirlwind.

The following legend illustrates her cunning qualities. Oyá was the first wife of Shangó, the *orisha* of fire, thunder, and lightning. One day, Shangó sent Oyá on an errand to bring him a special potion that would give him the power to spout fire. He asked her not to open the potion along the way. Oyá, not one to take orders, decided to taste the preparation; as a result, she acquired the ability to spout fire before Shangó. Shangó was angered by Oyá's disobedience, so he consulted Olodumare. Since Oyá already possessed the power to spout fire, Olodumare determined that she would appear before Shangó in all ceremonies. Olodumare recognized that once you have acquired a talent, you will possess it forever.

In another legend, one that teaches us to be continuously wary of the potential for trickery and deceitful actions, Yemayá tricked Oyá into becoming owner of the cemetery. Yemayá, weary of being in charge of the cemetery, invited Oyá to see the beauty and vast quantity of land she owned. However, in doing so, Yemayá failed to show Oyá the cemetery, which was in reality her home. Oyá, tired of living in the ocean, then agreed to switch homes with Yemayá, because she had fallen in love with the beauty of the land.

It was not until after they had switched homes that Oyá realized she had been tricked. Outraged, she confronted Yemayá, but Yemayá refused to take back the cemetery. Oyá went to Olodumare to resolve the problem, but Olodumare ruled that Oyá had to abide by her agreement to switch homes. He reminded her

that, in the future, she must examine all facets of an agreement before proceeding.

To this day, Oyá and Yemayá do not get along. In ceremonies when initiates are possessed with these *orishas*, they must be kept apart to avoid a confrontation.

The kitchen came alive with the laughter of *santeros* and *santeras* as Doña Rosa continued her dance and they jubilantly followed her to get their spoonful of honey. When Doña Rosa got to me, she paused and said, "Marta, I remember your first trip to Cuba in 1979, when you knew very little about Santería. You were like a thirsty child asking questions and drinking up all the information you could find, as if it were water. Today, almost eighteen years later, you have grown into a knowledgeable adult spreading our religion through international events around the world, and you are preparing to initiate others."

Doña Rosa placed the honey on the table and then placed her thin hands on each side of my face; in that instant I felt as if my *abuela* was present. Looking into Doña Rosa's aged eyes I noticed tears gathering on her lower lids as I stood up to embrace her. She said, "I have never traveled outside of Cuba and do not know much about other countries, but through your work the world has come to my doorstep. In the photographs you brought me I have seen *orisha* worshipers in Africa, Latin America, the United States, and other Caribbean islands. I now know that my religion belongs to me, Cuba, and to the world. Like Oyá's whirlwind, the religion is everywhere."

Ma Mina, a daughter of Oyá, seemed to be preparing to make her transition into the spirit world. As we left the apartment, she said to Zenaida, "I would like to visit the cemetery this week, my

child. Will you take me? It is time for me to visit my husband's grave. I want to let him know that soon I will join him."

Zenaida quickly responded, "Old one, you will be with us for a long time." Escorting Ma Mina to her downstairs apartment, we carefully guided her along the narrow stairs. Leaning heavily on Zenaida's arm, Ma Mina was brought safely to her home. I marveled at her agility at the age of eighty—obviously she navigated these steps daily on her own. Ma Mina's inviting apartment was like a gateway to the past. Its walls were covered with antique sepia-tone photographs of family and friends who had joined the spirit world. The baroque sofa was covered with faded, wine-colored velvet and trimmed with intricately carved dark wood. Two large, Chinese-style porcelain bowls were placed on a table surrounded by many more faded photographs. Filled with memories of loved ones, Ma Mina's home was a memorial to the deceased, as she herself prepared for her own passing to another level of spiritual existence.

Ma Mina noticed me gazing at the soft glitter of the porcelain and gently commented, "Those bowls were a gift from my deceased husband. He was Chinese and loved to decorate our home with artwork from his home. His family was brought to Cuba as indentured workers during the abolition of slavery. The Chinese were treated like slaves. They suffered the same mistreatment that we did." Catching her breath, she continued, "My husband was crowned with the *aché* of Oyá, by an old African woman, before we married. Mmmm, he was even more devoted to the *orishas* than I. How I miss him." Pausing, she added, "My beloved died ten years ago. His spirit visits me almost every night. He wants me to join him. I know that we will soon be together. For now, I have placed his Oyá and mine next to each other as a symbol of our unending marriage and love."

Laughing softly, she continued, "The divinities of the Chinese community are very similar to the *orishas*. People like to argue about the difference between the *orishas*, the Catholic saints, and the Chinese divinities. For me, they are different roads to the

same destination." Her statement was made matter-of-factly, without any sense of sadness. It seemed that Ma Mina was ready to place herself in the hands of Oyá. As we left, she embraced each of us.

We proceeded carefully along the dim hallway, down the hazardous steps, dodging exposed electrical wires until we reached the front of the building. The warm air was momentarily refreshing. Ernesto, our driver, proudly waited alongside his vintage car. His eyes signaled weariness, but his military posture indicated his resistance to fatigue. He was a former soldier who had studied engineering; he had been stationed in Russia during most of his military service.

Now retired, he supplemented his pension by using his car as a private taxi service. The car was a hand-painted, sky blue 1955 Chevy with a flowered chenille bedspread used as seat covers. Clearly, this car was Ernesto's proudest possession. On the floor of the car were blue-painted wood planks; the window handles were missing and had been replaced by knobs of wood held together with a thin woven wire cable. On the dashboard, Ernesto had installed a small window fan and displayed a red-and-gold crown that had originally been an air freshener and now represented his devotion to his *orisha* Shangó. He projected the warrior spirit of Shangó in a subtle yet strong and masculine manner. However, like his divinity Shangó, Ernesto could be playful one minute and erupt like thunder the next.

After many years of observing initiates, I now understand that practitioners often take on the characteristics of the *orishas* whose *aché* they possess. In many ways, the *orisha* and the initiate become one. Or perhaps it is that the initiate is born with the qualities of the *orisha*, and the *babalawos* discern which *orisha* is suited for that particular initiate. It is believed that we all are born with a patron *orisha*.

A godson of Elpidio, Ernesto was devoted to his Santería family, running countless errands for them. During our ride, he provided an update on the preparations for Javier's initiation, sharing the news that the sacrificial animals had been purchased;

Elpidio had selected the *babalawos* to participate in the initiation, and the food had been gathered for the ceremony. He stressed the difficulty of finding animals and the necessary food, because of the United States' embargo and the mass reduction of Russian assistance. Javier and Ernesto chatted away for the full forty minutes it took the 1955 Chevy to reach Zenaida's home. The car was straining at its maximum speed—according to Ernesto, we were traveling at thirty miles an hour. Zenaida silently guided my eyes to the speedometer and gas indicator, both of which were broken. We both started laughing as we realized that we really didn't know the speed of the car or whether or not there was enough gas to get us to the apartment.

Surrounded by old cars, vintage furniture, outdated fashions, and tropical decorations reminiscent of the early 1950s *I Love Lucy* television series, I felt as if I were traveling back in time in Havana. It was becoming exceedingly difficult to draw a line between my developing spirituality and reality, as my journey into the past blended into the present. I realized that my understanding of Santería was too limited even to know the right questions to ask Elpidio and Zenaida. All at once, I believed that my mother's visitation and Javier's initiation made it necessary for me to understand more about Santería. No longer wanting to be an outsider looking in, I decided to ask Zenaida and Elpidio to guide me. I was surrounded by spiritual activities, and this caused my interest to evolve, reawakening fond emotions and memories. At last, I wanted to understand the meanings of the images that had been an integral part of my youth.

My mother's spiritual presence triggered memories and emotions that had long been buried, forcing me to recall my childhood encounters with the spirits. My mother's instructions were clear—it was time to face my past so that I could step into the future. It was time to learn the beloved spiritual traditions of the family so one day I could pass them on to future generations. The comforting words of Ma Mina and my mother's spirit circulated in my mind, helping me shed the fear of venturing into the spirit world. Instinctively, I knew that my inner healing would occur.

The familiar warrior *orishas* who guarded the door of Zenaida and Elpidio's apartment became the symbolic threads that immediately connected my childhood in East Harlem to the home of initiates in Cuba. The sacred objects of the warrior *orishas* were similar to the ones that had protected my *abuela's* apartment. When I asked the meaning of these intriguing objects, I learned that the warriors are four separate and powerful protector *orishas*. Together, Oggun, the *orisha* of iron; Ochosi, the hunter *orisha*; Osun, the *orisha* that represents the sacredness of our heads and the seat of our wisdom; and Ellegua, the *orisha* of the crossroads, form a stabilizing force for the practitioner, bringing balance and the courage to confront difficulties.

Similar to the cosmology of *feng shui* in the Chinese community, one of the objectives of Santería is to create a positive balance between heaven and Earth, man and matter, creating the flow of *aché*, which is the equivalent of *qi* in Taoist philosophy. These variant *orishas* exist together, reminding us that living a balanced life requires cooperation and understanding.

It is the ability to create an energy flow that brings balance in our homes and contributes to our well-being. A home that is welcoming and organized certainly helps place us in a comfortable and receptive spiritual space. Ellegua's energy insists that we find resolution at the crossroads. Ochosi's hunter energy encourages us to seek opportunities that will yield peace. Oggun reminds us to always follow the path of truth and justice, while Osun prompts us to view our intuitive mind as a source of divine intelligence.

Residing behind the main doorway in the homes of Santería initiates, the warrior *orishas* guard their families. Placed in the most active location in the home, the entrance, the warriors create a sense of balance between the visible and invisible worlds.

The warriors Oggun and Ochosi are symbolized by a black iron pot filled with farming and hunting tools that embody their presence in the home. Within the cauldron are placed the sacred stones that represent the *orishas*. Ellegua was symbolized by the triangular stone, which was placed on a clay plate next to the

other *orishas*. When I asked about the importance of the stones as sacred objects, the response from my godfather, Elpidio, came in the form of a *pataki*.

"It is said that for a short time the *orishas* came to live on Earth among their people. The people, accustomed to their presence, began to ignore the contributions of the *orishas* to their daily lives. One day, the *orishas* became upset with the disrespect of the people and decided to return to heaven. Whenever they wanted to visit Earth from then on, it would be only in the form of rain. They fell into the rivers, forming sacred rocks in the colors that represented each one of them. Some rocks were white, which represented the creation *orishas*, yellow for Ochun, brown for Oyá, red for Shangó, and so forth. This is why the sacred stones are the representation of the *orishas* on Earth."

Often, beautiful *patakís* of Santería provided a direct explanation to my questions; at other times, the stories required a leap of faith. When I would mention to Elpidio that occasionally the *patakís* did not seem to make sense, he would respond confidently, "They will."

I tried carefully to observe and comprehend the whirlwind of information that was engulfing me. Perceiving my exasperation, Zenaida, with her sympathetic humor, commented, "Relax, everything will soon make sense to you. Life does not follow sequential chapters like a book. Sometimes you have to arrange the chapters in a way that works specifically for you. Santería is a learning process that guides you and helps you create a sacred space that works for you."

My spiritual experiences in Cuba brought with them a feeling of familiarity. The community of initiates felt like dear old friends eager and willing to make me feel welcome and a part of their family. To become a part of the religious community, I was required to take the first steps in my spiritual path, which meant receiving the *elekes*, beaded necklaces, and the warrior *orishas*. The *elekes* represent the colors of the major *orishas* that are received upon initiation. The *elekes* are worn daily and are a source of personal protection for the practitioner. When an *eleke* breaks,

it is an indication that negative energy is surrounding the initiate. The *elekes* are white for Obatalá, yellow for Ochun, blue and white for Yemayá, red and black for Ellegua, and white and red for Shangó.

On the way back to Zenaida and Elpidio's apartment, I asked them to mentor my journey. Following the advice of my mother's spirit, I decided I was ready to enter the world of Santería and Espiritismo.

Although he did not work directly with the spirits, Elpidio stressed, "When I see a spiritual problem in my godchildren, I send them directly to an *espiritista*—a medium." *Babalawos,* like Elpidio, are members of an all-male society of diviners in Cuba and other African Diaspora locations. They are the keepers of the wealth of knowledge that is locked within the *odus,* the symbols. The *odus* are like the keys that open the meaning of our oral bible of *patakís.* The *patakís* explain the complexities of both the spirit and secular worlds, providing initiates with explanations and solutions for the problems afflicting them.

Diviners are trained to interpret the intricate messages of Orula, the *orisha* of divination, by using the symbolic patterns cast by the *ikins,* palm nuts, and the *oguele,* the divining chain. This knowledge is deeply respected and guides the lives of initiates.

One day, I discreetly watched as Elpidio cast the *oguele* for one of his clients. The young man named Bebo, a friendly bundle of energy, was distraught because a series of promising job opportunities had ultimately led nowhere. Casting the *oguele,* Elpidio carefully took notes, listing the symbols that appeared in the patterns of the divining chain. Elpidio's chain was made of eight circular pieces of the hard shell of a coconut intermittently separated by a thin chain.

Finally, he looked into the young man's eyes and said, "Oyá is angry with you. What did you promise this powerful *orisha* that you have not given her?" Elpidio carefully explained that the *orishas* hold practitioners accountable for their obligations. Bebo sheepishly responded that he was supposed to have initiated the previous year, and it was Oyá who had claimed him. However, he confessed that he had squandered the money he had saved for his initiation ceremony.

Elpidio smiled as he scratched his cottony hair, and said, "Well, Oyá is telling you that she will wait no longer. If you are to solve the problems in your life, you must initiate as soon as possible." With a slight frown, Elpidio explained, "Never make promises you don't plan to keep." Again casting the *oguele* on the straw mat, he thoughtfully looked at the pattern made by the shells. "Take nine eggplants to the door of the cemetery and leave them at the gateway for Oyá. She will momentarily accept this gift while you prepare for your initiation. Oyá will help you find a job. However, she will not forgive you breaking your promise to her again."

With a knowing glance, he told Bebo to balance his life by paying more attention to finding a job than to his many girl-friends. Closing the session, he good-naturedly remarked that the girls would leave him anyway once they found out he did not have money. Blushing with embarrassment, Bebo accepted the advice and promised to change his behavior. With grandfatherly affection, Elpidio assured him that when he followed the advice of Orula, he would have more job offers than he could handle. He assured Bebo that once he completed his obligation to Oyá, he would see an immediate change in his life. Reminding Bebo of Oyá's importance both in the spiritual and *orisha* realms, Elpidio suggested that Bebo pay immediate attention to his initiation preparations. Elpidio's nonjudgmental approach was comforting, and his expertise attracted people from all walks of life seeking the guidance of Orula.

Sitting around the kitchen table drinking coffee, listening to the teachings of Elpidio and Zenaida, I felt as if I were back in my home in El Barrio, and I easily entered into a casual conversation. Javier, amused by the meandering way his godfather dispensed his wisdom, remained quiet. "My daughter, today you witnessed the power of the spirit world. Your mother's spirit touched you. It is ultimately your decision if you accept her guidance. As you

are a studious person, I know you want a precise account of what occurred." Trying to find the right words, Elpidio hesitated, then cautiously said, "You want an analytical explanation that makes scientific sense. This is not possible. When you live with the spirits, when you embrace *orisha* and feel it work, then you know they exist."

He explained that spirit visitations are generally made by family members and close friends. Elpidio further explained that spirit-time spans generations. Therefore, possession by spirits who lived long ago is a common occurrence. When I asked how the *orishas* differ from the spirits, he smiled and said, "Think of them as spirits that reached the highest level of evolution and were transformed into the forces of nature. They are the elements that give us life. They are nature itself."

Inspired by his explanation, Zenaida said, "The paths of the spirits and *orishas* require lifelong study, dedication, and commitment. When you are claimed by the spirits and *orishas*, you are destined for a divine journey filled with spiritual responsibilities. Today was just the beginning."

Continuing his orientation session with me, Elpidio said that we are all born with guardian angels and *orishas*. "It is our task in life to connect both to our spirits and to nature's energy forces in order to have health, happiness, and prosperity in our lives."

Zenaida added pensively, "When the soul and body are healthy and your state of mind is positive, everything is possible; nothing can stop you."

I was gradually coming to understand that when the spirits and *orishas* claim you, it is a blessing that brings significant responsibilities. Both Zenaida and Elpidio assured me that there was nothing to fear. It was their belief that a positive religious journey opened up pathways to new knowledge that helped the seeker find prosperity on Earth and in the spirit world.

Elpidio and Zenaida's love of Espiritismo and Santería was evident in their dedication to protect and pass on the religion through both their natural and religious families. Throughout the day, people came seeking advice and guidance from both of

them. Their home was a meeting place and a temple, a cross-roads for Santería worshipers, who ranged from teachers and artists to government workers and community folk. I could feel the apartment vibrating with *aché*, facilitating conversations among divergent groups, providing direction and information that could assist initiates in finding out about future rituals and social events.

Elpidio would generally sit in the back bedroom with his godsons, discussing at length the complex and profound meaning of the *odus* and *patakís*, the literary poems of Ifá. He explained that it is the responsibility of the Ifá priest to study each of the sixteen major *odus* and their meanings, in order to develop the skills necessary to help solve the problems of clients. He explained that the patterns represented by the *odus* allow the diviner to identify the *pataki* that will provide a solution to the practitioner's problem. He also confided that while it is important for the priest to have an engaging and tender manner in order to put his clients at ease, ultimately it is the success of his predictions that makes people return for advice. Elpidio's manner was usually very soothing; however, I noticed that when the situation required his admonishing a client for not following Orula's instructions, he did not hesitate to show great strength and determination. I was discovering that the philosophy embodied in the legends of the *orishas* remained central to the religion. In my later travels to Brazil, I found that diviners there also hold an esteemed position in the religious community. Unlike in Cuba, women in Brazil are prominent members of the circle of diviners. Casting cowry shells and *obí*, four coconut pieces, women in Brazil are equal in skill to their male counterparts.

According to historians, the Portuguese in Brazil feared the power of the *babalawos* among enslaved Africans, and they hunted the holy men down and killed them. Priestesses in Brazil rose to fill the void. When I visited the Yoruba sacred city of Ile Ife, Nigeria, in 1981, I learned that unlike the Cuban religious system, women were allowed to initiate in the Ifá system once they had completed menopause. Observing Zenaida as she assisted

Elpidio in his preparations, it was evident that she had mastered the meaning of the patterns formed by the *oguele*. Her eyes sparkled with understanding, as she silently formed the names of the *odus* that appeared on the divining tray—the *opon* Ifá. For me, the varying ways that practices have survived in the Americas reflects the strength of the *orishas* to adapt to the conditions they found in each country.

Other times, Elpidio would show his godsons how to consult with the divining chain for a client. As the elder, he would watch as his godsons divined and provided the advice that was dictated by the symbols of the *odu* and accompanying poems. Always pushing the boundaries of his godson's studies, Elpidio would then add poems and possibilities for interpretations they had not considered. A loving father and mentor, he made certain that all of his students continued to think and expand their information base. Elpidio constantly indicated to us that Santería is a religion that requires study.

"The more we learn, the more we understand what we need to know," was Elpidio's mantra. His favorite way of stressing the point was to say, "No one knows what is at the bottom of the ocean—Yemayá is the only one who knows what is in her house. It is up to us to discover what secrets she holds, if she allows us to. All the *orishas* have a wealth of information to offer us, and we can figure it out only when we dedicate ourselves to studying."

Often, he would show us his library of books and endless files of stories he had accumulated over the years, all neatly catalogued according to the symbols of divination. Since he had godchildren and friends spread throughout the world, Elpidio constantly received books and research papers that further expanded his studies. When he locked himself in the back room, everyone knew to remain quiet and respect his study time.

In the living room, Zenaida would generally gather with women friends as they cleaned the rice and black beans and seasoned the meat for ceremonial feasts. In the kitchen, men and women gathered to prepare objects that were needed for rituals.

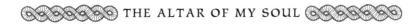

Sometimes *elekes* were strung; other times they made raffia curtains to cover the entrance of a ceremonial room.

The evening after the *misa* in which my mother's spirit had come to speak with me, I asked both Elpidio and Zenaida to be my godparents and mentors. We talked late into the night. Finally, Elpidio started feeling the weight of his long day and suggested that we continue our conversation the next day, since he still had to run an errand with Javier and Ernesto before retiring to bed. After they left, Zenaida secretively informed me that Elpidio had commissioned a craftsman to create a specially designed divining board for Javier. This would be their last stop before Javier went into isolation to prepare for his weeklong Ifá initiation.

To me, Javier's isolation meant that I would not see him for a week, when he would be presented to the Santería community in a public ceremony called *El Yoye*. Sensing my concern, Zenaida smiled and said, "Now we can really concentrate on your learning about Santería."

In retrospect, it amazes me how natural these first spiritual encounters in Cuba felt to me. Rather than experiencing any apprehension or fear, I felt a part of my new environment. My mother and Ma Mina had both been correct. I felt at home. Zenaida was like a sister, mother, and friend, all rolled into one. Elpidio was an elder father, grandfather, and uncle who was always available. Instinctively, I knew that if I were blindfolded and asked to fall backward, Elpidio and Zenaida would be there to stop my fall. Zenaida, delighted with my request, was thrilled that I would be her first godchild.

Given my short stay in Cuba, Zenaida decided that we would have similar learning sessions every evening. She lovingly admonished Elpidio by saying, "Marta is my first godchild, and she will be living far away from me. I want her to learn as much as possible before she leaves. We are her godparents and must properly prepare her in the ways of Santería—*La Regla de Ocha*."

Elpidio nodded his head in agreement, and with a crafty

smile he added, "I always do what she says; tomorrow we will discuss the *orishas*." Then, before leaving the apartment, he said, "Mark this date in your calendar. Today was an important day in your spiritual development. From now on your *madrina* and I will guide your development in the religion. Remember you are now a representative of this religious family, and we expect that you will study and follow the teachings of our home."

After the men left, Zenaida suggested that I spend the night. She reminded me that Santería was an active experience, something you live and breathe, not merely something you experience through books. "This week will be your introductory course in Santería." Having me close to her meant that I would be learning by observing and assisting her in the basic tasks that noninitiates were allowed to perform. Then she explained that as I advanced in the steps of initiation, my responsibilities would grow. She found a notepad and a pencil for me and instructed me to take notes and write down questions in preparation for our nightly meetings. In addition, she wanted me to keep a journal of my daily experiences and feelings, so I could create my own manual, to which I could always refer.

It seemed strange to me that Zenaida didn't have god-children, since she was at the center of her Santería community. When I asked her about this, she explained that the responsibility of a *madrina* is even greater than that of a natural mother, since the *madrina* cares for both the spiritual and daily life of her god-children. She stressed that it is a serious commitment and a responsibility that cannot be taken lightly.

However, she went on to explain that at a recent *registro*, divination session, the *orisha* Orula indicated that she had to accept the next person who came to her in search of a *madrina*. She could no longer refuse her destiny; it was time to give birth to a Santería family of her own.

"I always follow the advice of the *orishas*," said Zenaida emphatically. "They have saved me from death several times." She explained that it was due to the *orishas* that she was able to walk so soon after a spinal operation. The doctors had predicted that

she would be crippled. Obatalá, the *orisha* who claimed her, told her that he would heal her completely, and indeed he had. She patted my hand and beamed with delight. "One day I will tell you the many stories of how the spirits and *orishas* have performed miracles for me."

Clearly, Zenaida was eager to begin her mentoring. To start, she prepared a spiritual bath to cleanse my aura and attract positive energy. I immediately started taking notes. "My daughter, learn to listen with your heart and then you will remember everything. First let yourself feel, and then write it down. Then the words will be filled with meaning."

She explained that when I felt emotionally weighed down, or "just not right," a spiritual bath would help to clear away negative forces. I watched as she went about preparing the spiritual bath. She filled a large bucket with cascarilla, powdered eggshells, cocoa butter, Florida water, perfume, and the petals of white tuberoses. She told me that I was to slowly pour the mixture over my head and body, after I had showered. As I did this, I should also pray, freeing myself of all troubling thoughts and problems, and focusing on positive solutions instead.

"After you finish, dress in this white nightgown, wrap your head in this white cloth, and light a white candle before going to sleep," she instructed. "You will sleep like a baby in the calming color of Obatalá, the father of all the *orishas*."

The small, sparsely furnished room was painted white. There was a single bed covered with white sheets, and an old-fashioned, intricately carved bureau that stood out against the crisp, stark white walls. The well-worn room had a charming quality that was comforting and inviting. Sandalwood incense filled the apartment with aromatic smoke, and the scent of Florida water began to spread throughout the rooms. The sweet, enchanting fragrance of tuberoses filled the air as Zenaida emptied the small white petals into the spiritual bath. The intoxicating combination of scents swiftly began to ease the stress of this nearly overwhelming day.

I made a brave attempt to sort out the day's events, but my

 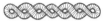

head was throbbing. Following Zenaida's instructions, I showered, then slowly poured the mixture of flowers and fragrances over me, asking the spirits for clarity of thought and greater awareness for my spiritual journey. Afterward, wearing the white nightgown and head scarf, I got into bed. I very quickly began to feel the heaviness of sleep claim my mind and body. Zenaida had lit a small white candle in the darkened room. The flickering candlelight spread a soft yellow-white glow that was very soothing. Sleep came quickly. Soon a marathon of images and scenes filled my dreams. The most vivid was the one of my grandmother.

My *abuela* was standing before her *bóveda*, lighting a white candle to her guardian spirits. Dressed in her usual white loose-fitting cotton dress and white scarf, she silently prayed, ignoring my presence. Abuela's beaded necklaces peeked out from the collar of her dress. Her sacred room, which had been a tapestry of shimmering color, was bathed in a soft, white, iridescent light suspended in space. After completing her prayers before the *bóveda*, she walked slowly to the mural of Saint Michael, the archangel, holding a bottle of *aguardiente* in her hand. Pouring the rum into her mouth, she sprayed the mural with a thin misty cloud. Droplets of rum ran down her chin, reflecting the white light in the room. Lighting a white candle before Saint Michael, she bowed her head reverently in prayer. In this way, Abuela appeared as a guardian angel, teaching me through my dreams the ritual I would also follow.

Then Abuela's image slowly began to shrink. The next thing I knew, she suddenly appeared on the table cluttered with the statues of the Indian, the Gypsy, and the African man and woman. But these ancestors were now alive, moving on the table as if they were walking freely in their own homes. The old man's eyes gleamed with the wisdom that Ma Mina's eyes now possessed. The warrior Indian's body, strong with the power of his youth, moved cautiously, quietly hunting for his prey. The Gypsy, caught up in the silent music that only she could hear, swayed rhythmically, moving her large satin skirt in a soothing movement that reminded me of pouring thick, sweet honey. The large

African woman stood next to Abuela, like a mother protecting her daughter. Alert and immovable, she was a pillar of strength. But she seemed to possess a silent power that could quickly explode in order to protect her family.

In her space, comfortably positioned between the African man dressed in white and the African woman in her contrasting red and white dress, Abuela stood erect. Then she cast her glance toward the door, finally acknowledging my presence. Her mischievous smile let me know that she had been aware all along that I stood watching by the door. It had been her intention to reveal this scene to me, to let me know that the statues that had been part of my childhood were reminders, representations of family ancestors who once lived and continued to protect our family. Like them, she would always be present in my life, protecting and guiding me. As she called to me with her smiling eyes, I knew to go before her and light a candle. I saw her smile as she said, "Don't forget the candy for Ellegua." Suddenly, I felt a strong ribbon of whirling colorful wind engulf my grandmother, carrying her out of my sight. Entranced by the beauty of the colors, I let my grandmother fade away.

A Message from My Elders

My *madrina*, Zenaida, explained that dreams are an important means of gathering information from our spiritual guides. Sometimes they provide a complete story that can easily be interpreted. Other times they provide symbols that, like pieces of a puzzle, come together to form a story. In my dream the figurines let me know that they were spirits that were actively involved in my life. The whirlwind and the many colors represent the symbols of Oyá.

Madrina Zenaida explained to me that I should re-

member my dreams and work to find their meanings. She suggested that I try to interpret each dream individually, but also try to analyze them as a unit because dreams often are interconnected.

The spiritual bath described in the chapter is an essential, basic way to open the channels for communication with your spiritual energies. Always try to relax and be in a meditative mood after the spiritual bath, especially before retiring for the evening. The basic ingredients are always powdered eggshells—cascarilla, which can be purchased in any botanica or religious store—cocoa butter, Florida water, perfume, and flowers.

Chapter Seven

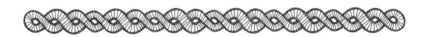

SHANGÓ

BORN TO
MAKE WAR

The parables explain the goodness and imperfections of humanity through the stories of the *orishas*. In understanding the meanings of the legends, we can also better comprehend our own behavior. One of the legends that explains the *aché* of Shangó tells us why he gave up the gift of divination to save his brother Orula. It is said that Obatalá was furious with his son Oggun for having raped his mother, Yemayá. He vowed that he would destroy any male child who was conceived by his wife. Soon after, Yemayá gave birth to a male child whom she named Orula. Obatalá ordered that Orula be taken to the forest and buried up to his neck near a ceiba tree.

After some time, Obatalá forgot about Orula and his vengeful decree. Time passed, and then Yemayá gave birth to another son, Shangó. The name Shangó means the one born with war in his head. And the special gift that Olodumare endowed him with was the *aché* of divination. Shangó grew into an attractive, gregarious young man who enjoyed the merriment of music and dance. He disliked the tiresome work required of the diviner.

Yemayá then had a fourth son, whom she named Ellegua. One day, Ellegua found out about his brother Orula. Curious, Ellegua led Shangó into the forest and together they found their older brother Orula. Shangó took pity on Orula, and both Ellegua and Shangó unburied him. Shangó then gave to Orula his divining board, *opon* Ifá, and the art of divination, so that he could earn a living. Shangó then went to Olodumare and asked to be made the owner of the sacred *batá* drums. Like Shangó, we must learn to share our gifts, and in the process we will find our happiness.

When I shared my dream with Elpidio and Zenaida, they were elated that both my mother and grandmother had come to guide me. The presence of the spirits was a sign to both Elpidio and Zenaida that my instruction in the way of Santería should start immediately.

The following evening, Elpidio and Zenaida carefully placed a set of newly crafted miniature tools of the warrior *orishas*, the *herramientas*, on the kitchen table. This was to be my first formal lesson in Santería, and it meant that they were officially my godparents: Elpidio, my *padrino*, and Zenaida, my *madrina*.

Elpidio set up an elaborate demonstration to begin my training. He started with the warrior *orishas, los guerreros*. He placed a black pyramid-shaped stone on the table. Embedded in the stone were cowry shells. The open side of the cowry was visible, giving the impression of facial features, like the stone I had seen in my *abuela*'s apartment. Then he placed next to the stone small farming tools: a small metal shovel, an anvil, an ax, and a stone pick. Carefully, Elpidio selected several small river-worn stones from a clay bowl.

I watched patiently from the living room door as he took out a black iron cauldron from a burlap bag. He then placed a small silverlike sculpture of a bird next to the other items. Elpidio took great care positioning the objects, and when he was pleased with his arrangement, he asked Zenaida and me to join him at the table.

"Do you know what these implements are, my daughter?" Elpidio asked. I responded confidently, "They are the warrior *orishas*—Ellegua, Oggun, Ochosi, and Osun."

Enjoying his mischievous Ellegua-like trick, he looked at me and said, "These objects are nothing. They are not sacred. They are not *orishas*." I looked from the warrior *orishas* protecting the door of the apartment to the ones on the table, and there seemed to be no difference. I remained silent and waited for an explanation, wondering what was going on.

Zenaida started explaining the sacred principles and practices that I should consider incorporating into my life. She began with *aché*, telling me that *aché* is a life force that receives its power from nature, and it is the flow of this energy that makes things happen. She went on to say that one of the objectives of Santería is to learn how to activate and attract this energy, which is limitless and spans space and time. In order to stimulate this energy force within, it is necessary to learn the sacred rituals and undergo the ceremonies of Santería. Zenaida discussed the varied levels of initiation.

In the first level, an initiate receives the sacred glass beaded necklaces, *elekes*. The second tier involves the ritual of receiving the warrior *orishas* that help the initiate to stimulate and heighten the *aché* that surrounds all of us. Zenaida visibly enjoyed Elpidio's little performance as he indicated that the objects on the table had not undergone the necessary sacred rituals in order to stimulate their deep-seated energy force. Consequently, they remained commonplace items. I asked how the energy force was stimulated.

"Through animal sacrifice," my godparents responded in unison. Watching my startled reaction, their eyes sparkled with amusement. "Listen to me carefully," Elpidio said as he looked toward my journal on the table. "Better yet, take notes," he encouraged. "An *orisha* is born very much like you were born. It was the union of your parents that conceived you. It was your mother who gave birth to you. In the act of giving birth, blood was spilled to facilitate your birth. So it is with the *orishas*. They are born from other *orishas*, and the sacrificial animal blood is symbolic of the blood that is spilled at birth. It is the blood that gives life. Blood is the force of life." He further elaborated, "When you receive the warriors, for example, they will be born from my warriors. During the ritual, you will witness that my warriors will receive the first animal sacrificial blood and then yours will be born. Eventually, when you are fully initiated, it is from Zenaida's *orishas* that yours will be born. The birth of an *orisha* represents a long ancestry."

Knowing the adverse reaction many people have toward animal sacrifice, Zenaida wanted me to understand the necessity of it. She carefully explained, "Just as we need daily nourishment to fuel our bodies, so the *orishas* need to be 'fed' in order to activate the energy force *aché*." Elpidio explained, "Sacrificial blood of the animals is the element that gives birth to the *orishas* and passes on *aché*." Passionately, Zenaida continued to share her

thoughts. "Not only are the *orishas* 'fed' through this process, but the community of initiates also eats, ensuring that members of the family will never go hungry. This divine, vital cycle links the *aché* of the *orishas* and humans, creating a complementary balance that maintains health and prosperity." The respect and honoring of animals in Africa continues in the lives of African descendants in the Americas. In the Santería religion the life force of animals used in rituals is revered because it brings spiritual rebirth as well as nourishment to the community.

"Santería is about building family and community, and creating a strong society," Elpidio added. "Both the spiritual and physical self must be fed, which contributes to the soundness of the body and mind of the individual. Since we do not live in isolation but in a society, a healthy individual contributes positively to the family and community at large. Santería teaches us to build a humane and loving society in which we clearly understand that none of us are alone."

Throughout my stay, the words of my godparents came to life. The animals used in ceremonies became a source of nourishment for children, adults, and elders. The meat of the animals sacrificed is considered sacred and provides both spiritual and physical nourishment.

Later that week, I attended a ceremony in honor of Shangó, in Centro Havana, where we were invited to stay for dinner. It was amazing that more than seventy-five people could jam into a *solar*—a single-room apartment complex connected by a narrow pathway—but they did. At the end of the pathway were the kitchen and bathroom facilities, which the residents all shared. Everyone was enjoying the mouthwatering beef stew and rice prepared by Elpidio's oldest goddaughter, Eugenia.

As visitors praised Eugenia's cooking, an undercurrent of social tidbits filled my ears. The woman next to me commented, "I went to claim my ration of chicken this week, and the butcher told me no deliveries had been made." Another commented, "Forget it, there is no meat to be had, not even on the black market." Someone else chimed in, "In my section we haven't seen

meat for the past four weeks. I have a collection of meat coupons that mean nothing. What is the point of rationing our food, giving us coupons, when there is no food?" Suddenly, a roar of laughter erupted, as everyone added their stories of unsuccessful attempts to find meat. A voice at the end of the corridor shouted out, "*Que viva Shangó;* Shangó lives! Today we are eating meat thanks to Oba Koso! Praise be to Shangó." In my first lesson, Elpidio had referred to this ceremony when he explained the important role of sacrifice in nourishing a community. Now he began to explain the reasons why Santería has been misrepresented.

Elpidio said, "Too many people who seek to undergo initiation have been fooled by unscrupulous ignorant charlatan priests giving them fake *orishas* like the ones here on the table. They are part of the reason that Santería has acquired a bad reputation. It is difficult for the novice to detect when the priests or priestesses they have selected as mentors lack the necessary knowledge. To make matters worse," he explained, "the persecution the religion has endured through the ages has caused practitioners to hide their ignorance behind the cloak of secrecy." Almost as an afterthought, he added, "No one is bothered by the notion of drinking the blood of Christ, in the form of wine, in church every Sunday. I find this practice startling."

I understood his deep-seated anger. Researching the history of African belief systems in the Americas, I have found significant evidence that these religions were persecuted from the time they arrived on our shores. Christian missionaries, together with the Spanish, Portuguese, and other European governments, actively sought to destroy all belief in African gods. In Puerto Rico, as in other countries, the Spaniards forcibly baptized Africans, in part to destroy their beliefs but, more important, to bring in greater profits. Africans who were not baptized were considered savages, *bozales,* and were worth less, while baptized Africans brought higher prices.

As a result, the Africans created inventive methods of protecting the *orishas,* turning the tables on their enslavers by using the religious imagery of their captors as a disguise. In Cuba and

Brazil, Africans used Catholic brotherhood and sisterhood societies, *cabildos* and *irmandades,* as safe places to hide their African gods, to continue their African rituals, and to re-create families and communities. One of the oldest *cabildos* in Cuba was dedicated to Shangó, using the image of the Catholic saint Santa Bárbara to hide the warrior *orisha.* Often created around African national groups, these societies served to rekindle a sense of community. Nevertheless, these societies in Cuba and Brazil, as well as in other locations throughout the Americas, were unable to protect priests and priestesses from persecution, imprisonment, and execution at the hands of their colonizers. There was no thwarting the colonizers' desperate attempts to stop the preservation and continuity of African religions. In spite of these atrocities, the warrior spirit of Shangó thrived in the African people of Cuba, who led slave revolts spurred by the *aché* of this warrior *orisha.*

For practitioners in Cuba, the *orisha* Shangó is the ultimate warrior. He punishes by hurling lightning and thunderbolts. Independent and elegant, Shangó was king of the city of Oyo in West Africa. When he died, Olodumare transformed him into an *orisha.* He possesses the intensity of fire, represented by the color red, but he also carries the calming energy of the color white.

According to the *patakís,* Shangó, when angered, never took prisoners during his battles, because he killed them all. The fury of Shangó is to be feared because he destroys with fire and is unforgiving.

Listening to Elpidio's explanations helped me understand the importance of accurately interpreting the philosophy, legends, and practices of Santería and its practitioners. There are historians who still describe slave revolts as acts of savagery, often recording only the lost lives of plantation owners. Little mention is made of the daily acts of abuse and degradation committed by colonizers toward their slaves. The lives of slaves who fought for their liberation will for the most part remain unrecorded in the annals of history. In his roundabout way, Elpidio was telling me that history is still the story of the conquerors.

Elpidio's deep sorrow also testified to the reality that African religions continue to be persecuted throughout the world. The irony is that while the religions are attacked, they are also being used in many of the same countries as exotica, something to be exploited in nightclubs and in public performances as tourist attractions. In a recently staged Brazilian production on Broadway, the female *orishas* were represented by women dressed in *tangas*—thong bathing suit bottoms—with pasties covering their nipples. Priests and priestesses throughout the world continue to fight against misinformation and the defamation of their ancient religions.

But my discussion with Elpidio opened other areas of thought. Was Santería more than a religion? Was it a means of maintaining a philosophy? A lifestyle? A new way of re-creating and defining family and community? A way of life that honored nature above all else?

Elpidio continued to teach me; he explained that it required long years of in-depth study to learn the intricate rituals that foster the positive energy flow of *aché*. He commented that as a young man he often studied by candlelight, writing out by hand pages of information from the books of elder priests. With a merry twinkle in his eye, he wondered aloud if I would have the same dedication and willingness to sacrifice in order to learn. Scratching his woolly hair, Elpidio lamented how many priests did not take the time to learn the profound teachings from their elders and therefore lacked the necessary knowledge to pass on to their godchildren.

"A priest or priestess with *aché* is a wise and knowledgeable person who has developed divine power within and can also pass it on," he said. "You can give only that which you have acquired. If you do not have food, you cannot share it. If you do not have knowledge, what can you share?

"Everything we need to know resides in nature; this is why all rituals and ceremonies in Santería use nature's riches and are a tribute to, a celebration of, the forces of nature," he went on. "Rituals include prayers, chants, the use of medicinal plants, and

oftentimes they include animal sacrifice, which is necessary to enhance *aché*."

Zenaida then stressed the importance of connecting the underlying lessons we learn from nature to our daily lives. She began by pointing to her Ellegua positioned behind the door, surrounded by children's toys and candy. "It is my opinion that Ellegua is both the most important and the most misunderstood *orisha* in Santería," she told me. "All ceremonies start and end with him. This informs you of his central role in our religion. He is the messenger between heaven and earth; he connects the divine cycle of our existence with the balance we seek." She walked to her Ellegua and rearranged the toys around the clay plate.

Elpidio agreed with Zenaida, explaining that Ellegua's youthful energy reminds us of the importance of flexibility and courage in seeking solutions, just as Oggun and Ochosi seek to instill the spirit of truth, justice, and cooperation into our lives. Each *orisha* possesses a particular power. They share these powers with us, explained my *padrino*.

"Please give me a clearer explanation of how an *orisha* can have many different qualities?" I asked, trying to follow his meaning. Zenaida continued the lesson. "Understand, my daughter, that Elpidio and I are discussing the basic role of the *orishas*. But we do not want you to think that they are one-dimensional or shallow. Just as you embody many roles in your daily life—for example, mother, grandmother, sister, aunt, professor, and lover—each *orisha* has many different roles, which we call *caminos*, or roads. Ellegua has twenty-one roads; Obatalá has eight roads; Yemayá, seven; and so on. In each road, they have different names and perform different functions, although they are all part of the same *orisha's* energy field."

It was clear to me that my godparents were working hard to provide information that was simple enough for me to understand. Yet they did not want me to receive the false impression that I could understand the complexity of the teachings of Santería in one week. Sitting in their kitchen in Cuba was like sitting on the lap of my mother as she lovingly swayed back and forth in her rocking chair. I felt as if I had known my *padrino* and *madrina* all my life. Our souls had connected in a very short time, and the trust we developed facilitated my learning. Their guidance made me more receptive to opening my inner self. In only a few days, dreams were awakening my intuitive abilities, my third eye, my sixth sense. I was allowing my mind to reach beyond the invisible barriers that I had unknowingly allowed to build over time.

Carefully pondering the iron objects of Oggun, Elpidio explained that all the divinities possessed human qualities, since they had once walked the Earth themselves. Again, he reiterated, "It is through the *orishas'* virtuous behavior, and their imperfect actions as well, that we learn the ethical and moral behavior that is essential in guiding our society." Suddenly I realized that when my godparents spoke of the spirits and *orishas*, they referred to them as living human beings. This is when I began to understand that their energies are part of our daily existence.

To illustrate this point, Zenaida—while packing dishes for use at Javier's initiation ceremony—began to tell me about the powers of the hunter *orisha*, Ochosi. Zenaida always spoke freely, unlike Elpidio, who carefully selected his words. She enjoyed elaborating on her stories, using her expressive, dark eyes to emphasize a point. "Ochosi is the divine hunter," she said. "He has the unique task of bringing his prey to be eaten by Olodumare and Obatalá. Ochosi is the only *orisha* with the directions to the secret house of Olodumare, as well as the power to administer justice. He acquired these powers directly from Olodumare.

"It is said that each morning Ochosi would disappear, taking food along the secret road to the home of Olodumare. All the *orishas* were curious to know where Ochosi went each morning. His mother, Yemayá, also curious to know where Ochosi went, decided to follow him one day. She made a hole in his pouch and poured cascarilla inside, which would leave a trail on the dirt road for her to follow. When she arrived at the tree trunk where

Ochosi left the animals he had killed, she decided to drain their blood. Daily she followed the same pattern of draining the blood of the animals left by Ochosi for Olodumare.

"Finally, one day Olodumare asked Ochosi why he was leaving the animals drained of their blood. Ochosi responded that when he left the freshly killed animals, the blood had not been drained. When Olodumare asked who else knew the secret path to his home, Ochosi assured him that he had told no one else.

"Embarrassed and upset, Ochosi did not want Olodumare to think he was untrustworthy. He put an arrow in his bow and released it into the air, shouting, 'It is my desire that this arrow land in the heart of the one who is causing Olodumare to distrust me.' When he returned home, he found his mother dead, with his arrow through her heart. Seeking justice above everything else, Ochosi had unknowingly killed his own mother. Ochosi's tears swept Yemayá away to the bottom of the ocean, where she was reborn and now lives. As a result, in honor of his devotion, Olodumare gave him the power of justice."

"When living in a society," Elpidio mindfully added to Zenaida's explanation, "there are rules that must be followed, or else there will be chaos. Ochosi reminds us that above all things there is the divine power of justice, from which no one can escape. Misdeeds can be hidden from the eyes of mortals, but not from the Almighty."

Zenaida then turned to face me, placing her hands on her hips. Her strength suddenly reminded me of the African woman ancestor who protected my *abuela*—clearly, Zenaida was as strong as a rock and would not be budged. "My daughter," she spoke passionately, "Ochosi reminds us to be aware of the actions of our friends and families. Ochosi's own mother did not respect her son's sacred mission, and this caused her own death. Envy, jealousy, secrecy, and deceit are human failings that exist within families and other relationships. This story tells us to be cautious of these unfortunate traits."

Zenaida's passion raised the temperature in the room, and I could only assume that there was a personal story that had caused the emotional intensity of her response, but I did not think it appropriate to ask. For me, the story struck home. Memories of my own family's breakup immediately came to mind. Viewing my family's turmoil through Ochosi's tragedy was helpful, yet I realized that the lessons in the *patakís* carried various meanings, dependent upon the interpretations brought to the stories.

My godparents enjoyed telling the stories of the *orishas*. We talked late into the night, sharing stories that helped to reveal the logic behind Santería. Enthralled by the beauty of the *patakís* and their messages, I lost track of time. Coming to the close of our session, Elpidio said, "Let us not forget Osun. We must always remember that we have an *orisha* that resides deep in the recesses of our minds. It is the intuitive spirit that saves or destroys us. Our challenge is to know how to respect and use this sacred gift wisely. We must use common sense, and the gift of logic mixed with faith."

Touching his head, Elpidio said, "Our head is so sacred that it must not be touched by just anyone. My daughter, remember these words: Hold your head up high, respect your *orisha*, and make certain that you know who touches the crown of your head. Osun is the messenger of Olodumare and Obatalá. When an initiate receives the warriors, Osun represents his personal guardian angel."

The long day had taken its toll on Elpidio, and it required all of his strength to pull himself up from the chair. Zenaida suggested that he take a nap before returning to the site of Javier's initiation. Although he was exhausted, Elpidio explained that it was his duty and responsibility to make certain that his godson's initiation was proceeding accordingly. Giving Zenaida a tender kiss on the forehead, he commented, "You know that we must follow our tradition to the letter. I will spend the evening with my new godson."

Deciding that it was too late for me to return to the hotel by

myself, Zenaida encouraged me to stay the night. I agreed and re-mained seated while she gathered the items Elpidio had left on the table. Pleased with the results of my first class, she took the opportunity to reemphasize parts of our discussion. "Remem-ber, my daughter, the *patakís* help us look at situations we often do not want to confront. All these stories exist in life," she said, nodding her head. After cleaning the kitchen, Zenaida lit a stick of sweet-smelling incense. "Oh, how I love the way the apart-ment feels and smells when I burn sandalwood fragrance," she commented on her way to prepare my bedroom.

Too excited to sleep, I jotted down the information that would become part of my personal journal. What impressed me most about my first lesson was that all the stories were applicable to incidents in my life. All of the stories touched upon different experiences I had had.

As I sat on the bed, a tingling sensation slowly started climb-ing from the tips of my toes to the top of my head. Unable to move because of the numbing sensation, my vision became ex-ceedingly detailed and clear. The image of my *abuela* in her usual white clothes gradually appeared at the foot of the small bed. She had a slight smile on her lips, looking younger than I remem-bered, her skin, youthfully soft and wrinkle-free, glowing like polished mahogany. Surrounded by a glistening aura, the white of her clothing sparkled with a pearl-like radiance. Soon, the whole room began to glow.

I watched motionless as another figure began to emerge alongside Abuela. Much older, slightly bent, the woman's small thin body was leaning on a hooked wooden cane made from the branch of a tree. She was dressed like Abuela, but her darker skin was heavy with wrinkles and stood out starkly against the white of her long cotton dress. Her small eyes, the color of roasted cof-fee beans, glimmered as she looked my way. As I searched her face to see if I recognized her, the tribal marks etched on her face began to shed tears of red blood.

Slowly, Abuela and the older woman walked toward me, the elder woman leaning heavily on the arm of my *abuela* for support. As they moved closer, the beaded necklaces around their necks began to radiate a blinding light. My *abuela* was wearing the red and white colors of Shangó, and the older woman was wearing white, the color of Obatalá. Then the older woman's cane transformed into a white horsetail whisk, the handle shining with opalescent beads like the ones that encircled her neck. As they came within arm's reach, the older woman raised her arm to hand me the beaming whisk. Sensing my *abuela*'s approval, I felt my arm reach out and accept the gift. And as I did so, I felt an electrical shock rush through my body. My arm, the whisk, and the older woman's arm became one.

A Message from My Elders

In our first session, Elpidio gave me a small, smooth, flat stone, *piedra de rayo*—a lightning stone. It is believed that these are the stones that Shangó hurls to Earth from heaven when he is angry. The second gift was a double-headed ax, covered with red and white beads, the symbol that represents Shangó in his path as a warrior. He advised that I place the ax in a prominent location in my home and always carry the *piedra de rayo* to protect me from the wrath of war. He cautioned me to remember that we all carry the warrior spirit of Shangó; therefore, we must learn to control and direct our tempers effectively in order to win our personal wars.

Before my initiation, I collected small stones that possessed a special attraction for me. Wherever I traveled, somehow I would find a stone that seemed to carry a "special something." On the beach of Loíza Aldea, I found a beautiful polished black stone that I treasure to this day. In Bahia, I found a piece of coral that reminds me of the African rhythms that permeate that beautiful

city. During my sessions with my mentors, I came to understand that there are stones that are alive; when they are part of ritual ceremonies, they become sacred symbols of the *orishas*. It is important to bring natural elements into your home. Seashells, rocks, flowers, plants, and similar items bring nature's positive energy into a home.

Chapter Eight

ORULA

GUARDIAN OF
KNOWLEDGE

Orula is the *orisha* who divines with the oracle system of Ifá. He has the skills to read the *odus* and to interpret the myriad *patakís* that reveal our destiny. It is he who teaches us the lessons of the *orishas*. The *babalawos* are the sons of Orula. Like him, they interpret the divining signs. And based on these signs, the *babalawo* selects a *pataki* that offers a solution to the client. The *odu* is determined by the *babalawo*'s manipulation of sixteen palm nuts, *ikins,* between his right and left hands. The *babalawo* covers a round wooden divining board, called an *opon* Ifá, with a powder made out of pounded yam, *yefá.* Depending upon the palm nuts remaining in his left hand, he identifies whether one or two lines are to be drawn on the pounded yam with the middle finger of his right hand. The resulting pattern defines the *odu,* as it identifies the appropriate *patakís* that the *babalawo* should discuss with his client. The diviner knows if the symbol carries positive energy, *iré,* or negative energy, *osogbo.* If the client's symbol reveals *osogbo,* the *babalawo* then prescribes an *ebó,* a sacrifice that the client must make in order to bring a positive balance into his or her life.

Just as there are many versions of a single fairy tale, there are many approaches to teaching these legends. The explanation of an *orisha*'s role in a story or even the final outcome of that story may change, depending on who is telling it. This multifaceted approach is an important aspect of Santería, suggesting that there are many truths, directions, and solutions in any one story.

It was wonderful to share my experiences in Ile Ife with Doña Rosa and to learn from the perspectives of the many initiates there. Over the past eighteen years, I have had the opportunity to gather knowledge from the many priests and priestesses who opened their hearts and homes to me in Africa and the Americas. It felt wonderful to have the chance to open my own heart in return. Doña Rosa was fascinated by a photograph I gave her portraying an African *babalawo* sitting behind his *opon* Ifá. The

round board was covered with sacred powder, and it was similar in shape and form to the *opon* Ifá seen in Cuba. Doña Rosa asked, "Is he Cuban?" After many years of research and meeting with international representatives of the *orisha* community, I felt privileged to have the opportunity to connect my global experiences and share them with the beloved Doña Rosa.

The morning of Javier's initiation, Zenaida was busy in the kitchen, filling large burlap bags with rice, beans, and potatoes for the ceremony. The overflowing bags of food reminded me of Elpidio's teachings about how the Santería community must feed not only the spirits and *orishas* but also the community.

Each time we visited the house where the initiation was taking place over the course of seven days, we found rooms bustling with members of the religious family, both young and old. People were cooking, cleaning the house, serving food to large groups of people, washing mountains of dishes, cleaning again, cooking some more, serving another group of people, and washing more dishes, all in what seemed to be an endless, dizzying cycle.

The honored elders sat on old rockers, observing the endless traffic of visitors and initiates, casually commenting on the degree of efficiency of the chores performed. Occasionally an elder would call out, admonishing a younger initiate for carelessly performing a task. They would then teach her the correct way in an effort to maintain the standards of the Santería house.

In Santería, novices select their godparents and accept the responsibility of functioning within a religious family. This has important implications for repairing the often devastating effects that result from the increasing disintegration of families. As a part of the Santería community, I have come to understand that the concept of family extends beyond my immediate family ties. When I was initiated into the religious family of my *padrino*, Elpidio, and my *madrina*, Zenaida, I acquired a familial community of initiated brothers and sisters who live throughout the

globe. Although my godparents never left Cuba, they had an international community of godchildren who provided a world-wide network of support.

In 1995, I traveled to Puerto Rico to begin researching my family's roots. During my travels, I arranged meetings with elders who had contributed to the growth of Santería in New York. I went to a housing complex in the outskirts of Caguas, Puerto Rico, to meet with Doña Cato, a Cuban woman in her early eighties. I telephoned in advance, requesting to meet with her. She reluctantly accepted, saying, "I am an old woman, and my memory is failing me. I probably will not remember very much."

When I arrived, Doña Cato was sitting on her porch, leisurely swaying on her rocking chair. She was a tall black woman, dressed in white from head to toe. She greeted me civilly, but with cool reserve. After exchanging pleasantries, I asked how she had become involved in the religion. "Oh, my dear, that was so long ago, how can I possibly remember?" she quietly replied. Then, noticing my *elekes*, she asked, "Are you involved in the religion?" When I mentioned Elpidio and Zenaida, her memory suddenly returned.

Explaining that she and Elpidio were old friends, Doña Cato requested that I enter her home and pay my respects to her *orisha* Yemayá. Again, the feeling of familiarity embraced me when I walked into the sacred altar room of Doña Cato's Yemayá. As I had done in Brazil, Cuba, and Trinidad, I saluted Yemayá. Afterward, I was embraced by Doña Cato warmly. I found it personally empowering to feel that I belonged to an extended supportive family, because it created a sense of historical and cultural continuity that I had not understood in my youth. I felt I was part of a spiritual legacy.

My sense of this spiritual legacy was really awakened for the first time at Javier's initiation ceremony. The old farmhouse where the initiation was taking place was located in a rural farming community outside Havana. Surrounded by an ample field with lush green trees, rich soil, and a small stream, the broken-down home was transformed by the ritual activities.

It was bursting with love and attention from devotees in the community.

The room where Javier was undergoing initiation was barred to all but initiated *babalawos*. Intermittently, we heard the *babalawos'* sacred prayers sanctifying the ritual. As the *babalawos* entered the room, we could hear their greetings. "*Iború, Iboya Ibo Cheché*, Blessings to all in attendance." My godfather taught me that when in the presence of a *babalawo*, I was to acknowledge the *aché* of his Orula by bending down and touching the floor with the fingers of my right hand. Then I was instructed to kiss my fingers and recite the greeting while the *babalawo* offered me his blessings.

Suddenly, all activity ceased as the Yoruba chants from inside the initiation room grew louder, indicating that Javier was receiving the oracle *orisha*, Orula. From outside we heard, "*Orula Iború*, Blessings to Orula." Then a stillness fell over the house as we heard the chants that signaled the crucial moment of initiation, "*Orunmila* [another name for Orula] *taladé; Baba moforibale*, Orunmila, we honor you; Father, we salute you." Suddenly everyone in the courtyard burst out singing, "*Orunmila taladé; Baba moforibale*, Orunmila, we honor you; Father, we salute you."

Outside on the patio, *santeras* and *santeros* waited attentively to assist in cleansing the sacrificial animals and began to prepare the evening's dinner, which would feed more than sixty people. They chatted among themselves, discussing the difficulty of finding basic products in the poorly stocked stores of Cuba. They unhappily complained about the lack of food, bath and dish soap, toilet paper, sanitary napkins, deodorant, aspirin, and, most important, medicine for children.

Despondent about the difficulties of finding rice, beans, milk, and meat on the black market, they asked themselves, "How much longer must we live like this? Even when we have money to purchase these items at higher prices on the black market, we cannot find them."

One of the elders chimed in, asking, "Is it worth being caught and placed in jail?"

Methods of Divination

Divination with a <u>babalawo</u>

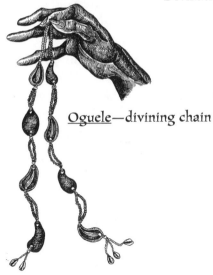

<u>Oguele</u>—divining chain

<u>Obi</u>—four pieces of coconut

<u>Dilogun</u>—cowry shells

<u>Ikin</u>—palm nuts

Olga, the medium, shrugged her shoulders, saying, "Vieja, old one, how can I let my grandchild go hungry? I must struggle along with his parents to find his nourishment."

Erica, the other priestess, responded, "How can I let my child go without milk? As it is, we eat only one meal a day."

The hurt and desperation in their voices filled me with grief. For the first time, I understood the full meaning of Elpidio's words, that the rituals of Santería were also saving lives. The food and the animals sacrificed to feed the *orishas* functioned as a lifeline, nurturing the life of the Santería community. In the worst of times, the only food that was available to members of the religious community was the food distributed at ceremonies.

A makeshift kitchen had been built on the patio. Six large metal drums had been turned into charcoal-burning stoves to cook the food. An unsteady wooden table made from old planks served as the surface for cutting meat and cleaning the rice and beans, as well as a storage space for the burned pots, pans, old cracked dishes, and bent silverware that was carefully guarded and put away. The sink, made of stone, served to clean dishes, wash the food, and even to wash clothing. There was always a *santera* or *santero* working by the sink, making sure it was clean and ready to be used for the next meal. The busy work area was outside, and it was burning hot from the sun, the crackling fire, the coal stoves, and the steam rising from the boiling pots.

Most everyone seemed not to notice the suffocating heat, continuing to perform duties long into the night, their work illuminated only by candlelight. The harmony of the group reminded me of the strength of a family, something I remember experiencing as a child. Whenever a job had to be done, someone would quickly jump into action in a selfless act of spiritual cooperation.

After the ceremony, when the sacrificial animals were brought out, an assembly line formed before them. Some *santeros* skinned or plucked the animals; others boiled them in hot water; and still others seasoned the meat and continued with the cooking. The *santeros* and *santeras,* accustomed to the long hours and hard

work of ceremonies, moved with a rhythmic gait that was as elegant as the movements of gazelles.

The following year, in Nigeria and Brazil, I would witness the same cool elegance in the stride of elder practitioners. According to Mãe Lucia, an elder in Brazil, the settling of *aché* in the bodies of initiates creates this grace. It is the process of becoming whole, of melding with your spiritual power. She stressed that when we learn to work with our spirits, understanding their likes and dislikes, our spiritual and our physical selves begin to merge. She used a Yoruba legend to explain this to me:

"Once upon a time, heaven existed on its own, as did Earth. Then, like two halves of a calabash, they joined and formed heaven and Earth. So it is with humans. When our spiritual half connects to our physical part, we are complete."

Surrounded by the elders, the history of Santería came alive for me. The caramel-soft skin of the matriarchs radiated with the wisdom of ancient knowledge. Their bodies were like boats gently swaying on the smooth waters of heaven, with silver hair sparkling like foam on the crest of oncoming waves. They had a particular cool, an *itutu*, displaying strength and self-confidence and good character, *iwa*, respected qualities to Yorubas in Africa and the Americas. It was as if the elders were cradled in the arms of Obatalá and Yemayá, possessing purity, wisdom, and motherly love. Despite the whirlwind of activities around them, they were able to sit quietly, observing and waiting.

Elpidio had again arranged for the use of Ernesto's car to pick up more bags of food required for the ceremony. Zenaida took advantage of the availability of the car to arrange for us to visit the homes of the elder *santeras* and *santeros* who lived in the area. Brimming with energy and excitement, she believed the best way to help me understand the meaning and power of the *orishas* was for me to meet with her mentors.

"My daughter, it is important that you hear the stories of the elders. They are each a storehouse of information; they are living *patakís*," she said. With a week left of my stay in Cuba, Zenaida was including me in as many experiences as possible.

"The best way to understand the religion is to learn from the old ones, *los sabios.*"

Zenaida took care of the elders, attending to their needs and basking in their friendship. She believed her guardian angels were old spirits, and they drew her to the company of the elders. The elders loved and cherished her in turn. They were recognized by the Santería community as possessors of ancient knowledge and traditional ways. Quite often, they were pursued for their advice and guidance when there were questions about correct procedures in rituals. They loved Zenaida and showered her with praise, treating her as their beloved daughter. They expected her to preserve and uphold their sacred teachings, passing them on to other generations.

First we went to Guanabacoa, to the home of a Yemayá priestess named Chela. Chela lived in a five-room wooden house at the end of a dusty road; she had an undistinguished home with a large porch along the front. Chela passed the day in her rocking chair, greeting passersby. The planks of the porch creaked and groaned with our weight as we sat down next to her.

Chela wore a starched white dress with a delicately embroidered collar, and a blue-and-white gingham apron that proudly announced she was a daughter of Yemayá. Though the edges of the collar and apron were frayed, her crisply ironed and precisely creased clothing revealed her pride and self-respect. Her wrinkled skin glowed softly, reflecting her inner light of profound knowledge and an all-encompassing peace. Chela's small, thin, slightly bent body made her look very fragile, and her arms brushed her apron as she spoke to us, wiping away the flecks of ashes dropped by her Cohiba cigar. The pungent aroma of tobacco and smoke floated around her blue scarf, which was wrapped high around her head, covering most of the puffs of her gray hair.

Since Chela did not have a phone, Zenaida could not give her any notice of our visit, and she was surprised and overjoyed to see us. Embracing first Zenaida and then me, she chuckled, explaining that she had been thinking about us. "Yemayá brought you to my door," she said matter-of-factly.

Zenaida explained the purpose of our visit. Chela giggled like a child, and said, "Why do you want to hear from this old woman?"

Her eyes twinkled as she sat back in her rocking chair. Rocking slowly to and fro, she fell into a pensive mood. Zenaida and I sat quietly next to her, waiting for a response. Chela appeared to have fallen asleep.

Then, softly, Chela started speaking. "I was a child of twelve when Yemayá claimed me. My parents were born in Matanzas, of African parents." She laughed lovingly when she spoke of her dear grandparents. "They barely understood Spanish; they spoke to me in *lengua*, in Yoruba. All members of my family were initiated into the religion, and all were ardent devotees.

"I was the youngest of seven children, and I did not want anything to do with Santería. I wanted to play. Working in rituals was too much work for me then. When there was an activity that had to do with the religion, I would leave the house and hide in the home of a friend. Then one day, Yemayá came down in a ceremony in my home and told my parents that she claimed me as a daughter. I had to initiate immediately. She said she would take care of me. My parents consulted with a *babalawo* to confirm what had been said in the ceremony. Again, Yemayá spoke through the *oguele*, the divining chain, affirming through the *odu* that I was Yemayá's daughter.

"I knew nothing of Yemayá's declaration. Later, my parents told me that Yemayá had spoken these words at three o'clock in the afternoon. At that same moment, at my friend's house, I had been possessed, controlled by Yemayá's spirit. She was in complete command of my thoughts and body.

"While in possession, Yemayá took me to the house of an African priestess named Juana, eleven miles away from where I lived. I was in possession for several days, but Juana took care of me, not knowing where my parents lived. My family and friends looked everywhere for me and were convinced that something terrible had happened. They thought I had run away from home to escape the proposed initiation. When I regained consciousness, Juana took me home to my parents.

151

"Two months later my parents held another Santería ceremony in our home. As a child, I did not know any better, and again I sneaked out of the house and went to hide in a friend's home. At the ceremony, Yemayá possessed an initiate a second time and told my parents that she would wait no longer. This time she was taking me, and I would not return. Once more, she possessed me at the time of the declaration. Yemayá again took me to the house of Juana, where I remained. Following Yemayá's wishes, Juana became my *madrina* and trained me in the ancient rituals of the Lucumís-Yorubas. Periodically, I visited my parents, but my home was now in the house of Yemayá.

"When the *orisha* claims you, it is because you need her *aché* to guide you, protect you, and bring you health. The *orisha* wants you to become a sacred vessel for her powers. Don't get me wrong, you can't sit back and think that the *orisha* is going to bring you riches. The *orisha* lets you know what will save you and what will destroy you. Ultimately, it is your faith in her guidance that determines your destiny. The initiate ultimately decides if she is going to follow the advice of the *orisha*."

To Chela, Orisha Yemayá was like a best friend whose guidance she welcomed and followed. As I listened to other stories of the elders throughout my travels, it was apparent that initiates believed the *orishas* were always present. They were not distant deities who were unreachable. Instead they were energy forces that resided within one's home and one's body. When I initiated, I finally understood the balance that the *orishas* provide. Suddenly I became aware of the immediacy of sacred powers in my home and in my life; in turn, I received daily spiritual reminders of how I must honor my home, my self, and my surroundings.

"The *orishas* reflect all of the peculiarities of humans. Since we were created in their image, we also have positive and negative energies that we must accept in our daily lives. We are fortunate because through the *patakís*, the readings, and the Ifá divination of the *orisha* Orula, we are taught how to handle the changing currents of life. Ifá offers us the opportunity to balance all that comes our way. But it is Yemayá who has me sitting here with you

today. To me, there is nothing greater than what I have learned from my *orisha*, Yemayá."

What I remember most about Chela was the passion in her eyes when she spoke. She possessed an intensity and faith that could not be shaken, and I wondered if I would ever feel similarly. Eighteen years after our conversation, I can understand her devotion to the *orishas* and how it deepens with time. I witnessed the spirits and *orishas* save my mother and niece. Later, as an adult, the *orishas* saved my son Omar from seizures and my sister-in-law from a near-fatal disease. I have witnessed the empowerment of my sons, Sergio and Omar, as they grew up. Like Chela, I have felt the elusive power of the *orishas* intervene many times in my life. Some say that this is simply my imagination; others ask me to prove it. But I cannot prove it logically. I just know.

Through the process of divination, the *orishas* "speak" to initiates, and it is the *orisha* Orula who interprets the message and provides a solution for clients' dilemmas. During my visit with Chela, she was eager to demonstrate the intelligence of Yemayá, so she shared with me the following *pataki*:

"Yemayá was married to Orula, the *orisha* of divination from the sacred land of Ile Ife. A famous and renowned *babalawo*, Orula had performed many extraordinary feats. He had amassed a large community of followers due to the success of his divination skills.

"One day, Olodumare called Orula to a meeting in a distant village, so causing Orula to be away for a long time. When Orula's clients came to Orula's home in need of assistance, Yemayá felt sorry that she had to turn them away. Since shells come from the sea, she instinctively possessed the knowledge of divination with cowries. And as the wife of Orula, she had observed him when he divined, and she had learned from him.

"When clients came to the door looking for Orula, she convinced them that she was as knowledgeable as he in the art of divination with the *ikins*, palm nuts, and *oguele*, the divining chain used as a substitute for the *ikins*. Her predictions and solutions were so successful with Orula's clients that the word quickly

spread of her wondrous skills as a diviner. Soon, lines of people seeking advice gathered daily, and she developed an even larger following than Orula.

"On his way home, Orula heard stories of an extraordinary woman diviner in his village who had the same—if not greater—powers and skills as he.

"Upset and angered by the stories, he decided to disguise himself, and he asked one of his former clients for her address. He was unpleasantly surprised to be given the address of his own home.

"Arriving home, he angrily admonished Yemayá for her behavior, claiming she had no right to infringe upon his domain. Yemayá, equally angry, responded that she could not let his clients suffer, defending her decision to use her powers to help them.

"Unable to resolve the conflict, they went before Olodumare. Olodumare decided that he would divide the divination system, allowing them both to use their skills. Yemayá's domain would be to divine with cowry shells until she reached the twelfth symbol, and Orula's domain would be to divine with *oguele*, the divining chain, and *ikins*, palm nuts, from that number on."

Chela then laughed, adding, "Do you think Yemayá forgot all she learned before Olodumare imposed his order?" Then, answering her own question, she said, "Of course not. Yemayá's knowledge is as deep as the ocean and has no end. Like the ocean, she is constantly moving and acquiring knowledge, and she uses her information wisely. This is the quality that makes the children of Yemayá so powerful. *O mio Yemayá!*" Chela exclaimed, looking toward the Yemayá altar in her house.

Chela's story reminded me of the powerful women I met in Brazil, Trinidad, Haiti, Puerto Rico, Africa, and the United States who were keepers of the tradition. The story that kept circulating in my thoughts as Chela spoke was how three enslaved African women bought themselves out of slavery and established the first Candomblé house in Brazil. Although I heard various versions of this story, it was clear from my photographs documenting the Candomblé houses that women were and continue to be at the forefront of preserving the traditional ways. In New York I had

the honor to meet Sunta, one of the first Puerto Rican priestesses in the city. She lived close to me, and I visited her often as I planned the first international conference on the *orisha* tradition. Well into her eighties, she had traveled to West Africa many times over the years to learn about the origins of the religion and its practices. A quiet woman, she did not boast of her achievements; however, it was evident that she had developed a strong following based on her knowledge of the religion. Chela, Mãe Lucia, and Sunta were all principled women who above all else believed in the power of their *orishas*, and without fear defended their beliefs.

Without uttering a word, I marveled at the beautiful *pataki* that addressed the role of women in Santería. At first, I had been fearful that Santería would replicate the machismo common in the Latino community, but this *pataki* was a wonderful example of how each *orisha* has an equally important role in the religion.

Excusing herself, Zenaida asked Chela if she could salute the altar of her Yemayá. She explained to me that this is the first thing she should have done upon arriving at the house. Zenaida was upset at herself for forgetting and asked Chela to forgive her oversight. Slowly, Chela got up from her rocking chair, and we all followed her into the house.

Chela's entire home was a shrine to Yemayá. The many shades of blue that are seen in the ocean were painted on the walls of her living room. Images of fish, seashells, and coral reflected the mysteries of the deep waters. The tall blue-and-white porcelain bowl, the *sopera*, which held the sacred implements of the queen of the sea, was placed on a specially designed stool painted with the image of a mermaid. Draped from the ceiling, covering the *sopera*, were two interwoven fishing nets that reached to the floor. On each side of the *sopera* were two large anchors that guarded the *orisha*. In front of the altar on the floor was a straw mat covered with fruits and pastries, *una plaza*, celebrating the seventy-second year of Chela's initiation as a priestess of Yemayá.

Our second visit was to the home of Guillermo, a Shangó priest who lived four blocks away from Chela. Now seventy-five,

Guillermo had been initiated in Havana at the age of eight. His stucco house was painted white and red in honor of Shangó, and a white-and-red flag greeted all who entered. A spry, energetic man, Guillermo was at least six feet tall and slightly heavyset. His richly tanned skin, the color of sweet caramel candy, stood out against his shocking white hair. Guillermo, immaculately dressed in a red polo shirt, white pants, and white patent leather shoes, clearly took pleasure in his suave, youthful appearance. He welcomed us warmly. Zenaida had telephoned him earlier, and he knew the purpose of our visit.

Inside, his house was designed in the shape of an *L*. The rear room, next to the backyard, was where he had constructed his ornate temple to Shangó. It was a large castle of white bricks, housing a life-size statue of the Catholic divinity Saint Barbara, the syncretic image of Shangó, as well as the altar where his Shangó lived. Saint Barbara's dress was red and white, and she was wearing a crown and carrying a sword; she was the perfect image for enslaved Africans to hide the *orisha* Shangó because she possessed the objects that symbolized his kingship, his colors, and his warrior status. The sacred stones, *otanes,* of Shangó were in a wooden bowl on top of a wooden stool dedicated to the warrior thunder god. The altar was covered with red-and-white satin material that hung luxuriously from the ceiling and fell to the floor in a cascade of soft, rhythmic folds.

Zenaida immediately asked permission to salute Shangó. She prostrated herself again, and Guillermo placed his hands on her back, blessed her, and then lifted her, just as Chela had done.

Embracing Zenaida, he said, "May the *aché* of Shangó always keep you safe and strong. You know that Obatalá [who was Zenaida's *orisha*] and Shangó are close."

Turning to me, he said, "My daughter, Shangó blesses the initiated and noninitiated, the *aleyo,* as do all the *orishas.*" He looked at Zenaida, and she agreed that I must also salute the altar. Then we went out into Guillermo's backyard, where Zenaida elaborated on the purpose of our visit. In his yard, Guillermo had planted

Shangó's favorite palm tree. The palm leaves provided much-needed shade, protecting us from the bright sun. The yard was so densely filled with hanging plants that we seemed to be in a small forest. We sat in a small alcove Guillermo had created with dried palm leaves. Eager to speak of his beloved Shangó, Guillermo told me about the special blessing of his *orisha* through the following story.

"There was a time that Olodumare was very unhappy. Although he controlled the world, including the *orishas*, he refused to rule. The *orishas* were free to do as they wished, happy that they did not have to abide by any rules.

"The only exception was Shangó, the god of fire, thunder, and lightning, who was traveling around the world. In his travels, he found a beautiful white parrot and immediately decided that he would take the parrot to Olodumare. Upon his return, Shangó presented the bird to Olodumare.

"Shangó said, 'My father, look what I brought you.'

"Olodumare responded, 'I already have everything, yet it does not bring me happiness.'

"Then the parrot surprised Olodumare and spoke. 'You have never had a talking bird to keep you company and be your friend. Now you will never be unhappy again.' Olodumare's mood suddenly changed, and he was overwhelmed with joy. From that moment forward, he actively began to rule the world and the *orishas*.

"The *orishas* were furious. Since they had once been free to do as they pleased, they now refused to follow Olodumare's orders. Meeting in secret, the *orishas* decided to steal the parrot and called upon the trickster Ellegua to carry out their plan. Ellegua took the parrot to a remote part of a distant jungle and released it. In the forest, as the parrot flew from plant to plant, it became covered with many colors.

"Without his beloved bird, Olodumare again fell into a depression and refused to rule the world. Again, the *orishas* were free to do what they wanted.

"Then one day Shangó decided to take a walk in that forest. There, he heard the call of the parrot. When he looked around, he saw a bird of many colors, but he did not recognize it as the one he had given to Olodumare. But the parrot told Shangó how the *orishas* had plotted against Olodumare, conspired with El-legua to kidnap him, and released him in the forest.

"Shangó took the parrot back to Olodumare and had him explain what had occurred. Delighted with the return of his parrot, Olodumare again regained his strength and power. Again, he decided to take control of the world and the *orishas*. Calling them together to admonish them for their misbehavior, he proclaimed that they would always carry the stigma of his displeasure and punishment by each having to wear a red parrot's feather on his or her head. Olodumare decided that Shangó, because of his faithfulness, would be the only *orisha* who did not have to wear a parrot feather."

Guillermo ended the story with a mischievous smile. "This is why Shangó is the only *orisha* who went unpunished by Olodumare. The children of Shangó are blessed by Olodumare."

Guillermo then added, "The Africans who brought the religion to Cuba kept the religion alive so we could defend ourselves against injustice, racism, and cultural genocide. Today, there is no stopping the beliefs that originated in Africa, came to the Caribbean, and are now practiced throughout the world. Santería has spread to Mexico, Venezuela, Uruguay, Russia, China, Spain, Canada, the United States, and many other countries. No one can stop it." The strength and power of Guillermo's voice roared like the thunderbolts released by Shangó.

Then he, like Chela, told me a story of his childhood. "I was a weak, sickly, skinny child, given to blackouts. My parents took me to see doctors and specialists to find out the cause of my weak condition. My parents were not Santería practitioners, nor did they attend ceremonies. They were faithful Catholics.

"One day, our next-door neighbors held a ceremony for Shangó. The drummers were playing the *batá* drums with so much power that the walls by my bed vibrated. The rhythm of the drums and Shangó put me into possession. Shangó took me into the ceremony, saying that I must initiate immediately in order to save my life. He wanted to cure my sickness.

"Friends at the ceremony told my parents of Shangó's message. Desperately concerned about my worsening health, they decided to follow Shangó's instructions. My parents arranged immediately to have our neighbors perform the initiation ceremony. Shangó kept his promise; he cured me during the first week of my initiation. The blackouts stopped, food remained in my stomach, and soon I regained my strength. Let me tell you, by the end of the week I had gained five pounds. When I was presented to the community at the coming-out ceremony, *el día del medio*, everyone was amazed at my healthy, robust appearance. *Maferefun Shangó*, praise be to Shangó. To this day, my *orisha* has kept his word.

"In life, Shangó was a king of the city of Oyo," Guillermo told me. "Shangó was born a warrior, and that is why he carries the *oché*, the double-headed ax, on his head. Shangó is amiable, loves to dance, and is the owner of the *batá* drums. He celebrates life to the fullest and, therefore, does not want to know of suffering or death. He controls fire and manifests in nature through thunder and lightning. One of the powers of Shangó that is not often spoken of is his generosity. When his children are in trouble, he comes to their rescue." As I listened to Guillermo that day, it occurred to me that *patakís* are a way of establishing a common set of values, and a code of ethical behavior for the international community of initiates. Through these stories, issues that most of us face on a daily basis are addressed and resolved. The *orishas'* escapades are very human and provide ways of addressing interpersonal relationships.

Our time with Guillermo was part of a centuries-old process of sharing and building community. He knew that Zenaida would bring only visitors that she deemed worthy of his knowledge and time. As it came time to leave, Guillermo reminded us, "*Orisha* is

love, faith, and commitment." Zenaida told him we were going to meet with Panchita. As Guillermo escorted us to the door, he waved good-bye and told us to give Panchita his regards.

A priestess of the *orisha* Ochun, Panchita lived just three blocks away, and we walked along the unpaved road to her home. We found her placing sunflowers on Ochun's altar. Though Panchita was seventy-five years old, her agile movements, youthful appearance, and constant laughter made her appear to be in her early sixties. She was dressed in a white-and-yellow gingham dress with embroidered trim, her head wrapped in a scarf of the same material, and her blue-black skin was radiant.

Panchita's small, four-room frame house, similar to the others I had been in, showed the ravages of age and the lack of raw materials available to mend deteriorating fences and freshen up peeling paint. Inside, the walls, which had once been a vibrant lemon color, were now discolored.

Over the years, Panchita had collected an array of utensils and furniture that celebrated the golden color of Ochun. On the wall over her stove, she had a decorative yellow teakettle clock that no longer worked. Flowers made of yellow tissue paper were placed throughout the house. Stiffened, hand-crocheted yellow doilies in the shapes of flowers were displayed on her kitchen table. Her home, like the others, was cozy, warm, inviting, and charged with spiritual energy.

In all of the homes we visited, the extraordinary will of the initiates was obvious in their attempts to surmount all barriers and adversity in order to gather the objects that celebrate their *orishas*. Their undying faith in Santería provided the inner strength to win the small daily victories they faced in acquiring the objects that reflected their devotion. With each visit, my desire to learn more of this devotion grew, as the beauty of spirit and faith unfolded before me through the worlds of the elders.

Panchita welcomed us warmly, rejoicing in the opportunity to share her unending love affair with Ochun. She led us immediately to the altar to salute Ochun. Panchita's altar was in the living room for all to see. In a sunburst of yellow, a tureen that held the sacred stones of Ochun was placed on a large wooden bureau. Her altar was decorated with yellow fans, peacock feathers, and sunflowers. It was surrounded by a golden yellow cloth covered with sequins. The light from the two burning candles shining on the cloth gave the altar a sparkling effect. Following Zenaida's lead, I prostrated myself before the altar and saluted Ochun. Panchita gave me her blessing and hugged me when I stood up.

Then we sat on overstuffed cloth chairs that Panchita must have purchased in the early fifties. Zenaida, animated by the success of her day's mission, told Panchita what had happened with Chela and Guillermo. Panchita nodded her approval.

Then Panchita turned to me, her eyes riveted on mine. "Yalorde, another name for Ochun, lets us know that she is a queen. Like Yemayá, she is royalty. Yalorde is loved by everyone because of her delightful manner. Her domain is fresh water, and she loves gold, sweet candy, perfume, and romance. She knows the secrets of all the *orishas*; therefore, they have great respect for her." With her fingers to her lips, Panchita whispered, "The *orishas* don't want her revealing their secrets. This is why she is the savior of the world." Laughing delightedly, Panchita told me this *patakí*.

"When the sky fought with the Earth, the sky decided to teach Earth a lesson. So the sky created floods that caused all of the riches on Earth to be destroyed. Earth soon realized her folly, and asked the birds to take a message to the supreme god, Olodumare. The message was that Earth wanted Olodumare to forgive her, and she promised to always listen to the sky.

"Although the birds tried and tried, they could not get to Olodumare with Earth's message. When the vulture heard about the other birds' failed attempts, she volunteered to go to Olodumare's home; the birds laughed, saying it was impossible that such a dirty, ugly creature would be allowed into the beautiful kingdom of Olodumare.

"Ah, but the proud birds were unaware that in one of her many transformations, *caminos*, Ochun takes on the form of

a vulture. And so it was that Ochun, as a vulture, took Earth's message to Olodumare. It is in this story that Ochun becomes the messenger of Olodumare and saves the Earth."

Pausing to catch her breath, Panchita then explained, "People are too often guided by the exterior, by how a person looks. They don't take time to look within. Ochun reminds us that beauty comes in many forms. That ultimately, true beauty is found in the loving behavior and care that is shared among people. Too often, initiates look only at the surface frivolity of Yalorde, ignoring the fact that through her sweetness she can often accomplish the impossible."

The power of the religion is that the *orishas* address the concerns faced by ordinary people. No issue is insignificant if it creates a problem in the life of the initiate. In my opinion, the power of the religion lies in understanding that we all have strengths and weaknesses and that we must learn to accept them and then work at changing our frailty into a source of power. Santería recognizes that even a source of strength can turn into a deficiency if improperly used. So it is important for the practitioners to understand the source of their *aché* in order to nurture and keep themselves spiritually balanced.

I smiled to myself. The *pataki* was enchanting and reminded me of the old line, "You can attract more bees with honey than with vinegar."

The duality of *aché* is explained in one of the stories of how Ochun enticed Oggun, the *orisha* of iron, out of the woods. According to the *pataki*, Ochun is the owner of honey and it is with honor that she conquers all her battles. It is said that Oggun took refuge in the mountains because he didn't like the way the *orishas* were behaving on Earth. One by one, all of the *orishas* tried to entice him out of his hiding place, but each of the *orishas* failed to find the secret hideaway Oggun had made deep in the mountains. When, at last, Ochun fearlessly ventured into the mountains, she found his hiding place. She tried to persuade him to come with her, but Oggun refused to leave. However, when Ochun seductively placed honey on his lips, he followed her straight out of the mountains. The moral of the story is that gentle strength is a source of power; it is important to recognize when to use gentle persuasion and when to be direct. Through the *patakís*, I was understanding a new way of looking at situations, one that made it clear that life is not black and white, but has many shades.

Panchita then told me she was born into a family of initiates and had always been involved with the Santería community. Surrounded by the *orishas* all her life, she spoke of them as if they were part of her immediate family. Her parting words to me were: "Remember that the *orishas* teach us about the world. They are the world to me."

Walking to our next destination, Zenaida and I relived the conversations we had been having that day. As we laughed like childhood friends, I was truly enjoying a new spiritual lightheartedness. And Zenaida was pleased that I had established a wonderful affinity with the elders, encouraged that I valued the importance of the stories.

In the two weeks I was in Cuba, Zenaida made certain that I experienced as much as possible. Within those two weeks, my life was transformed, and the separate pieces of my life—my growing experiences, my work, and my spiritual quest—finally came together. I felt complete. It felt as if I had known Elpidio and Zenaida all my life. I was home.

A Message from My Elders

The objective of divination is to solve a given problem. Elpidio explained to me that four basic systems of divination have survived in the Americas, and all have their origins in West Africa. Each of the systems uses different objects to divine. All of the systems were derived from the same stem, sixteen *odu* symbols that require that the diviner commit to memory the knowledge contained

in the *odu* patterns; a wide knowledge of many *patakís*; and *ese*, divination verses and their myraid variations. Diviners are trained experts in reading the *odu* that identify the particular *pataki* to help resolve their client's problem.

Depending upon the pattern formed when the objects (*ikins*; divining chain; cowry shells; or *obi*, coconut pieces) are cast, the diviner is able to identify the particular pattern and find the corresponding *pataki* to solve the client's problem. The most intricate systems are the ones used by the *babalawo*, who divine with sixteen *ikins* and the divining chain. The next is the system used by trained *santero* diviners, *oriates*, who use sixteen cowries. The basic system used by most initiates is divining with four pieces of coconut, *obi,* or kola nuts.

Other systems used in Santería include messages through dreams and possession by spirits and *orishas.* Answers to problems can also be acquired from elders, who have developed a high level of intuitive power and are able to interpret the energy field that surrounds you.

The process used to answer basic questions is generally the *obi* system, which uses four pieces of coconut or four pieces of kola nut. The patterns made by the four pieces when tossed to the floor determine the answer to the question.

○ ○ ○ ○

Alafia is the term used when all the white pieces of the coconut fall faceup: When the four white sides are visible, the answer to the question is yes. However, it is recommended that the *obi* be cast again to confirm. This pattern indicates that the energy surrounding you is positive.

○ ○ ○ ●

Etawa indicates that three white sides and one dark side are visible. When this is the outcome, the response is probably yes. Generally positive, but something is missing. Another toss of the *obi* is required to determine the final answer. The energy surrounding you is positive, but caution is indicated.

○ ○ ● ●

Eyife is the term that indicates that two white sides and two dark sides are visible. The response when this occurs after a toss is a definite yes. Everything is perfect, and positive energy surrounds you.

○ ● ● ●

Ocana Sorde indicates that three dark sides and one white side are visible. This means a definite no. Caution is advised. Further tossing of the *obi* is necessary to determine how to balance your energy.

● ● ● ●

Oyekun indicates that four dark sides are visible. When this is the outcome, the response is no, and that a spirit needs to be attended to. The *obi* must be thrown again to determine what the spirit requires. This pattern requires immediate attention to the spiritual problem negatively affecting your energy field.

Chapter Nine

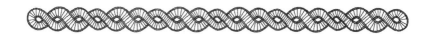

ORÍ

WE ALL HAVE
OUR PERSONAL ORISHA

Accoording to our legends, Orí went before Olodumare and asked to come to Earth. Olodumare granted the wish with specific conditions. Before birth, every soul would be summoned before Olodumare to select an Orí. The Orí selected by the soul would determine that person's destiny. This destiny would never change. If the destiny selected determined that the person would live for fifty years, this would not vary. However, Olodumare agreed that the person's life could be influenced, for the better, if he or she followed the teachings of Ifá, Orula.

Olodumare further decided that, when the person came to Earth, all memory of having selected the Orí would be forgotten. And upon the person's death, Orí would be required to return to heaven to await being selected by another person about to be born.

Doña Rosa, enjoying our conversation, said, "Do you realize that throughout the world there are millions of initiates who have the sacred *aché* of the *orishas*? I wonder how many there are." Teasingly, I said, "Doña Rosa, if everyone has Orí, then everyone has *orisha*." Pondering my comment, she responded seriously, "You say this in jest, but this is true; we all have Orí, we all have a destiny. Eighteen years ago, did you think you would be sitting in my humble kitchen preparing to become a *madrina*?"

As we walked toward the site of Javier's initiation, where we planned to meet Ernesto and Elpidio, Zenaida and I were elated by the words the elders had shared with us. She told me that sometimes the elders refused to talk with beginners. We were lucky that they had been in a sharing mood and obviously thought it was worth their time to speak in my presence.

When we met Elpidio, he was delighted and surprised that

our conversations had gone well. As we headed back to their apartment, Elpidio and Zenaida got into a friendly competition. Teasing her, he said, "I hope the conversations left *orishas* for me to discuss with my goddaughter."

Zenaida quickly responded, "There is so much to be discussed in this short week." Opening her eyes wide, she continued, "I want my goddaughter to receive as much information as possible before she leaves us."

They functioned as one person, starting and completing each other's thoughts, and it seemed that since Elpidio and Zenaida were crowned with Obatalá, they both possessed the wise characteristics of this *orisha*.

We sat around the kitchen table, tired but still excited by the wonderful day we had had. Elpidio rested his head in his hands as he watched Zenaida place glasses of cool water on the table. "My daughter, there is one concept that I want you to take with you, and it is that we all have *orisha* and are sacred," he said enthusiastically, as if the words themselves carried energy. "I do not care what religion a person follows, all I know is that each and every one of us is sacred because we have Orí," he continued, his face taking on a stern expression. "Each one of us has come to this Earth with a destiny that must be fulfilled. Santería helps us understand our destiny and how to best live out our destiny on Earth." Tapping his hand on the table, he concluded, "Learn why you came to Earth. Understand what you must accomplish while you are here. Listen to the teachings of Orula so you can achieve the most from your life. This is the power of Santería."

Zenaida nodded her head in agreement and said, "There is so much to learn in this religion." Looking toward the tureens that held the sacred stones of her *orishas*, she added, "There is nothing greater than to understand your destiny. When I initiated, my Orí and each of the five *orishas* that were given to me spoke through the *odus* cast by the *oriate*'s cowry shells. Together, the *odus* formed the text, the bible, that I follow."

Elpidio then quietly added, "This is why Zenaida and I wanted you to speak with the elders, so you could see for yourself how they have lived out their destinies by following the teachings of Ifá and the guidance of their *orishas*. Santería is a religion that holds you accountable for your actions on Earth, here and now. How you live your life on Earth will determine how enlightened your afterlife will be."

I was exhausted and ready for bed. Zenaida smiled, then said, "Your room is ready."

Lying on the neat, white bedcovers, recording my notes for the day, I began to feel the now familiar pins-and-needles sensation rising from the bottoms of my feet to the top of my head. This time I was not apprehensive, letting the feeling take over my body. Slowly, the room filled with a soft, shimmering white light that told me my spirits would soon appear. Then my *abuela*, the older woman, and my mother appeared, all dressed in immaculate white clothing.

The three of them were moving slowly in a tight circle, almost as if they were floating above the floor. Holding hands with their backs to me, they seemed to be deciding whether they would change the direction of the dance.

They opened the circle, and the older woman with the tribal markings on her face looked directly at me with piercing, glowing eyes, her gentle expression both commanding and loving. I saw etched on her cheekbones the deep black scars of her tribe.

She quietly approached me, placing my hand in hers. As I joined the circle, she said, "Welcome, my great-granddaughter; I have been waiting a long time for you. I have traveled a long way. I am María de la O, your great-grandmother." The soft, soulful penetrating beat of the *batá* drums played in the air, and in the distance, voices of women began singing one of the songs of praise to Obatalá.

Baba Elerífa Odúmila Gbogbo Iworo Baba Elerí Ifá . . . Father, owner of privileged heads, give blessings to all who eat sacrificial meat. Father, owner of privileged heads, give blessing to all who follow the teachings of Ifá.

The ceremonial drums used in Santería are called *batá* drums. Shaped like hourglasses, the double-headed drums are covered

with goatskin on each side. The three ceremonial drums vary in size. The largest drum is called the *iya*, followed by the *itotele* and the *okonkolo*. Lying horizontally across the knees, each drum has a distinct sound. During ceremonies they enter into a rhythmic call and response, in the tempos of the particular song of the *orisha* to be called to Earth. In the Santería religion only men are allowed to play in ceremonies. Sacred *batá* drums and drummers undergo a special ceremony in which Añya, the *orisha* of the drum, consecrates the instruments and the drummers. The *batá* drums are original to the Yoruba of West Africa and were re-created in Cuba by enslaved Africans. Following the journey of Santería initiates, one can find *batá* drums throughout the Americas.

The dreams were vivid and real. I felt the touch of my spiritual mothers, my guardian angels, as they entered, guided, and filled my dreams with divine inspirations. The dreams unfolded like scenes in a film, but they had no logical sequence. Since I did not have the full script in my hands, the ending was still unknown to me. What was clear, however, was that a new order was emerging in my life, and it would soon be revealed. Eager to understand what was going on, I looked forward to a forthcoming divination session that Elpidio was organizing for me before I was to leave for home. I tried to remain calm, though I was very curious to know the revelations Orula would have about my life.

The spiritual past that was coming into the present through my dreams was opening a series of inner doors, each connecting me to my unknown family lineage. I hoped that through divination I would gather information on my family's spiritual legacy, whether my family would reunite, and what my destiny would be.

In the meantime, Zenaida continued to organize our daily activities, filled with learning opportunities that revealed the complexities of Santería. She would advise me: "Never go into a situation blind. The more information you have, the better your decision. I consult the spirits, Obatalá and Orula, when there is a major

problem or decision I must make. I always seek *confirmación*, confirmation, from the higher powers; that is why they are there." This belief, I felt, explained her unshakable confidence.

For the next phase of my training, Zenaida decided we should visit a *tambor*, a drumming ceremony, in celebration of her god-sister Justina's fifth year of having been initiated with the *orisha* Obatalá. Zenaida was particularly eager to attend, wanting to know if Obatalá had a divine message for her. She advised that I dress in my best white clothing.

Zenaida wore a layered cotton skirt trimmed in white lace. The hem was cut into eight-pointed, petal-like leaves covered with layers of white lace that were woven with threads of silver to catch the light. Her blouse, trimmed with the same silver thread, created a continuous shimmer around her robust body. Her cotton scarf, covered with rows of silver lace, was carefully wrapped around her head and appeared to be the feathers of a bird in flight surrounding her dark shiny skin. With white mule sandals also trimmed in silver, she looked magnificent. As I was unprepared for such a grand event, Zenaida lent me a white flouncy skirt covered with lace, and I wore my white T-shirt, white sneakers, and a matching head wrap. My informal style was no match for Zenaida's luminescent grandeur.

The aim of the drumming ceremony was to have the *orisha* possess a designated Omo Obatalá, a child of Obatalá, to speak to the religious community. The ceremony took place in Old Havana, which was a short distance from Zenaida's apartment. A large crowd had already gathered outside the street-level apartment where the drum ceremony was being held. The narrow street with its endless line of worn colonial buildings was overflowing with restless initiates dressed in an array of white clothing, like restless doves ready to fly into the distant blue sky.

The front room of the apartment was filled with practitioners dressed in beautifully designed, handmade white clothing. The ninety-five-degree temperature, mixed with the sizzling heat released by the dancers, created a wall of humidity that hit us as we entered. Zenaida wedged through the crowd, making space

with her ample body. I followed her lead, stepping into a sliver of space as she quickly maneuvered through the web of dancers. Zenaida searched the crowd and quickly found Justina at the far end of the room.

Justina led us into the adjacent room, where a magnificent altar in the room's west corner had been erected in honor of Obatalá. Like a vast wedding cake with innumerable tiers, yards of white satin had been wound around a porcelain bowl, which was placed on top of the sculpture of an ivory elephant. Obatalá's bowl was immediately the center of attraction. Before the *orisha*, there was a dazzling mosaic design of fruits, food, and flowers in a festival of colors. There was a tower made of mashed white yams in a large white enamel basin; dishes of *merengue,* a candy made from whipped egg whites and sugar; *dulce de coco,* coconut candy; *arroz dulce,* rice pudding; and many other sweet treats. On the floor was a large two-layered birthday cake with apple-red jellied writing that read: *Felicidades, Mi Padre Obatalá,* Happy Birthday, My Father Obatalá.

Two large white candles had been lit on either side of the altar, shining their sacred light and blessings on the initiates who came to pay their respects. Zenaida prostrated herself before the altar, then I followed, praying for our families and blessings for all.

Justina was a gentle fair-skinned woman who appeared to be in her late forties. Her chestnut-colored hair was flecked with bronze highlights that cast a golden shimmer around her face. She seemed worn beyond her age, her tired skin and tightly drawn mouth registering years of exhaustion that her carefully applied makeup could not hide.

Zenaida, overwhelmed with the beauty of the altar, compli-mented Justina on her hard work in gathering Obatalá's favorite foods. With a sad smile she said, "In Cuba, where it is so difficult to find anything, you were able to find everything. Obatalá will see your sacrifice and bless you." Stepping back into the room where the drumming ceremony was in progress, I felt the intense spiritual vibration that was about to take over. Faces glistened with perspiration as drum rhythms drew the dancers closer into the world of the *orishas*. It was clear from the faces of the initiates that they were oblivious to their surroundings—they were engrossed in singing the songs, following the precise step patterns and hand movements that would create the ambience in which the *orisha* would select and possess their bodies.

The room vibrated as the dancers' voices became one with the movement of their bodies, "*Babá Alaye O Babá Alaye O . . .* Father, owner of the world, Father, owner of the world . . ." As the drumming intensified, the vocalist, the *arpon*, beseeched the *orisha* by talking into the ear of a dancer who would soon be touched by Obatalá's *aché*. The *arpon*'s voice became stronger, more forceful and intense, as he teased and enticed the *orisha* to possess. "*Baba Pe Wuró Obi Eyó Araye O . . .* Father, they called you because of your grandness. He who has brought happiness to the world."

His vocal cords were stretched tight against his maple-colored neck; his eyes opened wide as the force of his voice exploded in his body, sending out renewed energy. His hands pointed nervously in the direction of the dancer, urging, begging, nagging, enticing Obatalá to enter. The urgency in his voice continued to escalate, soaring like an arrow shot into the sky. The penetration of the drumbeats shook the sacred dancer, rippling through his body, as the insistence of the *arpon*'s voice sent chills down the spines of all present, taking us to higher and higher spiritual levels.

Zenaida, hearing the rhythms of the song to her *orisha* Obatalá, started dancing before the drums. Gently she pulled me to her side, coaching me to follow her lead. Bending low, we performed the slow, swaying steps of the dance to Obatalá. Following the steps, I watched for the moment the *orisha* decided to materialize. Caught in the high-pitched fervor, I felt my head swirl with the repetitive rhythms and movements. The dance steps to Obatalá came naturally as my body joined the flow that

united me to the other initiates. The step-by-step beat released by the *batá* reached into my heart, manipulating, caressing, opening my soul to spiritual energy.

The room seemed to move in a delirious unison as the dancing bodies called upon Obatalá. We moved like soft, rippling waves waking at sunrise. The selected dancer, named Jaime, was a slim man in his late forties. He was wearing thick glasses and oversize white baggy clothing that hung from his thin body, and his shy, nondescript manner made him almost invisible. However, as he began to enter into a state of ecstasy, his personality blossomed. When the *aché* of Obatalá began to touch him, he fought fruitlessly, trying to stop the energy that was overtaking him.

He jerked, he ran, he shook his head, and he held his hands to his ears in an effort to keep the begging voice of the *arpon* from entering his inner psychic realm. Like the persuasive, alluring voices of Puerto Rican soloist Marc Anthony, the African American singer Luther Vandross, and Brazilian vocalist Gilberto Gil, the *arpon*'s voice lovingly cajoled Obatalá, mesmerizing him with the sweetness of his song. Jaime's body moved more erratically as his conscious and unconscious fought for their space within his body. A woman from the crowd quickly stepped forward to remove Jaime's eyeglasses, protecting him from possible injury.

The dancer's anxious face searched briefly for refuge, but his vision was already blinded by the divine radiance of the *aché* of Obatalá. Then his bulging eyes seemed to acquire divine sight as he effortlessly moved about. He was enraptured by the spirit force. The dancers surrounding him had built up their own divine power, and now they moved together like a rushing, rumbling tidal wave. The insistence of the drumbeats summoned Obatalá, while simultaneously the trembling voice of the *arpon* reached yet a higher level of passion.

"*Okú Ni Baba . . . Babá Wu Olowo eee Babá Wu Olowo eee . . .* Father, may you have a long life; Father, who looks after his venerable flock."

The chorus of initiated dancers responded, "*Okú Ni Baba . . .*

Father, may you have a long life . . ." The driving, pulsating beat of the drums made his body move like a puppet controlled by an unseen hand.

The *arpon*'s demanding voice rose higher as he stared into the eyes of Jaime, who was trying feverishly to escape his gaze. "*Babá Pe Wuró Obi Eyó Alayé O* . . . Father who calls us; who gave birth to the happiness of man . . ."

The initiates in the room, as well as those outside, were touched by the spirit of the ceremony. The overflow of people stood in the street, hoping to eventually find a bit of space in the room to slip into, as everyone wanted to be part of the spirit energy that was about to erupt. Anxiously, they looked through the entrance door and into the two front windows, trying to get a glimpse of the *batá* drummers, the *arpon,* and the sacred dancer who was ready to receive Obatalá. The voices mixed in a forceful chorus that Obatalá could no longer resist. The dancer's slim body shook like a leaf caught in the violent winds of a storm. He swirled before the *batá* drums, then leapt as if he were held by a thread that would take him through the ceiling right to heaven's door. When he descended, he was strong, composed, calm, and cool, the adored regal king of purity and creation. Before us now stood a giant of a man, confident and commanding.

Jaime would soon be dressed in the ritual pristine clothing of Obatalá. The crowded room seemed to sigh with relief and gratitude that Obatalá had finally been persuaded to make his appearance on Earth. The room was filled with enthusiastic congratulations for the drummers and the *arpon,* who had worked so hard to secure the spiritual connection. Immediately, they were overwhelmed with offers of cool refreshments, dollar bills were placed on their foreheads, and the small empty calabash on the floor in front of them was filled with money, tokens of appreciation for their special musical gifts. Designated initiates quickly guided Obatalá to the back room, where they would dress him. Happily, everyone waited for Obatalá to appear in his full regalia.

Obatalá, the king, made his regal entrance dressed in a white satin Nehru-collared jacket. The sleeves were gathered at the

shoulders and bloomed into long bells of cloth that came to-gether at the wrist. The pant legs were also bell-shaped, stopping at midcalf. On his head, Obatalá wore a royal white crown intri-cately decorated with silver thread and rhinestones. It was clear that Jaime was no longer in his body. He was now the embodiment of Obatalá.

The design of the ritual clothing resembled the dress of colo-nial times. Like the Catholic saints that hid the *orishas*, the imita-tion of colonial elegance served to conceal the identity of the *orisha*. The ceremonial clothing of both male and female *orishas* continue to recall the royal dress of sixteenth- and seventeenth-century Spanish royalty. The ingenious methods used to camou-flage the *orishas* I found fascinating. Before me was Obatalá in the colonial dress of the culture that had tried to destroy him. His defiance demonstrated that nothing could stop the *orishas*.

Starting with Justina, the people in the room went forward and lay on the floor before Obatalá so as to be lifted by his divine *aché*. Unconcerned about getting their clothes dirty, the initiates lay on the floor before the divine power, hoping to receive advice that would help them to overcome their daily struggles. The divine eye of Obatalá read the minds of those before him, generously greeting, advising, and even admonishing when necessary. The clarity of his vision was so startling that many hesitated before ap-proaching him, afraid to hear the truth of Obatalá's words.

Zenaida whispered in my ear, "When Obatalá speaks, it is law. You must follow his advice to the letter. Sometimes he tells you what you do not want to hear, but you must still follow his instructions. He knows what is best for you."

Obatalá hugged Justina, thanking her for the wonderful, elabo-rate ceremony. Rising to his full impressive height, he said, "You do not need to shower me with gifts that you cannot afford. It is your heart, spirituality, and pure love that I want. Remember that I never want more than you can give." Pausing a moment as he con-tinued to embrace her, he said, "Do not worry, you do not have cancer. Go to the doctor, get an examination; all you have is a female problem." He held her hands and looked deep into her eyes and said, "This is the second time you have been advised to go to the doctor. This time it is minor, but do not wait to be told a third time. Then it will be serious, and I will not help you."

Justina's eyes filled with tears and confirmed the words of Obatalá, agreeing that she would immediately make an appointment to be examined by a doctor. Obatalá patiently spoke to all who came before him. On occasion, he would shout out to an initiate who was avoiding him and respond to an unasked question. In particular, I remember Obatalá looking at a young man who was standing by the door, trying to decide whether to enter to go before the *orisha*.

Obatalá looked his way and said, "It is time you assumed the responsibility of your actions. You are going to be a father. Do not hide from me. I am the father of creation; I created you, do not offend me by abandoning the child and your responsibility." The startled man blushed, turned, and ran away, causing all the gathered initiates to burst into laughter.

Zenaida then decided to go before Obatalá for her blessing. Embracing her gently, he held her at arm's length, and then said mischievously, "Well, you finally decided to listen to me. You are starting your own *orisha* family, your *familia santoral*. I am glad; it is time. Soon you will have a house full of godchildren who will bring you greater health and happiness. Your *aché* is in giving birth to the future generations of the religion." He smiled as he twirled her around, then, facing her, said, "I have never failed you. You have no need to doubt me."

Turning in my direction, he beckoned me forward, but my legs refused to move. I was frightened, and my feet felt as if they were nailed to the floor. Wanting Zenaida to guide me, I stared at her, feeling fear mount inside my stomach as my body remained frozen. Obatalá laughed out, "Come to me, my child, why do you fear your father?"

Barely breathing, I followed the reverent actions of others and lay down on the floor to await his blessings. When Obatalá

lifted me, a tingling electrical sensation raced through my body, stopping deep inside my head. Obatalá delicately hugged me.

Then, holding me at arm's length with his left hand, he brought Zenaida forward with his right hand. He swayed back and forth on the balls of his feet, and with an authoritative look in his clear eyes, he said to Zenaida, "Understand the power of my will. I brought this young woman, *obini*, from another country to be your first goddaughter. You have been running away, avoiding your own salvation, refusing to give birth to children in the religion. You cannot run from me."

My heart was beating hard inside my chest when Obatalá's unwavering eyes fell upon me, and he spoke. "You also have been running from me, ignoring the spiritual signs I have sent you. I brought you here from your country to show you my power. You are my child, and you cannot turn your back on me." Still standing on the balls of his feet, he continued to sway back and forth, looking from Zenaida to me. With a knowing smile, he said, "I have brought you together to help each other and to spread my *aché.*"

Suddenly, he turned to the drummers and hugged each of them. Then he embraced the *arpon*, who had started to sing and was encouraging everyone to join in, signaling to the drummers to start playing as he began to dance before the *batá* drums. "*Okuni Bamba, Okuni Bamba . . .* That you live a long life, that you live a long life."

Soon another initiate rose into the spiritual world, bringing down the blustering energy of the whirlwind with the female warrior, Orisha Oyá. Oyá descended into the body of an older woman named Mari. The music continued to drive its sacred message as it found a willing receptacle in her willing body. The *arpon* quickly went to Mari's side, cajoling the *orisha* to possess her and signaling to the drummers to play the special rhythms of Oyá. The *arpon* joined in with his magical song, enticing the *orisha.* "*Oyá de Ariwó, Oyá Nsan Loro Sokotó . . .* Oyá, the one who arrives making noise, Oyá, that one who comes with the wind . . ."

The slow, halting steps of the older Mari were soon transformed into the youthful, explosive steps of the whirlwind that signified the presence of Oyá. The *arpon* came closer to sing into Mari's ear. Shaking her head as she covered her ears tightly with her hands, Mari began to twist and strain, fighting to regain control. The *orisha* could no longer be resisted, and suddenly Mari's soul was set aside and Oyá joined the ceremony. This time, women attendants gently guided the *orisha* to the back room to prepare her ritual dress.

Oyá soon reappeared, resplendent in her multicolored colonial-style gown, whirling a fly whisk of dark brown horse hair around her head. She stopped at the door and looked at those gathered with fire shooting from her eyes. As she walked into the room, it seemed to shake with the strength of her divine power. Her bare feet hit the decorative tile floor like the beat of the drums and resonated throughout the apartment. Oyá's voice burst out over the room from her deeply heaving chest, announcing that the purpose of her visit was to clean the environment with the windstorm power that was her particular *aché*. She indicated that death was circling the house and explained that she wanted to cleanse the environment and that we would be protected. Greeting Obatalá, she asked his permission to perform the ritual. As in the calm before the storm, the room fell silent. Obatalá nodded his approval. Then Oyá danced, gathering the negative energy of death until she swept into the back room like a cyclone. The room quickly became animated as the fear of death was appeased.

Obatalá asked the drummers to play his sacred rhythms to guide him back into the spirit world. Slowly the *batá* drums began to play. The room of initiates began to move in unison to help build the sacred intensity Obatalá and the spirits needed to ascend back into the spirit world. Then the energy in the room began to quiet down. The ceremony had been successful, and the room was now filled with chitchat and excitement. With a slow, deliberate beat, the *batá* drums started to announce the closing of the ceremony. As I watched a daughter of Yemayá dance around

the room with a pail of clear water, I felt the intensity in the room lessen.

Even before the *tambor* ended, the practitioners began to discuss the advice of the *orishas*, interpreting how they would apply Obatalá's warnings to their lives. Yemayá's daughter continued her circular dance with the pail of cool water as she worked her way to the door, cleansing the environment. When she threw the water into the street, the other practitioners cleared the way, not wanting to be splashed with the negative energy that Yemayá had gathered in the bucket of water. Once the water splashed onto the sidewalk, everyone relaxed and turned their attention to their hunger.

Although others lingered, Zenaida suggested that we return to the apartment to wait for Elpidio. Walking into the cool evening breeze, we felt invigorated. Zenaida was delighted; Obatalá had spoken to her, and she vowed to obey his instructions. Overwhelmed by his affirmation, she rejoiced in the knowledge that she would eventually have a large religious family. "My daughter, do you realize that I've never met the dancer who was possessed by Obatalá? There was no way he could have known that you are my goddaughter." Shaking her head, she chattered on about the power of the *orisha*. "We must believe; we must believe," she kept repeating as we walked to her apartment.

Elpidio was already waiting for us when we arrived. Anxious to get to Javier's initiation site, he seemed agitated. Tired of waiting for Zenaida to bring food, he was munching on an old piece of bread. Zenaida quickly opened her bag, filled with an assortment of food from the ceremony, and spread it out on the table. Realizing that this was his only meal for the day, she encouraged him to eat. Planning to stay at the initiation site for the evening, he packed clothing while he intermittently took bites of food.

"The ceremony ends in three days, and there is much to do," he said absentmindedly as he picked at the food. Zenaida quickly joined in, reminding him to make time for my divination session. Since two *babalawos* were coming to the apartment, she concluded that the session should take place as soon as they arrived. Elpidio then finished his meal and went into the living

room to prepare. Smiling at no one in particular, he commented, "The work of *orisha* is never done."

When his godsons Chino and Eddie arrived, Elpidio instructed them to complete setting up the consultation area. When they finished, they called Zenaida and me into the room. Elpidio and his godsons were dressed in white. On their heads were yellow and green caps, the colors of Orula. Elpidio, sitting on a straw mat on the floor, was flanked on either side by his godsons. His legs surrounded the *opon* Ifá, which was covered with a fine dust of pounded yam, *yefa*, *aché* of Orula. Elpidio held a deer horn in his hand, an *idrofa*, that he used to tap on the board as he said his sacred prayers.

I was instructed to sit on a low wooden stool before him, and Zenaida covered my knees with a white towel. Then I placed my bare feet on the straw mat. Elpidio proceeded to guide me through the steps of the session, explaining that I was to let my breath and thoughts fuse with my energy once he gave me the objects I was to hold. In preparation for the session, Elpidio poured libation on the space, thereby sanctifying it. Holding a small gourd filled with cold water in his left hand, he put his right index finger into the water and let a few drops fall to the floor. Then he prayed to the ancestors, calling the names of his blood and religious family.

He placed a small stone and tiny bone in my hands and asked me to shake them as he gathered the *ikins* in his hands. Elpidio gathered the sixteen *ikins*, which represented the major *odu* symbols, and, after manipulating them between his hands, he asked that I shake the small rock and bone again in my hands. Then he asked that I separate my hands, making certain that I had one of the objects in each hand. He asked that I repeat the process each time he shook the *ikins*. Sometimes he asked for my right hand other times for my left, depending on the *odu* pattern that determined which hand he should select. The stone represented positive energy while the bone represented negative energy. A pattern developed in the dust that defined the symbol that would begin to explain my destiny. Finally the process ended, and the three

babalawos started reading the sign that had emerged on the board.

Elpidio cautioned me before he started reading the *odu*. "Orula tells you what you need to know, not necessarily what you want to hear." Pausing for a moment, he continued, "Sometimes people have a problem that they think is important. But since Orula sees everything, he will address the problem that he deems crucial to your life." Apprehensive, I listened, wondering what he would say. "My daughter," Elpidio began, "Orula says that you were born into this religion. You have a long family history of practitioners. Did you know this?" I responded that this information was beginning to surface in my dreams.

Elpidio continued, "Orula says that you have had many problems with your family. Don't worry. Your family's problems will be solved. Orula says you will be very successful. He is not talking about money. He says your future success is directly tied to understanding and learning about the religion. Orula is telling you that you will be respected because of the important work you will achieve in spreading information on this religion. Respect is something that money cannot buy, and this is why it is important. In fact, Orula says that you will travel internationally, spreading the word of Santería. Orula states that it is necessary that you initiate for your health, and for the stability of your family and your future." Elpidio provided details that were impossible for anyone to know. He spoke about my failed marriage. My growing interest in African culture. The need for me to research my family's history. I was surprised and startled by the accuracy of the information he revealed about my family, friends, and my personal life. Orula talked about the organization I had recently created, the Caribbean Cultural Center. Orula said that this organization would grow into an international institution. This was hard for me to believe, given that our budget was so small that we had a staff of only two, a secretary and myself.

"This *odu* states that you have spiritual gifts that must be developed for your own health. Like your godmother, you will

be an *espiritista* and a *santera*. You must learn and practice both systems. Godchildren will come to your door, and you cannot turn them away, because you will lose your *aché*. It is important for you to begin this process as soon as possible because eventually you will have many godchildren," he explained. Surprised at Orula's prediction, I frowned and looked inquisitively at Elpidio.

Although I did not want to offend him, I asked questions to clarify my understanding of Orula's predictions. How could I spread the teachings of Santería when I knew nothing? Patiently, my *padrino* explained that time would confirm the words of Orula. Elpidio and his godsons said that they had spoken the words of Orula. Then I asked about my work.

"The center is a small organization with little money; we cannot assume the cost of international work," I said.

They all agreed that Orula never makes a mistake. Padrino added that I should write down all that was said to me. He wanted me to remember word for word what had been divined. "A few years from now, you will come to Orula and thank him for the words that have been said to you today," Elpidio prophesied. "Orula has spoken. It is by your initiation that your *aché* will grow and bring your success," Elpidio said as he began to gather the *ikins*. I tried to hide my disappointment as the session ended. However, my spiritual awakening of the past week made it clear to me that I should begin my involvement in Santería.

Surrounded by spiritual energy, I asked if it was possible to receive my *elekes*, *Kofa*, *guerreros*, and Olokun before I left Cuba. Both Zenaida and Elpidio agreed that if it was my desire to follow Orula's words, they would prepare the ceremonies enabling me to begin the first stages of initiation.

The following day Zenaida arranged for Virginia, her godmother, and Justina to be part of the ceremony that would place the sacred beads around my neck. They prepared my spiritual bath, and the rogation for my head, *rogación de cabeza*, and then completed the ceremony before Zenaida's shrine for Obatalá. My old clothing was torn from my body, and I was given a spiritual

cleansing bath. Dressed in completely white clothing, we went before Zenaida's *orisha* altar. The placing of the *elekes* was a private ceremony, which included my *madrina*, Virginia, and her godsister and godmother.

As I knelt before my godmother, each necklace with the colors of the *orishas* was placed carefully by the three *santeras*. Each *eleke* was handed to Zenaida by her godmother, and she placed it on my outstretched hands, explaining the colors and powers of the *orisha*.

This ceremony helped me understand the importance of the ancestral legacy of Santería. When Zenaida assumed the responsibility of being my godmother, Zenaida's godmother became my grandmother in the religion. As the protective powers of each *eleke* touched my neck, the memory of the beads that surrounded my *abuela*'s neck filled my thoughts. I relished the spiritual comfort that now I, too, was protected by the *elekes* of Ochun, Yemayá, Shangó, Ellegua, and Obatalá.

Elpidio and his godsons moved quickly to prepare the sacred symbols of the warriors. They planned that the following evening I would receive the warrior *orishas*. Then the receiving of Orisha Olokun and my *Kofa* were planned for the end of the week. My Olokun, a road of Yemayá, would be born from Zenaida's Olokun. My godmother explained that Olokun is the *orisha* that brings health to the initiate. Elpidio made it clear that my *Kofa*, the facet of Orula that females receive from a *babalawo*, would be born at Javier's Ifá initiation ceremony. He added, "Javier's Orula will be born from my Orula at the same time yours is born." Explaining the importance of receiving *Kofa*, he noted that the oracle *orisha* holds women in high regard and actively protects them. He added that receiving *Kofa* required an added divination session that would determine which one of the *odus* would guide my life. Elpidio added, "Once you receive *Kofa* you will know what saves and what harms you. Also we will know the *orisha* that claims you."

These introductory ceremonies were the first steps of my growth into Santería. My godparents were my mentors and guides

into the sacred world of the *orishas*. The relationship that unites the novice, godparents, and spirits begins with these ceremonies.

When Elpidio and his godsons presented me with the *guerreros*, they explained that increasingly I would notice a growing stability in my life, that the warriors would help me center my thoughts and, therefore, my direction in life. Also the warriors would protect my home from negative energy. As I held the implements of the *orishas* in my hands, childhood memories once again emerged. I remembered my grandmother's apartment with love and a newfound understanding of the sacred beliefs she practiced. I could feel her presence enjoying the moment alongside me.

When Elpidio divined for me the second time, he teasingly asked if I wanted him to identify the *orisha* who would claim me. I agreed, curious to know if the messages in my dreams conveyed by my spirits were correct. Elpidio asked me to concentrate silently and name the *orisha* who would claim me. Then he turned to Zenaida and asked her to call out the name of the *orisha* she thought would call for me.

I felt my heart pounding as my dreams filtered through my thoughts. The image of my *abuela* appeared before me, tenderly transmitting her love. I felt a soft breeze waft across my body as the fragrance of Maderas de Oriente filled the air. My mother was also present. Growing light-headed, I began to hear the rhythms of the *batá* drums echoing distantly in my mind. My inner voice spoke.

Next I heard the snapping sound of the divining chain moving in Elpidio's hands. When I looked at the chain, it seemed as if it were moving in slow motion, as if suspended in midair, deciding in which pattern it would fall. Elpidio looked at the pattern and asked for my right hand. I held my breath as my hand slowly opened. The small stone was comfortably nestled in the palm of my hand.

Elpidio was overjoyed and Zenaida jumped excitedly out of her seat laughing. "My first child will have the same *orisha* as her godmother and godfather."

Obatalá had claimed me. I was elated, for here, at last, was the confirmation I sought. Elpidio, glancing at his notes, indicated that Orula had more to say. Concerned with the late hour, he explained that it was best to discuss the reading in full the following morning. As I was very tired myself, I quickly agreed.

"Do you have any pressing questions, my child?" Elpidio asked before closing the session.

A Message from My Godparents

My godparents explained that each and every one of us has the *orisha* Orí. We all have a destiny. Practitioners seek to enhance the positive energy of Orí by periodically having a *rogación*. The *rogación* includes grated coconut, powered eggshells, cocoa butter, and cotton. All these objects are the spiritually cooling color of white, sacred to Obatalá. The mixture is ceremonially placed on the energy points of the body, which include the top of the head, front and back of the neck, arm creases, knees, and feet. The priest who is performing the ceremony then divines with *obi* in order to determine if the Orí has positively accepted the *rogación*, which is designed to attract cool, positive energy. This ceremony brings peace, which allows the practitioner to perform his or her daily functions without turmoil. For noninitiates, my godparents recommend periodically taking a spiritual bath with cocoa butter, milk, powered eggshells, a favorite perfume, and petals of white flowers. They also recommend using coconut shampoo or coconut oil in one's hair following a spiritual bath.

Chapter Ten

OCHOSI

IN UNITY
THERE IS POWER

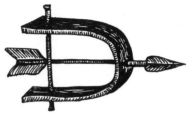

One morning, the *orisha* Ochosi, the hunter, set out early to go hunting. When he went into the forest, the foliage was so dense it took him a long time to reach the clearing where he could hunt animals. By the time he got to the clearing, the animals had left. In days that followed, no matter when he set out, he was unable to get through the forest in time to catch his prey. So he went to Orula, the oracle *orisha* of divination, to ask for help. Orula divined and told Ochosi to make an *ebó*, a sacrifice, with a plant at the entrance to the forest.

In another part of the forest, the *orisha* Oggun, the god of iron, was clearing a path through the trees. He was also trying to hunt for his food. He, too, was unsuccessful, because by the time he got to the clearing where the animals grazed, they had left.

He then decided to consult with Orula. Orula told Oggun to make an *ebó* at the edge of the forest with a plant, assuring him that his problem would be resolved.

The next day, when Oggun was clearing a path, he came upon Ochosi. They started fighting, each claiming the spot in the forest as his own.

But then along came Ellegua, inquiring why they were fighting. Ochosi shouted furiously that Oggun was interfering with his hunting. Oggun argued that Ochosi was the one interfering. Ellegua then asked how many animals they had captured. Both shrugged and said, "None." Ellegua wisely advised them to work together—Oggun could clear the path and Ochosi could use his bow and arrow to capture their prey. Oggun and Ochosi followed Ellegua's suggestion; as a result, they caught many animals, which they shared with the people of their villages.

While Doña Rosa busied herself organizing the plates on the kitchen table, she paused and said, "Marta, soon you will start another branch of our religious family. Being a *madrina* is an important responsibility and must be taken seriously. Your godchildren will come seeking advice, information, and solutions to

their problems; you must be prepared to share your knowledge with a pure heart, always making certain you have no hidden motives. When we try to fool others, we are only fooling ourselves. The unselfish guidance you have received from your godparents is an example you should follow. It is important to nurture a loving unified family." It was a lesson I had learned from my own godparents, over eighteen years before on my first trip to Cuba.

The evening of the ninth day of my first trip to Cuba, I stayed in Zenaida and Elpidio's apartment once again. I was so energized by the day's activities, sleep would not come to me, no matter how many incense sticks and candles I burned into the night. Writing about the day's events in my journal, I connected the messages of Orula and my dream. My spiritual path was unfolding before me. I knew now there was no turning back.

In preparation for my trip to Cuba, I had done extensive research on the religion. The images in the books recalled the objects I had seen in my *abuela*'s home; however, they seemed distant as I viewed them through the objective eyes of a scholar, rather than the eyes of my *abuela*'s granddaughter. The information gathered from my studies was coming to life in the vibrant stories of initiates who embraced the *orishas* as a way of life.

That evening my dream was a *prueba*, a confirmation, of the words of Orula. Madrina Zenaida explained that a spiritual awakening occurred with a flowing together of messages from different sources, like many rivers coming into one.

That evening the spirit of my great-grandmother, María de la O, came to sit by me. Her presence illuminated the room with clouds of white light. Her hand tenderly stroked my head, sending out smooth, soft waves of numbing electricity. For the first time, her face revealed a slight smile as she gently nodded her head in affirmation. Then she stood up and delicately lifted my left arm.

Magically, a white-beaded Obatalá initiation bracelet, an *ide*, appeared on my wrist, confirming the words of Orula in my dream.

The following day, Zenaida and I went to the public ceremony in celebration of Javier's initiation. The house, located an hour from Havana, was filled with initiates and overflowing with chatter; the smell of food permeated the house as children played tag in the overcrowded room. When we entered, Olga, the medium, waved to us from the far side of the room, signaling us to join her. No sooner had we squeezed into our cramped space than we heard the drummers begin to play.

The gradual, rolling drumbeats announced that a new *babalawo* was about to appear. The white curtains of the initiation room were gradually pulled to the side, and Javier could be seen walking at a measured pace surrounded by *babalawos* of all ages. All adorned in white clothing, they formed a calm, moving stream around Javier. Javier's clean-shaven, honey-colored complexion glowed with the spiritual cleanliness that magnificently heralds rebirth. His features had acquired the intangible, noble quality that new initiates exhibit when the *aché* of the *orisha* is newly crowned. He was now a *babalawo*, a father of secrets and an oracle in training to become a voice for the sacred knowledge of Orula. Although *babalawos* do not fall into trances, there was an aura that confirmed the radiance and presence of the divine oracle Orula.

Slowly the procession circled the room. Everyone present was resplendent in the glory of having given birth to another priest who would protect and pass on the sacred teachings of the ancestors and *orishas*. As the procession moved by us, I noticed the faraway look in Javier's eyes as he was led into the front patio so he could carry out the ceremony called *la siembra*, the planting.

Javier carried a hoe and a machete with which he would sow the earth in a symbolic gesture of his commitment to hard work and his intention to harvest the fruit of his labor. It is a ceremony that affirms the *babalawo*'s honesty and his desire to have the

religion grow and expand. This simple ceremony formed a promise to the community, a vow that he would diligently study the teachings of Ifá, would honestly interpret them, and would dedicate himself to promulgating the religion. After Javier sowed the earth, *santeras,* who were daughters of Orula, performed the dance of *los platos,* literally, the dance of the plates. In the Santería religion, women are not initiated as *babalawos,* since this priesthood is restricted solely to men. However, women do undergo a ceremony in which they receive the blessings of Orula, *Kofa. Kofa* bestows women with Orula's *aché* and designates women as daughters of Orula, *apitibisas,* who assist in ceremonies to Orula. The *apitibisas* danced around Javier holding white plates above their heads filled with different types of food, *adimu.* With slow, undulating movements, they rhythmically danced in a circle as other initiates watched jubilantly. The *babalawos* placed money on the plates as the women danced, singing, "*Orunmila taladé, Baba moforibale* . . . Orunmila, we honor you; Father, we salute you . . ."

Once *la siembra* was completed, the *babalawos* proceeded to the dinner table, where a lavish spread of food had been placed in honor of the new initiate, the *iyawo.* The metaphorical ceremony of *la siembra* revealed how the elaborate ceremonies of Santería served to rekindle memory and recommit the community to their ancient ethical codes.

The splendor of the ceremony was something I would come to witness in Trinidad, Brazil, the United States, and West Africa. Elaborate, lengthy ceremonial events serve as public declarations of commitment to the continued growth of the religion. Javier's glorious ceremony helped me understand the importance of having our communities witness rituals affirming our historical legacy.

The day after Javier's ceremony, I returned to the rapid, breathless pace of New York City. The frenzied environment of Kennedy Airport rapidly overtook me. Customs officials snapped, "What were you doing in Cuba? Did you bring back cigars and rum?" As they rudely shifted through my bags, my spiritual experiences in Cuba seemed distant, trapped much like the island's architecture in an antiquated past. The feeling of nostalgia and the nurturing spiritual memories I had experienced now felt as if they had all been part of a dream.

However, when I arrived home, I began creating my *bóveda*, placing it in my living room to honor the dear memories and presence of my mother and *abuela*. I wanted my *bóveda* to become the center of my family's lives, to give my sons the opportunity to be full participants in my spiritual growth, with the hope that they, too, would feel connected to our ancestral traditions. What was most important to me was that they learn to honor, respect, and rejoice in our cultural traditions. Unlike my mother and *abuela*, I did not want to hide or withhold my spiritual legacy.

With my sons Sergio and Omar beside me, I went through our old family albums, selecting photographs to be placed on the ancestor table. Looking through the albums was like reliving my childhood, and allowed me to introduce my sons to family members they did not know. They met my mother as a young woman; her gentle smiling eyes, filled with hope, looked at them from a small sepia snapshot, probably taken by one of those quarter machines at Coney Island. Then they saw her as a proud middle-aged mother, sitting beside my father and surrounded by her young children. My brother, sister, and I were dressed in our best clothes, staring stiffly at the studio camera with forced smiles. This was our one and only formal family portrait. They saw her as an older, tired woman, just before her death, wading in the water of Luquillo Beach in Puerto Rico. They were introduced to my brother and my sister, Alberto and Socorro, as healthy infants in vintage, straw baby carriages with large thin wheels. My sons laughed at the outdated outfits of Alberto as a teenager, who smiled confidently at the camera. They teased me when they saw the wide, heart-shaped brim of my Easter hat, which I wore when I was eight years old. For the first time in years, I dared to

look at my family photographs and allow myself to face the pleasure and pain they provoked in my heart. Omar asked about my sister: "Where is she? Can I meet her?" With unwanted tears in my eyes, I sadly said, "She is far away and we cannot visit her right now." "Can we write to them?" Sergio asked. "When I get their addresses, we will," I responded. Not knowing how to respond fully to their questions, I tried to hide the truth of our family's separation by avoiding direct answers. How could I explain my brother's and sister's behavior to my four- and nine-year-old sons?

I placed my *guerreros* behind the front door, just as my *abuela* and godmother had done. Every Monday, I woke up early and changed the water in the seven glasses on my *bóveda* and attended the warriors, stroking them carefully with palm oil, *manteca de corojo*; covering them with cigar smoke; spraying them with a mist of *aguardiente*; and offering prayers. As my sons watched me perform these simple ritual obligations, I explained each step to them. Using the simpler *patakís*, I introduced my sons to our spiritual family and the warrior *orishas*: Ellegua, Ochosi, Oggun, and Osun. Filled with my family photographs and the *aché* of the warrior *orishas*, our home acquired a feeling of ancestral warmth and spiritual solace.

The weekly rituals in tribute to my ancestors and the warrior *orishas* required that I stop and focus on my spiritual growth, setting aside, for those moments, other parts of my life. Meditating on the lives of my ancestors allowed me to relive the magical moments of my time in Cuba. And I also recalled my summers at Rockaway Beach with my family, Sunday dinners when my father and brother argued over what team would win the baseball series, and afternoons with Abuela, sitting in her sacred room and watching her change the glasses of water on her *bóveda*. But these ceremonies also brought back painful memories that I had tried to repress. Finally, I began to set aside the pain and follow my mother's advice by letting in positive thoughts. I meditated on my love for my children. I thanked the spirits for giving me two sons who brought me such happiness. By speaking to the spirits and the warriors, I was able to learn from my past actions and begin to consider various ways to handle similar difficult situations in the future. And I was able to accept what I had known all along.

Advice my mother had once given to me as a child came in a new light. "You cannot give what you do not have. If you don't have any candy, how can you share it?" Suddenly I understood that in order to give, you must first have something to contribute. My mother's words became the underlying principle of my work at the center—to gather information, you must be willing to share it with others. I was overwhelmed by the positive response of audiences, the large number of people desperate to find that missing part of their cultural heritage. I developed programs that included a balance of artists, scholars, and community leaders, thereby providing a rounded view of the cultural and religious themes we were exploring.

When I first returned from Cuba, I developed a concert in celebration of Shangó's day, on December 4. We invited an initiated scholar to speak about Shangó worship in the Americas, and had traditional drummers and dancers of Cuba and Brazil perform the music and dances of their countries for Shangó. The performance was sold out; we had a standing-room-only audience, as well as a long line of people hoping to enter the theater. We had priestesses and priests bring their godchildren dressed in ritual white to witness the beauty of their culture in an artistic setting. The audience and performers became one as the call and response to the chants and rhythm of the drums overwhelmed the concert hall. Initiates in the audience filled the aisles dancing to the rhythms of their *orishas*. Our religion was no longer hidden behind closed doors; it was on a concert stage for everyone to enjoy.

At the end of the performance, one of the older priestesses sought me out with her godchildren in tow. With tears in her eyes, she said, "In 1956, I was present at the Palladium nightclub when Mongo Santamaria, the legendary Cuban drummer, presented a spectacular concert in honor of Shangó. Since then, I have not witnessed a single public presentation honoring our religion in a respectful manner. Thank you."

Although I performed the ritual obligations for my *bóveda* and warriors, I set aside my journal, letting it gather dust on my cluttered desk. Promising to review the notes in my spare time, I became overwhelmed with the responsibilities of directing and fund-raising for the center's programs while performing the many chores of a single mother. A few months after the concert, I focused on re-creating Carifesta, the international African Diaspora festival of Cuba, for a New York audience. Using college conference rooms and major concert halls throughout the city, we transported the tropical extravaganza to our urban setting, and entitled the series the International Expressions Festival, October 1980.

Among the many concerts and performances, the center hosted a panel discussion featuring priests and priestesses from Africa, Brazil, Cuba, and Haiti. They compared the religions of the Yoruba in West Africa, Candomblé in Brazil, Santería in Cuba, and Vodun in Haiti. By the time the panelists completed their presentations, they had proposed and convinced the audience that a similar gathering should take place in 1981 in Ile Ife, Nigeria, the birthplace of the *orishas*. It was decided that an international conference would be organized, with the center as the coordinating institution, working with organizations in the Caribbean, Latin America, West Africa, and the United States.

Two months later, I was planning trips to Brazil, Trinidad, Haiti, Puerto Rico, as well as locations in the United States. When I called Zenaida to inform her of my new project, she immediately turned over the telephone to Elpidio; I repeated with tremendous excitement, "Padrino, I am planning an international conference on the *orishas* to take place in the sacred city of Ile Ife, next year."

Expecting a congratulatory response, I was surprised when he said, "I can see you have not been checking your journal. You have forgotten the words of Orula. Orula prepared you for this in the divination session. Remember, as I told you, Orula is never wrong." When I hung up the telephone, I ran to my desk and uncovered the journal and feverishly looked through my notes. He was right; Orula had said that I would travel internationally in celebration of the *orishas.*

Immediately, I started planning my trip and arranged for Tom to take care of Sergio and Omar. My sister-in-law, Laura, the deputy director of the center, would be responsible for the center's programs during my trip. As I stopped to take stock of my life, I noticed that Orula was proving his power to me in several ways. I was forced to delve deeper into my soul to determine my spiritual commitment as the business trips began materializing. I received calls from scholars and initiates in Africa, Latin America, Europe, and the Caribbean as word began to spread of plans for the upcoming conference. I received a call from a *santero* in Uruguay, who conveyed the sentiments that most were expressing. Explaining that he had saved his pennies in order to place the call, he said, "I do not have the money to be with you in Ile Ife, but my soul and *orisha* will be there with you. I had to let you know that there is a religious community in Uruguay, and we are also struggling to have the religion respected." Calls from the community of initiates affirmed the need and importance of uniting the varied branches of practitioners.

My journal became my bible, helping me to understand Orula's advice, and the guidance of the *orishas* that were now essential principles in my life. My studies intensified as I sought to identify the underlying commonalities that would assist in deconstructing the cultural borders that distance and time had created.

As I was doing this, I learned that in New York our own communities were divided. Cuban and Puerto Rican initiates were vying for recognition, arguing over which group was most influential in the Santería community. African Americans who were introduced to the religion by Cubans and Puerto Ricans in the late fifties were establishing independent *orisha* houses devoid of

Catholic images, correctly arguing that these church symbols had nothing to do with the Yoruba of West Africa.

The growing Haitian and Dominican communities were introducing the practice of Vodun into the city, first brought to the Caribbean by the enslaved Fon people of West Africa. A small and growing community of Brazilians from Bahia were also beginning to practice the rituals of Candomblé, introducing *orishas* that no longer existed in the other religious systems. New York was already a global village of initiates, and my task was greater than understanding what scholars had written about the religion—it was to understand how our communities perceived themselves and their role in the international community of initiates.

Like Oggun and Ochosi, I felt as if I were a warrior lost in the wood, still searching for more information on why people wanted to initiate into an ancient African religion. I began interviewing initiates wherever I traveled. It was important for me to understand why others sought out the spiritual forces of the ancestors and *orishas*. I wanted to understand how to bridge the varied *orisha* systems in Africa and the Diaspora. By speaking with practitioners throughout the world, I believed I could gain a better understanding of myself. Through their cooperation, much like that shared by Oggun and Ochosi, I could find what I was searching for.

I started gathering stories soon after my arrival from Cuba in 1979. The teaching tales of initiates in New York connected to those told by the elders in Cuba. For example, Norma—a producer of children's television programs who was a consultant for a book project on Yoruba folktales for children that we developed at the center—told me how her first trip to West Africa changed her life. She had seen the faces of her brothers and sisters in Senegal, Ghana, and in other countries throughout West Africa. Though she did not know the native language of these countries, she felt a deep connection with them that began to fill her soul.

As part of the black and Latino power movement of the seventies in New York, Norma had always been active in cultural ac-

tivities that celebrated her Afro–Puerto Rican heritage. But it was not until she traveled in West Africa that she began to understand her heritage through the symbols, dances, songs, and clothing that she recalled from her own childhood.

Norma's light-skinned face flushed with excitement and her body trembled as she described that special moment when she connected to the *orishas*. She had accompanied a college friend to a reading with an *oriate*, a diviner, in the Bronx. "Imagine going to an apartment far on the outer part of the South Bronx, walking up four flights in an unlit hallway to meet a stranger, because your crazy best friend wants to know if her boyfriend is fooling around," Norma told me, laughing. "Girl, was I pissed, after climbing all those stairs to see this priest.

"Well, let me tell you, my friend walked into the divining room that was closed off with this white sheet, while I sat in the living room surrounded by an altar that covered every wall in the apartment. Blue and white was everywhere, on the sofa, chairs, walls, curtains, carpet, and ceiling. The altar to the *orisha* Yemayá was like a queen's crown of silver and blue cloth, with a large Chinese enamel bowl decorated with blue-and-white fish. Blue metallic cloth hung from the ceiling, intertwined with a silver cloth to imitate a waterfall. When I sat down on the soft cushions, it felt as if I were going to drown in this beautiful sea of color. A feeling of tranquillity and serenity filled my inner being. The peace and spirituality that had begun to emerge in me in Africa were right there."

Excited by her friend's response to her reading, Norma decided to have the *oriate* consult the *orishas* for her as well. "After casting the cowries on the straw mat, he looked at the patterns and didn't say anything to me for a long while. This old Cuban man with shriveled hands and face totally ignored me as he went about tossing the cowries. I started fidgeting, trying to get his attention. He continued moving the cowries, ignoring my impatience.

"Then he looked me straight in my eyes and said, 'Why are you acting as if you want to leave when you know that here you

201

have found your inner peace? It is Yemayá who brought you here because she wants to save you from yourself.' He told me that my job didn't bring me the happiness I sought, nor would another pair of shoes or a car. He said, 'It is spiritual healing that you come seeking.'

"His words cut through me, cut through every inch of me, every year of my life, from my childhood all the way to my present life. When he finished his reading, my inner soul screamed yes!

"Then he smiled, and said, 'Always give thanks to the *orisha* Ochun for having brought you your happiness. Ochun, the *orisha* of fresh water, is the guardian *orisha* of your friend, and although both of you are always arguing, there is friendship. In the stories of Santería, Ochun and Yemayá protect and help each other.' "

Norma's self-commanding and decisive manner was helpful in allowing me to understand how to balance the power of culture with the strength of spiritual energy. I learned from her that this power and this strength are the same. The turbulence of the ocean surrounded Norma at every moment, making the spirit of Yemayá visible in her every action. Yet the calming quiet of a rolling wave that ended its journey on a warm shore was also Norma.

I met Warren, an engineer, when he attended a panel discussion on Santería and Candomblé at the center. He had just left a lucrative job to dedicate himself to his *orisha* and to his studies of the religion. It was incomprehensible to his family that he had achieved the "dream" and had chosen to toss it away. His family was up in arms, fighting his decision to enter into the *orisha* priesthood, leaving behind his "professional, successful position."

Talking with Warren was like drinking a glass of cool water in the middle of a desert. His composed elegance was in clear contrast to Norma's effervescent, stormlike energy. Like his *orisha*, Obatalá, the god of creation, he took great care in selecting his words and actions. He appeared to be a typical corporate type, with close-cropped, brushed hair and a careful, analytical style. When I asked about his dedication to Santería, he explained, "Life is about making choices that make sense. Choices that make you live a better life and allow you to be in the service of your family, community, and society.

"Working for a large corporation, I am an object, a thing, with no value. My value is based on the amount of profit I can bring to the corporation. The more enriched they are, the more value I am perceived to have. It's not about me; it's about my skills—if they could pull out my talents and put them in a box, it would be clear that I'm not needed. I found no humanity in the engineering positions I've held.

"Each of us has the responsibility of living a life filled with love for a better, more humane existence. If we do not do our part to create a more humane society—a society where a person is of more value than things—then we are fostering a mentality that supports the enslavement of others." Warren continued, espousing our need to foster values that place children and families first, education that provides opportunities for all, and jobs that contribute to the well-being of our community. He told me, "I have faith in my religion because it created a new reality for our people that negated the enslavement of our spirits. The *orishas* brought us to the Americas for a reason, and it certainly was not for me to be enslaved by corporate interests. It is our faith in the *orishas*, our faith in a new tomorrow, that will prepare us for the next millennium. And I believe it is my duty to prepare my community now."

Warren put into words the elusive drive that fueled my commitment to an organization that provided alternatives and solutions for my community. The feelings of Norma and Warren were my feelings as well. And I was assured that through my work, their vision of the world would find a wider audience.

One of the many things I have learned through Santería is that friendships develop magically. Conversations happen simply because someone may notice the beaded necklaces around your

neck or the bracelet you wear that identifies you as a member of the larger religious community. This is how I met Cudjoe, a middle-aged musician, on the bus on my way to the Caribbean Cultural Center in midtown Manhattan. He noticed my beaded bracelet and with a sly wink pulled up his sleeve, displaying his Ochosi bracelet of Prussian blue and amber. Slipping into the vacant seat next to me, he asked, "When did you initiate?" Before I could answer, he said, "I initiated in Brooklyn twenty years ago. My *madrina* is Ochosi Tafa; you must know her?" "Sorry, I don't," I responded, and he made me laugh with his impish manner.

"Well, I am a true son of Ochosi. No one can mess with me, because I'm always ready to fight and hunt them down. If you need protection, just let me know," he continued, laughing. "My *orisha* is the greatest blessing I have in my life. Ochosi protects me always, because I am a faithful follower. One day, I'm walking down my block, and this crazy man started shooting, just running out of a store he had just robbed. He wounded two people who were walking on each side of me. Miraculously, I was not harmed. Then he decided to come after me. I ran down the block trying to protect myself, and the police got there just in time and arrested him. Wheeeee, I love my Ochosi."

My interviews provided an understanding of the deep-seated commitment that initiates had for the religion. As I planned my trips to organize the First International Conference of Orisha Tradition and Culture, the interviews provided an important source of motivation. The planning phase of the conference occurred in 1980, over a three-month period. I traveled to Brazil and Trinidad to plan the conference, and during my travels had the opportunity to hear many more stories of how the *orishas* had been instrumental in saving initiates' lives and protecting their children.

Mãe Leila, a priestess of Candomblé whom I met through officials at the Bahia Cultural Foundation, lovingly escorted me into a temple where the *orishas* of her religious family were kept. Looking out over the vast land owned by the *terreiro*, the temple,

I noticed the slow, melodious movement of a sea of black Brazilian initiates going about their daily chores. In the distance, a young girl carried on her head a straw basket filled with newly washed clothing. A young man was repairing a fallen picket fence. Older members of the community were seated under large tree branches laden with lush green leaves, avoiding the burning sun.

In Mãe Leila's *terreiro*, each of the *orishas* had a small one-room house that could hold at least twenty people. When she opened the door to the house of Oxalá, the Brazilian name for Obatalá, I imagined that this is what heaven must look like. Exquisite, large bows of embroidered lace covered long porcelain bowls, neatly organized on white shelved walls that seemed to vibrate with spiritual energy. The spiritual essence of *aché* immediately embraced me when I prostrated myself in front of the *orishas*. Lifting me with her delicate hands, Mãe Leila warmly embraced me as if I were her long-lost daughter.

"My child, welcome to our humble home. This is your home away from home." When she learned that I was planning an international conference to take place in Ile Ife, Nigeria, the following year, her face lit up. Then tears of joy burst from her eyes as she again embraced me. "My daughter, this event will be very important. It is time that the world recognized the power of the *orishas* and the community of initiates. Look around; this is a small town. We live as a family. My child, you see the old woman dressed in white, sitting by the man with the striped shirt?" "Yes," I responded, then asked, "How old is she?" "We think she is ninety-two years old. Her birth was never officially recorded. What we do know is that she has lived her whole life on this *terreiro*. Like her, there are many men and women who have continued the ways of their ancestors, living in traditional communities. It pleases me to know that our belief system is in Cuba and the United States. No one can stop the *orishas*."

I laughed when she uttered these words; they repeated the thought of the Shangó priest in Cuba. Looking forward to my visit to Trinidad, I asked Mãe Leila if she knew anyone I should meet

with during my trip. "Ahhh, my daughter, make certain to meet with Mother Sheila. She is a dear friend who has been visiting Bahia for more than fifteen years. Take her address and tell her I sent you," Mãe Leila said, and she placed a beautiful white-beaded necklace around my neck. "You will need the patience of Oxalá, the *orisha* of creation and peace, to organize this conference and achieve success."

My travels to Trinidad were equally illuminating. There, I witnessed rituals similar to the ones I saw in Cuba and Brazil. I met and was accompanied by Mother Sheila, a Trinidadian priestess who was also a prominent choreographer and scholar of the African Diaspora cultures, and well known in the Shangó community of Trinidad. Our visits to the temples introduced another reality as I witnessed Amit, an East Indian Yoruba priest, include his Indian gods beside the Yoruba gods on his altar. The ornate beauty of Shangó resided alongside Shiva, the East Indian warrior divinity, as members of the same family. When I visited his home with Mother Sheila, Amit was comfortably dressed in the traditional clothes of West Africa, designed with East Indian red, white, and golden cloth. He was the head of a large family of initiates that included Trinidadians from all racial groups and economic statuses.

Amit blessed Mother Sheila and warmly welcomed us into his living room. After I explained that I was coordinating the First International Conference of Orisha Tradition and Culture, planned for the summer of 1981 in the birthplace of the *orishas,* he lowered his guard and quickly warmed up, sharing his thoughts and hospitality with us. Amit's home also reflected the unification of two religions, as the double-headed ax of Shangó was surrounded by the golden, red glitter of exotic silk cloth. Talking with him, I recalled the conversation I had had with Ma Mina about the photograph of her Chinese husband, which rested alongside the tureen of his Oyá. They both saw no contradiction in practicing these divergent beliefs simultaneously.

Mother Sheila then took me into the mountains of Port of Spain, to the temple of Gabby, a priestess of the Shangó religion.

Mother Gabby, a thin, dark-skinned young woman, had a large room filled with Catholic images representing the Yoruba gods and goddesses of West Africa. And she had another room filled with the "stools" of the *orishas*. Smiling shyly, she pointed to the stools and bowls that had large flags of pink, yellow, and white alongside. Pointing to the stools, she said, "There is where the true power of the *orishas* rests."

Walking back toward the room where she kept the Catholic saints, she motioned for us to follow. "Let me show you a portrait of a saint I recently purchased in Venezuela; it is an image of María Lionza. According to the blacks in Venezuela, she is the representation of an Indian goddess. The Catholic followers of María Lionza are spiritualists who, like us, work with natural elements of nature. Air, earth, wind, and fire, tobacco and candles, call the spirits in a similar way to our practices." Once again, the cross-cultural connections emerged, affirming that the American Yoruba belief systems are inclusive, embracing many traditions, yet maintaining the philosophical foundation, the *fundamento*, of the original African philosophies. In every temple I visited, I found testaments to the power of faith and religion in keeping a community united. This was also my experience in Haiti, which I visited in preparation for the conference.

Although the Haitians' religion emerged from the Fon people of West Africa, members of a sister religion, the Haitian practitioners would also have representatives at the conference. I wanted to be certain that we had the broadest possible representation of the many African religions that were thriving in the Americas. During my trip to Port-au-Prince, Haiti, I was taken to the temples, the *homforts*, of the *luas*, Fon divinities of the Vodun. Invited by the *hougan*, Vodun priest, Max Beauchamp and I toured the temples of Haitian African gods and goddesses. The *homforts*, equivalents of the *orisha* temples, were decorated with beautiful bursts of colors in celebration of the Vodun gods. Max's temple occupied a large area and reminded me of the Brazilian *terreiros*. The round, straw roof of the temple sheltered intricately designed, sacred altars. Standing among the mosaic of

sequins and satin cloth on flags and bottles on the altar was like being within a rainbow.

The temples were attended by priestesses, *mambos,* dressed in clothing that was so white it had an almost light-blue glow. When I met with a priestess named Paulette, she told me, "It is because of the *luas,* the African Vodun gods, that Haiti was liberated; they are so powerful." In Haiti, I was struck by the pervasive presence of the *luas* in all areas of life. Images of the *luas* were everywhere, just as in Bahia, Brazil, where African gods are openly celebrated. At the crossroads, offerings of rum, candles, and tobacco to the divinity Legba, the Vodun equivalent of El-legua, the trickster, professed the continued devotion of initiates to the mischievous divinity. The overwhelming presence of the *luas* in Haiti and the *orishas* in Brazil would not prepare me for the quiet energy of the *orishas* in Ile Ife, Nigeria.

For a period of three months, I was immersed in my travels and in planning the conference that would take place the following year. My travels culminated in Ile Ife, Nigeria, the site where the conference would take place. I was met at the Lagos Airport by the local coordinator of the conference, Dayo Otunde, a professor of philosophy at the University of Ile Ife.

The tropical foliage surrounding the airport made me feel as if I had arrived in the Caribbean or in Latin America. The rich, reddish brown of the earth and the deep blue-green of the palm trees were framed by the clearest blue sky I had ever seen. Riding in the van to Ile Ife, I trembled from shock as the words of Orula again reverberated in my mind. I would soon be arriving in the sacred city of Ile Ife, just nine months after Orula's prediction that I would travel internationally in celebration of the *orishas.* I felt as if I were dreaming with my eyes wide open.

The reaction of priests and priestesses in Ile Ife was inspiring. In the face of the relentless onslaught of the Christian and Muslim faiths, they were struggling to maintain the traditional Yoruba religion. Similar to the battle the Yoruba descendants in the Americas had with the Catholic church, the Yoruba of West

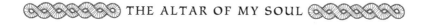

Africa were being ostracized for their desire to maintain their traditional beliefs.

When I visited the temples from which the *orishas* in the Americas had been born, I was saddened to see how the houses of our honored gods and goddesses had declined. When I asked why the temples were so poorly kept, Dayo explained that the traditional religions of the Yoruba were under attack by other religions. Most of the temples were administered by Muslim or Christian officials, who were not committed to preserving a religion that they viewed as incompatible with their own faiths.

This was why Dayo wanted the First International Conference of Orisha Tradition and Culture to occur in Ile Ife. He wanted the community to understand that the Yoruba traditional belief system was so powerful that it continued to be a strong force throughout the world. "How is it possible that in the birthplace of the *orishas* our worship is being stifled? We need to send a message to the people here and abroad that the *orishas* will always be present in our lives. Ile Ife is where the root first took hold on the Earth. We need our brothers and sisters from the Diaspora to come home to show our international strength," he told me, expressing such great emotion that I knew my work would not be for naught. As we visited the homes of traditional priests and priestesses in Ile Ife, the message was the same. I was moved to tears when we visited the house of a respected elder *babalawo* named Babatunde. When Dayo explained the conference project, Babatunde remained quiet for a long time. Then, signaling to Dayo to translate, he said, "Orula told me that one day soon our children would come back home. This is wonderful news. They are returning when we need them most."

When I returned home to New York, my heart and mind were filled with the images of Yoruba practitioners from all over the world. The traditions of the initiates were so similar in all of the countries that I would sometimes lose sight of where I had attended certain rituals. In each country, I witnessed variations of a tradition that had departed from Africa nearly five hundred

years ago. In reviewing my journal notes, I began to understand the historic significance the conference would have in mobilizing a global community of initiates and uniting the varied branches of the Yoruba religion.

Through the many conversations, I learned that the power of a faithful community can move mountains. How do you explain faith? Can you capture it, box it, sell it? No, I learned, faith lies within, in our commitment to our own sacredness. My experiences in Africa, Brazil, Trinidad, Haiti, Cuba, and New York taught me that the power of the *orishas* resides in each of us. There is no one faith that is superior, and this is why spirituality cannot be codified. So in their journey across the Americas, the *orishas* embraced all the diversity of racial and cultural traditions that Africans in the Diaspora represent. For me, this is the strength of the New World Yoruba religions—their ability to embrace us all.

I completed my trips in February 1980. On returning home, I realized how much I had learned and enjoyed on my first trip to Cuba and how much I missed the community of initiates. As the contemporary, impersonal rhythm of New York somehow drained my spirit, it was absolutely clear to me that Cuba—despite old-fashioned ways, cobbled streets, inadequate phone service, and poor transportation—held the wisdom of our ancestral elders. Like the other countries I had visited, there was a resplendent, magical feeling in the air that enlivened the soul. There was also a willingness to share a sacred knowledge, even in everyday acts.

As my revelations developed, the time came for me to take the next step. I called Zenaida and told her I wanted to return to Cuba to fully initiate into the Santería religion. She rejoiced, saying, "Yes, it is time you follow the prediction of Orula. It is time for you to advance to the next level of initiation."

We agreed that I should arrive in Cuba on April 1, 1981, and remain two weeks. It had been a year since my first visit. So much had happened in that brief time. So much had changed. I had changed in ways I was only beginning to understand. I felt a new awareness of my place in the world now that I had met my international community. I looked forward to my initiation, with the knowledge of the serious commitment I would be making. Santería is a religion that requires the study of the intricate rituals in honor of the many *orishas*. I was not frightened, nor did I have any doubts of what would be required of me. Initiation required that I dress in white for the first year, which, at first, was daunting. In the initiatory year, there would be restrictions regarding food, time schedule, and religious commitments that would require considerable changes in my lifestyle. Having had the opportunity to see the many branches of the religion, I knew I would find the spiritual fulfillment I was seeking in Santería. And that was more than enough for me.

The kinship with my godparents, my dreams, and my burgeoning spirituality all confirmed that I was on the right path, on my way to the *orishas*.

A Message from My Godparents

Zenaida patiently explained the importance of cooperation in achieving our desired goals. "This is why the religion has survived, my daughter. We have established a network of initiates who all work together. Like Oggun and Ochosi, we must understand that often the only way to achieve our goals is to work cooperatively.

"Remember that Ochosi is a hunter and his symbol is the bow and arrow. He is always vigilant, watching and analyzing the best path to take. With his bow and arrow, he eliminates any obstacles in his way. We must always be aware of our surroundings. Working cooperatively requires that we become fully aware of our responsibilities in the partnership with our community.

"My daughter, I am sure you have noticed that in your *guerreros* Oggun, represented by the iron farming

tools, and Ochosi, the bow and arrow, are together in the same cauldron. This is a symbol of their partnership. I suggest that in every home there be a bow and arrow and small farming tools to remind us to be vigilant as we work toward unifying our family, relationships, and community.

"Take this small bow and arrow charm that I had made by an artisan and put it on a charm bracelet or chain. It will serve as a reminder of the unity we must all strive for. Each *orisha* has symbols that represent it, that serve as reminders of the powers of each divinity. Objects from the ocean, for Yemayá; the double-ax sword, for Shangó; amber, for Ochun; ivory, for Obatalá. Specially designed amulets placed on charm bracelets or neck chains are good keepsakes and reminders of our ethical responsibilities."

Chapter Eleven

ORISHAOKO

GUARDIAN
OF THE EARTH

Orishaoko is the *orisha* responsible for the earth, agriculture, and the harvest. Orishaoko protects workers and is a faithful friend. Because he is so trustworthy, he is often asked to resolve disputes among the *orishas.*

One day, Obatalá came looking for Orishaoko, because he needed someone to care for his farm, where he grew sacred yams. These magical yams could speak at night, giving away secrets of how Obatalá created the Earth. Afraid to allow anyone to attend the yams, Obatalá would stay up nights to watch over them. But eventually he grew very tired and was unable to take care of his godly duties.

He asked Orishaoko if he could help him attend to his farm. Obatalá explained that he was afraid to have strangers look after the yams, because they were magical and talked at night, telling all the secrets of Obatalá's powers. Orishaoko went to Obatalá's farm and stayed the evening to care for the yams. When they started talking, Orishaoko asked them to stop. The yams refused to listen to him. Orishaoko decided to bury the yams. He explained to Obatalá that the yams would grow under the ground and would talk no more. The moral of the story is, Beware of people who talk too much and reveal your secrets.

On my second trip to Cuba, I initiated. Although it was only a year after Javier's initiation, many policies had changed in Cuba. The food, cloth, and other items necessary for initiation were even more difficult to find. The government had declared that an official permit had to be granted in order for Cubans to hold initiation ceremonies or rituals. In addition, it was deemed illegal for foreigners to initiate. The Cuban government had also added additional restrictions tightening the surveillance of Cubans in the country who initiated into the religion. Members of the government and the Communist party lost their positions if they were found to be initiates of Santería. Community watchdog groups were set up to report on foreigners visiting the homes of Cubans.

In addition, at this time there was a flourishing black market economy, using U.S. dollars, and the Cuban government wanted to control this illegal traffic. I knew not to bring U.S. currency into the country, but there was still the question of how the animals and foods would be purchased for the initiation ceremony. At the time Cuban money was worth twice as much as U.S. dollars, and the little money I had saved would be insufficient to cover my initiation expenses.

I could not help but have visions of landing in a Cuban jail, and this was my only hesitation. When I expressed my fears to Elpidio, he laughed and quickly responded that he would never place me in danger. He had already consulted with Orula, and he assured me that there would be no problems with the initiation.

Following the advice of Orula, I planned the trip. I arrived in Cuba on schedule, and Zenaida had arranged for my ceremonies to start on April 7. Laura, my sister-in-law, agreed to come to Cuba with me to support my decision. Since she had encouraged my spiritual growth, she agreed to be the family member who would witness the public celebration of my initiation; she made plans to meet me on April 6. At the advice of Elpidio and Zenaida, Laura and I divided up the ritual clothing that I was required to bring. Since Cuba did not have any department stores where cloth could be purchased, it was necessary for us to bring in the clothing for the week of rituals, as well as white towels, white sheets, slippers, underwear, castile soap, and other items. Laura decided to take the white sheets and decorative cloth for the altar, and I carried in the ritual clothing and other supplies for the weeklong ceremony.

I was a nervous wreck waiting for the airport attendants to look through my packages. The stern-faced young woman who was assigned to me asked in a dispassionate voice, "Are you Cuban?" "No, I'm Puerto Rican and have an American passport," I replied. "You look Cuban. Let me see your passport," she asked without looking at my face. When she saw my passport, her attitude altered slightly, and she rummaged through my bags. I held my breath, hoping she would not see my beaded

necklaces, initiation dress, and other scattered items. I knew she could not miss the piles of white towels. In between the white clothing, I had also hidden fifteen pairs of jeans. I prayed to the *orishas* to blind her eyes and let me get through customs. Not changing her expression, the young woman winked, pointed to the *elekes* hidden under the collar of her uniform, and let me through. I sighed with relief and walked out into the street to be greeted by my godparents.

Ernesto had driven my godparents, and he waited to drive us back to the apartment. To follow the regulations of my visa, I checked into the hotel, left some clothing there, and then immediately went to meet Elpidio and Zenaida at their apartment. I brought with me the white clothing, towels, soap, slippers, my dress for presentation to the public, shoes, and white underwear.

To avoid being caught purchasing items with American dollars, Zenaida asked that I bring fifteen pairs of jeans in various sizes. Though she would not provide details in our telephone conversations, I followed her instructions. Once we arrived at the apartment, Zenaida laid out my ritual clothing on one side and the jeans on the other side. "Guess why you brought these jeans?" she playfully asked. I shook my head. "We will sell these jeans for Cuban dollars to purchase the animals and food, to pay the drummers, and to buy whatever else is necessary for your ceremony. These jeans, *pitusas,* are gold, my daughter."

Shocked, all I could do was laugh at the thought that my initiation would be sponsored by American jeans. She explained that jeans were the *onda,* the current trend, and Cubans were eager to have "real" jeans from America. Although jeans were coming in from Mexico, Spain, and other countries, it was the ones from the States that were all the rage. Zenaida enjoyed bartering and looked forward to selling the jeans at the highest price.

I soon learned that the process would be time-consuming, difficult, and nerve-racking. Every time we sold a pair of jeans, we worried that the buyer might be a government official and we would both land in jail. But Zenaida assured me that nothing would happen since we were protected by the *orishas.*

It occurred to me that the creative ways of circumventing authority were similar to the inventive methods that had allowed the religion to continue. Just as people had hidden the *orishas* behind Catholic images to protect the religion, Zenaida was using American jeans to preserve it. Being part of this process was invigorating and made my faith even stronger. I had to believe and have faith in order to take these risks. Like others before me, I did whatever was necessary to preserve my faith.

But to further complicate matters, Elpidio and Zenaida decided that my initiation would have to be held at an isolated, rural farm in Lauto, an hour from Havana. While Elpidio's godchildren prepared the house for my initiation, I stayed at their apartment in Havana. Friends of my godparents visited daily, seeking to help with the chores in preparation for the ceremony.

Everyone in the Santería community was outraged at the new, strict regulations. The question on every mind was, How could the powerful energy of the *orishas* be relegated to appear according to the three-hour limit designated in the permit for *tambores*? To show me how destructive the new regulations were, my *madrina* took me to a *tambor* for Ellegua.

The *tambor* took place in the same apartment where the Obatalá ceremony had occurred during my first visit. When we arrived, the street was filled with guests entering the apartment. Unlike at the Obatalá ceremony, there were now two uniformed policemen guarding the entranceway. From the end of the street, we could see the difference in the body language of the visitors. The free-spirited feeling of community was gone. Suspicious of the police, the guests were self-conscious and uneasy throughout the ceremony. One of the initiates kept watch, following the movements of the police.

Zenaida, looking mistrustfully at a couple she had never seen before, whispered that she believed they were government agents. It seemed that everyone in the room felt the same. The couple were given the cold shoulder, and generally made to feel uncomfortable. Though they were not welcome, they chose to stay, and this served as confirmation to all gathered that they were under-

cover police. Zenaida explained that only the police would have *la cara*, the stone face, to remain.

Throughout this quiet test of nerves, my heart was paralyzed, and visions of being put in jail filled my thoughts. The drummers finally took their seats next to the elaborate altar of Ellegua. In keeping with the childlike, mischievous quality of the *orisha*, the red-and-black altar was piled with toys, lollipops, and *bombones*, hard candies.

Yards of red-and-black satin cloth had been pinned to the wall in swirls with *garabatos*, curved branches, reaching out from the center of a flowerlike spiral. The black-and-red porcelain bowl holding the sacred *otanes* was covered with rows of red-and-black beaded necklaces. A pointed red-and-black hat was placed on top of the bowl, reminding us of the precarious balance that Ellegua embodies.

In this environment of discomfort and suspicion, the *batá* drums slowly began. The drummers tried to build up their intensity with the drumbeats that would bring forth Ellegua. Finally, the power of Ellegua descended, as the *arpon*'s persuasive song took effect. The designated dancer for the *tambor* began to receive flashes of Ellegua's *aché*. The *arpon* called in his ear, "*Moforibale, Moforibale* . . . Praise be, Praise be," and the initiates responded, "*Mama Keni Irawó* . . . Bring us your goodwill." Spinning around the dancer, the *arpon* furthered his insistence, "*Bara Suwayó omo Yalawana* . . . The vital force determines our path." The call and response continued to build until the singer, now perspiring heavily, refused to let the dancer continue the cat-and-mouse game. "*Mama Keni Irawó* . . . Bring us your goodwill."

Suddenly, the mischievous Ellegua appeared in all his childish splendor, joining the ceremony in his red-and-black satin shirt and pants. With a burlap bag filled with candy hanging from his shoulder, he gleefully threw sweets to the crowd. Hugging children and picking up toys from the altar, his delightful antics made everyone laugh.

Then his mood abruptly changed, his joyfulness abated, and his decisive adult logic came into full play as his joyous dance

turned to the dance of a warrior. The branch became a dagger, poking the suspicious-looking couple that were still standing against the wall. Then Ellegua pulled the undercover couple to the dance floor and forced them to join him in his movements. The couple obviously did not know what to do, caught in a whirl of rapid dance movements and the provocative antics of Ellegua. Finally, the couple panicked and ran into the street with Ellegua in pursuit.

The crowd, enjoying Ellegua's prank, burst into laughter, hugging the *orisha* and asking for his blessings. "No one can fool the fooler," proclaimed Ellegua as the ceremony continued. When the end of the ritual neared, Pedro, who had commissioned the *tambor*, discreetly tried to convince Ellegua that it was time to leave. But Ellegua would not listen. He danced and played, obviously waiting for the police to reappear.

Promptly at four o'clock in the afternoon, the police arrived with rifles strapped to their shoulders. When they entered the apartment, Ellegua joyfully skipped out the front door laughing, and he danced down the street into the crossroads. The policemen foolishly stood by the door, not knowing how to react. Ellegua had again proven that he did not give in to the rules of man, that he made his own rules instead. "Nothing can stop the religion," initiates proclaimed as they left the ceremony.

With all this in mind, my ceremony was carefully planned in secret. We told only the members of the inner circle of our religious family. Zenaida called on the elders whom she trusted, knowing that, for them, no law was greater than *La Regla de Ocha*, the law of the *orishas*. I felt as if I had become part of a crusade, a warrior in the battle to protect my faith. And I willingly participated in the secret errands for the initiation.

When all the preparations were complete, Elpidio, Zenaida, and I sat in their living room enjoying the success of our week's work. Tired, drained from riding around at night in Ernesto's slow-moving car, walking the streets on various errands, ordering the animals for the ceremony, and purchasing candles, we were finally able to relax. The next day, Wednesday, we would hold the ceremony that would inform my spirits of the initiation. I learned that the ceremony would also identify my specific guardian angels.

As we sat together Zenaida said, "You have changed since our first meeting. You have acquired an indefinable strength." Almost absentmindedly, Elpidio commented, "Obatalá is already surrounding her. I see that she is already shedding her past and moving into the future. The trips she has taken have made her aware of the power of the *orishas* around the world. My daughter understands her mission. She understands that in unity, there is strength."

"Initiation is the process of shedding the past and welcoming the new"; those words of Elpidio rang in my ear throughout the week of rituals that would, no doubt, transform my life. The deliberate manner in which Elpidio uttered the phrase made it clear he would not be questioned about its meaning. His approach, like many African elders, was to let the power of his words become a reality in the lives of his godchildren.

I was learning that words carry power; they have their own *aché*; they cause actions and reactions. Elpidio was always very careful in selecting his words, and I knew this trait was an important one to acquire. To speak nonsense, to speak without thought simply for the sake of talking, was considered a defect that often resulted in disaster. The sobering weight of his sharp, tired voice made it clear that it was my responsibility to interpret his words based on the *pruebas*, the lessons of my life.

"In life, we are introduced to many roads, which we can choose to follow or not. What is good for me may not work for you. Each person comes with his or her own *aché*, which determines what is best for Marta, what is best for Zenaida and for Elpidio. If you try to imitate me or anyone else, you will fail

because you are denying your own divine gift. Until now, you have been floating, sometimes following the best path, sometimes not. You have no blueprint or guide for your life. It is as if you had an invisible blindfold covering your eyes. You will find that Santería removes the blindfold, as the *orishas* guide you in helping you to understand and confront everything that comes your way," Elpidio explained.

He alluded to the week of initiation rituals as a "rebirth," as laying to rest my past and allowing the flowering of my spirituality. Adding to his thoughts, Zenaida said, "Initiation is like a snake shedding its skin and acquiring a new one. It is a new beginning, the opportunity to start anew." The first ceremony before the initiation process began with a *misa*, a spiritual session, to identify and inform my guardian spirits. Zenaida prepared a small gathering with eight trusted women and men friends, all of whom were respected elders in the religion. Their status in the community would assure that the ceremony went according to tradition. In addition, their experience and very presence would protect us. The elders Zenaida selected would also participate in the mounting of my *orisha* during the final initiation ceremony rituals.

Elpidio left to complete a series of last-minute errands for Zenaida, as she carefully explained the importance of the *misa* before we began. "In some religious houses they do not hold a *misa* for the initiates. In our house we do. In this way, you are protected by both the spirits, who are closer to Earth, and the *orishas*, who live in the higher levels of heaven. This is the way it should be," she explained as she placed nine chairs in a semicircle around her *bóveda*.

Once the ceremony began, she placed another chair in the center, where I was asked to sit among the elders. Zenaida brought a white enameled bowl filled with water and placed it before the *bóveda*. She poured Florida water, petals of tuberoses, red roses, and cascarilla into the bowl, as the mediums and I spoke of my initiation. They took great pleasure in sharing the importance of being a child of an *orisha*. Ma Mina, the eldest, reminded me that during my first visit to Cuba she predicted that I would initiate.

She laughed, claiming that the spirits and *orishas* work in mysterious ways.

Zenaida then lit a white candle and placed burning sandalwood incense on the ancestor table. Lighting a cigar, she blew a cloud of smoke over Mama Chola, the small doll placed on the altar that represented Zenaida's primary guardian spirit. Dressed in a bright yellow and white dress, the doll was sitting on a small wooden chair and looked out at us with a shy grin. Zenaida asked me to stand next to her, then knocked three times on the ancestor table.

Looking at the image of Mama Chola, and then toward heaven, she prayed, "Mama Chola, my special angel, and my *cuadro espiritual*, my guardian angels, I come before you to ask, just as my godmother shared her sacred knowledge and spirituality with me, bringing me health, peace of mind, and family stability, that you give me the ability to pass on my spiritual gifts to my goddaughter, Marta Moreno Vega. As my godmother's hands have brought me sacred blessings, let my hands also pass on divine blessings."

In the tranquillity of the morning, the light of the candle seemed to jump higher; the fragrance of the tuberoses and incense grew stronger, as the aura of the room became spiritually charged. We stood before the *bóveda* in silence, receiving a sanctified clarity that let us know the words of Zenaida had been accepted by her spirits. The atmosphere in the room changed as it was touched by spirit energy. Again, I sat, meditating and waiting for the *misa* to begin.

Ma Mina, fidgeting in her chair, said in her amusing, fragile voice, "Imagine, this young woman coming from so far to receive *orisha* in Cuba. I'm so proud that our religion is touching the lives of teachers, lawyers, government officials, and the common people. *Orisha* is for people from all walks of life; neither their class nor money matter. The spread of the religion will change the public's misconception that this religion is for the illiterate. This religion is for everyone."

All nodded in agreement, commenting that divine knowledge and power are available to all who knock on the door of the

divinities' sacred houses. The head medium, Doña Melissa, sat with Zenaida near the *bóveda*, facing the center chair where I was seated. Slowly rocking back and forth as if she were sitting in her rocking chair, Doña Melissa said, "There is nothing more important in life than to have the spirits and *orishas* with you. When you walk with the divine, you know that your life is forever blessed."

One by one the mediums slowly walked to the *bóveda* and cleansed themselves. I was the last one to go before the *bóveda*, then I returned to my chair. Doña Melissa lit her cigar, gently blowing a cloud of bluish smoke into the room. Concentrating, she remained silently swaying. In a gradual, smooth whisper she began to recite the prayers that would attract my spirits to the *misa*.

"Our Father who art in heaven . . ." Her voice filled the room with a gentle murmur, as the other mediums joined in with their hypnotic, soothing voices. As veterans of many *misas*, they had all memorized the long prayers. I sat in the center, and the gathering's energy wrapped me in a warm blanket of words and songs as the spirits began to appear. At the beginning of the session, Doña Melissa implored the good spirits to instruct the gathering, to deflect selfishness, pride, and jealousy. She asked those mediums present to have clear hearts and humility in order to attract the positive spirits. She then asked that any medium who had not come to share holy teachings leave the gathering, for our spiritual guides would not permit people of ill will to remain.

Doña Melissa implored the spirits of goodwill to visit, to open our minds with good intentions. Then she asked that my spirits acknowledge that this *misa* was in their honor to inform them of my impending Santería initiation. She asked that they visit the *misa*, identifying themselves as the guardian angels in charge of guiding, teaching, and protecting me along my spiritual journey.

As Doña Melissa continued the prayers in her peaceful voice, Zenaida began to sway back and forth in a gentle flowing motion. Zenaida's eyes closed as her swaying picked up momentum. Suddenly, she paused and slowly opened her eyes wide. She had a

faraway gaze that signaled the presence of a spirit. "Good day, if it is day; good evening, if it is evening," the spirit said in a melodious high-pitched voice as she stood up to greet the gathering.

Doña Melissa returned the salutation, welcoming the spirit to the humble meeting. She then asked, "Please let us know your name, Good Spirit."

The spirit turned to Doña Melissa and said lovingly, "*Vieja,* old woman, I am Mama Chola, the guardian angel of Zenaida. I've come to bless my daughter and all the mediums gathered. Tell her not to worry, that the ceremony will be successful."

Turning to me, the spirit welcomed me to the family. She smiled warmly and continued her dancelike motion. "Don't be frightened, my child; you are loved. As I protect your godmother, I will also protect you," said Mama Chola, and her glazed stare reached into my inner soul.

Leaving almost as quickly as she appeared, Mama Chola said her task was done. She wanted to assure my godmother that the ceremony would proceed without interruption. Zenaida swayed back and forth until she gradually slowed down and then settled back into her seat as the spirit left her body. She returned to the session as if nothing had happened and continued to pray.

Then, on my right side, groaning sounds began to build up gradually in the body of Ma Estela. I felt a shiver climbing up my spine as her voice rose and the presence of the emerging spirit filled the room. Simultaneously, on my left side, I heard coming from Doña Bárbara a heaving sound, which soon exploded into a loud shout.

Both spirits emerged at almost the same time, surrounding me with their energy. Walking around me, they looked in my direction, smiling, with familiar love in their eyes. Although we could not touch, their comforting vibrations encircled me before they spoke. In the presence of my elders and mentors, I felt protected and safe. I was prepared to meet my spiritual guides and guardians.

My grandmother was the first to speak, through the medium Ma Estela. Walking with the halting small steps of age, chewing

tobacco as my grandmother once had done, the spirit faced me with a wide grin. "*Mi negrita,* my little black one, finally you come to me," she said as she continued to walk with her slow, halting steps. Then the spirit removed the scarf from Ma Estela's head and retied it in the same fashion my grandmother once had. She was looking at me as she performed this task, and the glazed twinkle in her eyes revealed my grandmother's spirit.

Doña Bárbara, also in trance, came to her side and intertwined her arm with my grandmother's arm, leaning heavily for support. Immediately, the dream with my mother, grandmother, and great-grandmother came to mind. I knew then that the spirit of my great-grandmother was present in the room. With her bent finger she made imaginary markings on her face. Unable to move, I watched my dreams come to life. "I am María de la O. Blessings to all the mediums present, and thank you for bringing me here." Turning to me, she said in a whisper, "Daughter, I am always with you, do not despair. Although many of us have left you, we are with you in spirit."

I remembered the feeling of increasing loneliness, and how much I missed my mother and grandmother and my other family members. Not wanting to share this feeling of loss with anyone, I had felt a sense of despair growing within me. Her words reached deep into my soul and started a fountain of tears rolling down my face. When I tried to stop crying, the tears only came faster.

Then I heard another familiar voice, "Thank you, my daughter, for completing the spiritual journey for our family." It was my mother speaking through the body of Doña Melissa. As she moved from the chair to join the other spirits, her right hand lightly rubbed the left side of her chest.

Before me stood a re-creation of my dreams. Slowly, they formed a circle and danced together. When they finished, they opened the circle and welcomed me in. And it was at that moment that my inner spirit took flight, leaving my body. I was transported into another reality, joining my maternal spirit guides in their sacred circle. As their spirits began to fade, they

gave me their blessings. When I regained consciousness, I was still seated on the chair. I was elated that my spirit mothers had appeared. Not having shared this particular dream with anyone, it was a confirmation, a *prueba*, of the existence of my spirits.

Looking around, I saw that the mediums had also returned to their own bodies and were softly reciting their prayers. My feelings of despair had disappeared, healed by the mystical powers of my ancestors. The inner feeling of weakness had been replaced by strength and the power of spiritual elation.

Then the mediums began to identify the spirits they saw standing next to me. Ma Mina looked to the side of me and asked, "Do you have knowledge of a large, strong, black woman dressed in red and white? She wears a red scarf around her head; her long red dress has a large white collar." "Yes," I responded. "She is standing next to you and acknowledges that she is part of your *cuadro espiritual*. To your other side is a strong, bronze-skinned, Native Indian warrior, wearing a headdress with beautiful plumage, holding a bow and arrow. Do you have knowledge of this spirit?" "Yes." I nodded.

Ma Mina then explained again that my guardian angels were making their presence known. Ma Estela, in conversation with Ma Mina, added that there was a messenger of Obatalá standing behind me, who was also one of my guardian angels. "He is tall, covered in shimmering white cloth. He is intelligent, maybe a lawyer or a teacher, a well-educated man who gives her clarity and brings her peace. This spirit advises her to be cautious and think carefully before she makes a decision. He says that she is too impulsive and gets angry too quickly. His presence will always remind her to be ruled by reason and not by impulse," Ma Estela concluded.

Surrounded by familiar childhood energies and other spiritual forces, I felt a path opening up for me that would protect and guide me and my family as well. The spirits I had seen on my *abuela*'s altar were protecting me. The guardian angels were now connected to me and I to them forever. Now I could talk to them.

Zenaida then confirmed the message of the spirits. With four

pieces of coconut she asked for verification that the spirits that came forward were, indeed, my guardian angels. When the *obi* fell in the *Eyife*, the affirmative pattern with two white sides and two dark sides facing up, it was clear that the *misa* was a success. Everyone rejoiced in the visit of the spirits and the feeling of enlightenment they left behind.

Slowly the mediums stood up, helping to spread a white sheet over my head. Each medium held a section of the sheet, and they danced slowly in a circle around me. Surrounding me, they praised my angels by singing, *"En coronación, en coronación bajan los seres, en coronación, en coronación bajan los seres.* The spirits come down with the purpose of mounting their initiates, the spirits come down with the purpose of mounting their initiates."

As the spirits left, the mystical cloud that had filled the room disappeared. The mediums then recited the final prayers to end the session.

"We thank the good spirits who came to communicate with us. We ask them to help us practice the instructions they have given us." Words were unnecessary at this point as joy radiated in the faces of the mediums. Clearly, they were all pleased and proud to have contributed their sacred skills in the creation of another member of their religious family. The success of the *misa* brought us all continued blessings. As the mediums left the session, they embraced and blessed me. They let me know that they would be present the next day for the beginning of my initiation rituals.

Zenaida, buoyant from the success of the *misa*, started packing the bags of rice, *frijoles*, garlic, onions, and other food items for the dinners that would be served during the weeklong ceremony. The kitchen looked like a grocery store, filled with overstuffed burlap bags of food. She suggested that I check my suitcase to make certain that my clothing and toiletries were packed for the following day. According to her time schedule, as soon as my sister-in-law Laura arrived, we should be ready to leave the apartment for the country.

When Elpidio returned home, I expressed my joy to him over the success of my *misa*, but also my remaining concern that my initiation might bring us serious problems. Rather than cause difficulties, I told them it might be better to delay the initiation until the Cuban government's policies toward Afro-Cuban religions became more tolerant. In his pensive slow manner Elpidio predicted, "The government will eventually establish a more lenient policy toward Santería and other African religions."

And indeed, over the past ten years there has been a resurgence of public celebration of African religions, particularly through the arts sanctioned by the government. The government has even sponsored scholarly conferences and training workshops that promote the diverse African religions of Cuba, and with the lifting of restrictions, the religious community has benefited.

"There are too many officials high up in the administration who are initiates and practitioners of Santería," Elpidio explained. "They would have to get rid of more than ninety-nine percent of their officials, and still no one could guarantee that the remaining one percent were not supporters of the religion. It is even rumored that Fidel initiated in Africa and seeks the advice of the *orishas.*"

Elpidio firmly believed, and time has proven him right, that the spirits and the *orishas* could not be stopped. "Can they get rid of the ocean? Will they destroy the Earth? Can they stop breathing? No, my daughter, the *orishas* cannot be stopped," he explained as we prepared for the ceremony.

Elpidio was deep in thought, lost in his own world, as he slowly settled onto the sofa. Finally, as if each word were being pulled out of him, he slowly continued, "It is your *orisha* that has brought you back to Cuba, and he will protect us. I have consulted with Orula, and we have nothing to fear."

While Zenaida and Elpidio planned my ceremonies with extreme watchfulness, neither showed any signs of being frightened or having second thoughts. Their *itutu*, their cool restraint, lifted

them above the fray, above fear. The cultivation of *itutu* and *iwa*, exemplary behavior, are the desired qualities of initiates, and I could see them radiating through the actions of my godparents. Watching them move in times of crisis was like viewing a slow-moving motion picture. Rather than be ruled by their anxiety, they were guided by the words of Orula.

With focused concentration, they moved as one in their own sacred dream space, checking and rechecking their thoughts and actions. They understood the need to follow tradition, as well as the need for flexibility when necessary, to protect the integrity of their ancestral beliefs.

Usually, the Santería community is informed of a pending initiation. In my case, care was taken not to inform the public until after initiation had taken place. Although my godparents anticipated public criticism, they decided that secrecy was a necessary precaution. Zenaida and Elpidio, with the guidance of the elders, relished the *prueba*, the test the *orishas* had placed before them. They saw adversity as a test the spirits and *orishas* were placing in their path.

As I watched my godparents, it was clear that they fully functioned within the cycle of divine give and take. Their strength instilled in me a sense of courage as they prepared for my ceremony with utter devotion and love. It was clear that the sacrifices being made for my initiation would have been made for any of their godchildren. At all costs, my *padrino* and *madrina* understood that the family had to be protected. That night, I rested peacefully, so tired from all the preparations for the ceremony that I quickly fell fast asleep.

The next day, the rays of the morning sun peeking through the shutters woke me. In the silence of the morning, I took a bath of tuberoses, Florida water, cascarilla, and Maderas de Oriente perfume to spiritually cleanse myself and to attract positive spiritual energy. Afterward, I put on a light yellow cotton dress and immediately felt an unusual stillness overcome me. It was as if I blended into the morning silence.

Zenaida was busy in the kitchen collecting the plates, pots, and utensils needed for the ceremony. Casually, she called out, "My goddaughter, don't wear any makeup. In your first year of initiation, you cannot wear makeup, so you better start getting used to it. Oh, did I tell you that you can't look into a mirror the first three months?"

"No, you didn't," I said, surprised that she had waited till the last minute to add this detail.

I quietly walked into the bathroom and looked into the mirror. What is the point of this? I thought as I tried to hold back my anger.

My hands, like an artist's paintbrush, carefully moved over my eyebrows, nose, mouth, and cheeks as I drew a mental picture of myself. In the mirror, I saw reflected the stages of my life. I saw myself as a child, in my *abuela*'s house hiding behind her skirt, afraid to look at the mural of Saint Michael, the archangel. I felt her hands on my arms as she tried to pull me from behind her. I remembered her letting me hold the fan of the gypsy and how we danced our own style of flamenco. I could hear the clicking of my heels against the linoleum floor when we danced to the *orisha* music of Celia Cruz.

I saw the bony face of my mother when she was near death, her hair glowing like a halo. The image of my brother, sister, and me sitting in the living room listening to the songs of the spirits, as we tried to control our fear over our mother's illness. The dreams of my spirit mothers flowed through my mind like pages turning in a book. I recalled my first trip to Cuba when my spiritual awakening began. Everything seemed as if it had happened to someone else a long time ago.

In reality, each one of us, regardless of our cultural traditions, undergoes rites of passage—special once-in-a-lifetime experiences that transform our lives. Sometimes it is a first kiss, or feeling the movement of our first child, or falling in love for the first time.

Unlike the other special moments in my life, the experience of initiation was a path that would fortify and expand my

spiritual self. Rather than a sad good-bye, my whole being was looking forward to the spiritual renewal and commitment that would change me forever. Looking into the mirror, I asked myself, "Are you frightened?" "No," I replied aloud. Then, glancing at my reflection for the last time for the next three months, I waved good-bye.

Zenaida called to me from the other room, "My daughter, instead of leaving this evening for the initiation site, we are going to depart this afternoon. Elpidio's godsons are waiting downstairs and will start transporting the elders to a new location in Guanabacoa. Ernesto went to the airport to meet Laura. When they return, we will go to the initiation site in Ernesto's car after Elpidio completes the first ceremony of initiation, *El Ebó de Entrada.*"

In the first ceremony of initiation, Orula would prescribe the items needed to properly cleanse me before beginning the ceremony. When I asked why we had changed the schedule and location, she explained, "Elpidio consulted with Orula this morning, and Ellegua came forth to speak through the *odu.*

"Ellegua advised that everything be turned upside down, that if things were to occur in the evening, they should take place in the morning. If events were to take place in one location, they should happen in another place." I had learned that Ellegua, the master of organized confusion, reminded us that in difficult times people will change their behavior and act contrary to their ordinary habits. So in the event anyone had leaked information on the initiation location, we would be protected.

In her mother-teacher mode, Zenaida continued to explain that the spirits and *orishas* provided information and knowledge that at the time might seem incorrect. However, it was important to remember that the divine sight and wisdom of the spirits and *orishas* gave them the ability to see the past, present, and future, placing all events in context, as part of a continuum. Therefore, their advice would not necessarily provide an immediate solution but it would a long-range one.

"Daughter, you must be like your godmother," Zenaida told me. "Learn to always question and find the best solution for your

situation. The spirits and *orishas* insist that you be constantly aware of what is happening around you. There are initiates who sit back, thinking that the spirits and *orishas* will do everything for them. But no, this is a partnership," Zenaida explained, as she finished organizing the bags of food for the ceremony. "We must internalize the teachings of the *orishas* and use them in our lives. The changing of the time and location of the initiation is a perfect example of how the *orishas* guide our lives."

At one o'clock, Zenaida and I began to worry about Laura's late arrival. Ernesto called from the airport and said she was nowhere in sight. Zenaida gave him the address of the new location and asked him to meet us there instead of her apartment. Finally, she determined that we should follow the advice of Ellegua and move ahead with our preparations. We waited for Elpidio, who soon returned with two of his godsons.

They quickly set up their divining trays in the living room. Consulting with Orula, they determined that the *ebó* prescribed should be disposed of in a grassy area in a nearby park. This would assure that the negative energy that was cleansed from me would be placed in a natural location.

Zenaida asked me to wait in the kitchen for a moment, because she had last-minute details to work out with Elpidio. As I sat at the table waiting, Zenaida came over and placed a heavy object around my neck. When I looked down, I saw it was a beautiful white-beaded necklace in honor of Obatalá. As of that moment, I had been taken into sacred custody and the initiation process had begun. From that moment on I was to be quiet, remain calm, and follow Zenaida's instructions.

At two o'clock, Zenaida decided we should go to Guanabacoa. Tato, Elpidio's godson, volunteered to drive us. I remained silent during the car ride, though I was wondering if something had occurred in New York preventing Laura's arrival. Reading my thoughts, Zenaida assured me that nothing was wrong. She reminded me that Ellegua had said that there would be some minor difficulties; however, everything would be resolved if we cleverly changed our plans.

"We have done everything according to the instruction of the spirits; nothing major will go wrong," she said with great confidence. "The *ebó* that Elpidio prepared is an added protection for us all, don't worry. The ceremony will be the best Havana has seen in a long time," she continued, trying to alleviate my concern. I looked out the window, recalling the similar landscape during my ride to Ile Ife. The swaying palm trees, rich soil, and small wooden houses painted a picture I had seen time and again during my recent trips.

Tato took us to a farmhouse in an isolated wooded area on the outskirts of Guanabacoa, quite a distance away from Havana. The old wooden building, in desperate need of paint, was much like the one Elpidio had used for Javier's initiation. This location had been selected because, although it was far away from the city, it was still close enough for people to travel back and forth without too much difficulty. Those who lived a significant distance away would be staying at the initiation site during the weeklong ceremony, while others would leave late and return early in the morning.

Soon after entering the house, I was instructed to sit in a chair facing a blank white wall and to wait for further instructions. Zenaida suggested that I meditate and relax. I tried to remain focused on the upcoming ceremony; however, my mind kept drifting. Had Omar gotten sick? Was Sergio involved in an accident? Had Laura missed the plane? Thoughts kept popping up that I just could not hold back, and it was impossible for me to relax.

We later found out that Laura had been detained at the Havana airport because of the white sheets, towels, and other ritual items she was bringing in for the ceremony. Since they were attempting to control the initiation of foreigners, they made her leave all these items at the airport. She tried to convince the officials that she had a skin condition that required her to use cloth that had no dye coloring. When she told us the story, we all burst into laughter.

The airport officials refused to accept her false claims. They promised that the items would be returned to her when she left

Cuba. Ultimately, however, the items were left at the airport because we were afraid to go back to the officials to reclaim them. The *santeras* and *santeros* were preparing the special initiation room, hidden by a white sheet, as I sat looking at the wall. I heard the low murmur of voices while secret preparations were made. Sitting on the chair, lost in my thoughts, I did not notice when eight *santeras* quietly surrounded me and gently asked me to follow them.

Like graceful white swans they surrounded me as Virginia, my *ayubona*, my second godmother, guided the procession out the door and toward the river. After we had left the house, I noticed that Madrina Zenaida had remained inside. Virginia, then, became the elder in charge of my purification ceremony at the river.

As the procession moved toward the river, we were surrounded by rustling old trees and a field of blue-green grass. The crumbling, colonial buildings of Havana seemed millions of miles away. A gentle breeze set the leaves whispering as it cooled the heat of the warm afternoon. The sky was a clear blue covered with white clouds moving slowly above my head. As we walked away from the house, glorious gifts of nature unfolded before me. The only thing on my mind now was the vividness of the trees, the intensity of the sky, the brightness of the sun, and the snapping sound of grass beneath our feet. The *santeras*, absorbed in their own chatter, seemed to be a significant distance away from me. I remember wondering, Why are they so far away?

When we reached the riverbank, we all paused to look at the beauty of Yemayá-Ochun. The spot to which I was taken was the point where salt water and sweet water came together. Then Virginia instructed all the *santeras* to surround me. She instructed me to remain silent, to close my eyes, and to follow her instructions.

As I stood by the river's edge, the soft earth enveloped my bare feet. Virginia, a daughter of the *orisha* Ochun, turned to the river and began praying. She tossed silver coins and copper pennies into the river as she informed Yemayá-Ochun of the purpose of our visit. She explained to the *orishas* that I was going to be initiated into the Santería religion, that I had been brought to

them to receive their purifying waters and blessing so I would be fully prepared for initiation.

Virginia handed me a calabash filled with oranges, molasses, and honey. At her instructions, I knelt by the water and carefully allowed the ingredients of the calabash to flow into the water as I prayed to the water *orishas* for their protection. Then I stood up and waited silently as Virginia chanted the songs praising the divinities.

Then Virginia and the other *santeras* began smoothly to rip away my clothes, tossing the shredded clothing into the river. My light yellow dress, my slip, my underwear flowed away in the lazy current, symbolizing the death of my old life. As I heard my old clothes fall into the water, feeling them move farther and farther away, a spiritual dream-state deepened within me. My mind was now filled with a white, iridescent haze.

Bathing in the sacred waters of the river goddess would be the final purification ceremony before entering the initiation room, the *igbodú*. Zenaida's assistant, my *ayubona*, led me into a shallow clearing by the river's edge and started bathing me from head to foot with castile soap. As I stood motionless with my eyes still shut, chants to the *orishas* filled the air.

The cold water against my skin made me shiver until my body gradually became accustomed to the temperature. I felt drowsy and separated from the physical world, as if a great force was trying to pull me deeper within myself. I struggled to hold my consciousness, praying to the water goddesses to care for me, to cleanse my thoughts and body in preparation for receiving Obatalá. Most of all, I asked Yemayá and Ochun to help me protect my family.

When the *santeras* dried me with large white towels, I felt as if I were watching myself from afar. The *santeras* then moved me to a nearby grassy area and dressed me. I stood still, both feeling and not feeling their touch. Soon, new white clothing covered me. When I was fully dressed to Virginia's satisfaction, the procession commenced. Virginia finally told me to open my eyes as we walked toward the house where my initiation ceremony was about to begin. A clay pot of cool river water was placed on my head by Virginia. At this moment, my soul felt even more detached from my physical body, as if it were suspended in midair. The feeling was similar to the sense of distance that had overcome me at the *misas*—as if there were two of me, the outer physical self acting as a container for my inner spiritual being.

When we neared the house, it seemed very far away. It felt as if we would never reach our destination. Finally, we were at the front door. It was opened by Madrina ringing the *agogó*, the bell of Obatalá. The ringing of the *agogó* filled my head with an overwhelming, metallic sound.

I vaguely remember Madrina taking me by the elbow as Virginia told her, "Here is your daughter." Then Zenaida led me toward the initiation room. From behind the white curtain a booming voice demanded, "Why have you come?"

I responded, "To find *orisha*."

"Which *orisha*?" asked the voice.

"Obatalá," I responded.

The spirit force of Obatalá claimed me as the white curtain was drawn to the side, and I entered the *igbodú*. As I was transported to the spiritual realm of my *orisha*, the physical world faded away.

A Message from My Godparents

My *madrina*, Zenaida, took great care in explaining that initiation into Santería is a serious, lifelong commitment. "My daughter, initiation is the process of having the *aché* of the *orisha* that has claimed you ceremonially mounted on your head. Identification of the *orisha* in our house is determined by Orula in a divination session with *ikin*

conducted by a *babalawo*. In some houses, *santeros* or *santeras* determine the *orisha* with cowry divination and also give warriors. In our religious house, this is the domain of the *babalawo*.

"The *iyawo*, the novice, during the first year must carefully follow the tenets prescribed by the religion. You must dress in white for a year. Until the ceremony that marks your three months is performed, women wear no pants, must always wear stockings and a shawl, and have their heads covered. Remember, the first three months you cannot look into a mirror. It is necessary that you get home before sundown. To eat, you will sit on the floor on a straw mat, using a spoon and a white plate, and you will drink from a tin cup. During this year you may not shake anyone's hand or accept anything given to you from a noninitiate." I understood that these changes in my lifestyle symbolized the process of shedding unconscious habits, spiritually centering while analyzing my daily behavior. The process developed greater awareness of every thought and action, forcing me to live in the moment, connecting the secular and spiritual realities.

"These restrictions assist you in concentrating on your new path and help you reexamine your previous lifestyle. Before I initiated I would often dress in white. It allowed me to focus and concentrate on my spirituality instead of worrying about my appearance. I recommend this for everyone. Remember, it is important to be faithful to the commitment you have made to yourself and your *orisha*."

Chapter Twelve

AYÁGUNA

YO TENGO MI ACHÉ
ON HAVING ACHÉ

Each *orisha* has different roads, *caminos,* on which to project a different aspect of her or his powers. On each road, the *orisha* has a different name, one that identifies the particular powers that are manifested. Obatalá has various roads in which he appears as a man, others as a woman, a young warrior, or a wise old man. In these varied manifestations, Obatalá is called Orisha Ayé, Obatalá Orishanla, Obatalá Igba Ibo, Obatalá Oba Lufon, Obatalá Ocha Grinan, Obatalá Ekanike, Obatalá Acho, Obatalá Oba Moro, Obatalá Alaguema, Obatalá Talabi, Obatalá Yeku-Yeku, and Obatalá Ayáguna.

Obatalá Ayáguna, the young warrior, is the road of Obatalá that claimed me. In this manifestation, he is a fierce young warrior, riding a white horse, swinging a staff in one hand and a sword in the other. He was once a king who fought in many wars until he reached Asia. His children are identified by wearing a white *eleke,* with one red bead. When he possesses his children in a drumming ceremony, he dances as if he were in a battle. The children of this *orisha* share his warlike qualities in their defense of just causes.

According to legend, Obatalá Ayáguna was challenged by an enemy to compete in a contest. When they saw how young Ayáguna was, his enemies assumed that Ayáguna did not possess the strength to meet the challenge. Angered by his enemies' disbelief, Ayáguna challenged them to prove who was the best warrior. His enemies went into battle and cut off 201 human heads by the following day, which they brought to Ayáguna to show their bravery. Ayáguna waged battle the same day and that evening brought 201 heads and placed them before his enemies. To make certain that there was no question of his valor, he proceeded to cut off the heads of his enemies.

Olodumare created Obatalá in his image. Obatalá is the father of all the *orishas,* and his word is law. In Obatalá, the day and night were born; that is, life and death, the good and bad. As a child of Obatalá Ayáguna, one possesses the warlike qualities of this *orisha,* but one must beware of controlling one's temper.

Pleased that the initiation of Paco, the Puerto Rican drummer, was about to start, Doña Rosa turned to me. "My daughter, it is time to reflect on the changes Obatalá has brought into your life. What has occurred to you in these eighteen years since Obatalá came into your life?" I explained that I realized that living with the *orishas* was a continuous growth process, one that encouraged me to understand myself so I could share my knowledge with others. Like placing the pieces of a puzzle in their proper location, the *orishas* had guided me to the areas of my life that needed attention and helped me find solutions. It is a never-ending journey. I am part of the process of regeneration. What my *madrina* has shared with me, I must share with others.

Although I knew that Obatalá had claimed me, it wasn't until the day of *itá*, the third day of the initiation ceremony, that the diviner El Chino identified the particular name of my *orisha*: Obatalá Ayáguna.

I entered the *igbodú* with my eyes closed. As is tradition, they remained closed throughout the initiation ceremony. I was seated on a stool and instructed to remain silent. I felt the gentle touch of one of the *santeras* as my hair was shorn. The snipping sound of the scissors echoed in my head, and the pungent scent of fresh plants tickled my nose. The sensation of the razor scraping against my scalp caused shivers up and down my spine. As I struggled to remain conscious, a light airiness filled my head and a numbing sensation spread throughout my body.

In the distance, an immense figure emerged from a shaft of intense light. He was dressed in a white iridescent robe that completely covered his body. Slowly, this majestic figure moved toward me holding an *iroke*, a white horsetail whisk, the symbol of Obatalá, covered with sparkling white beads. He radiated a pure calm that penetrated deep into the inner recesses of

my mind. A series of mild explosions went off in my head as Obatalá extended the whisk toward me, silently encouraging me to accept it. The last thing I remember was willingly reaching for the *iroke*. I was initiated with the *orisha* Obatalá Ayáguna on August 11, 1981.

The soft murmuring voices slowly woke me from my deep sleep. I felt myself swim up from the depths of an ocean of clouds to a clearing where the welcoming rays of the sun embraced me. In the background, the whispering voices of Zenaida and Virginia broke the silence and helped call me back to reality.

I had been sleeping on an *estera*, a straw mat, covering the wooden floor. The small bare room next to the *igbodú* would be my home for the rest of the week's rituals. The white room had a surreal quality. A candle flickered from the corner of the room, creating long, distorted shadows of Zenaida's and Virginia's bodies on the wall. The doorway, covered by a white sheet, isolated the room from the rest of the house. Zenaida and Virginia sat on low stools waiting for me to awake. When I awoke, Zenaida told me she was pleased that I had slept so peacefully. Enjoying my pampering, Virginia laughed as she fondly recalled the similar care she received during her first week as an *iyawo*, a new initiate.

Turning to me, she said, "You will always remember this week. Yesterday was the day of your rebirth. This is a week of introspection and revelations that will guide you throughout your life. You are our newborn child, and your mothers are here to care for you and teach you." Virginia opened the remaining window shutters, letting in the strong rays of the late-morning sun. She went to the closet and pulled out a change of clothing, towels, and soap in preparation for my shower. Zenaida went to prepare my breakfast. This was the day when I would be presented to the public, and they were both nervous and excited. Virginia helped me up from the floor and guided me to the bathroom because my light-headedness made me unsteady.

The first thing I noticed upon entering the bathroom was that all the mirrors had been covered with white towels. From a pail on the floor, the sweet fragrance of perfume, cascarilla, and

tuberoses filled the air. I showered and then followed Virginia's instructions to pour the floral mixture over my body as I prayed for the health and happiness of my family. The splash of cool water quickly cleared my head, reviving me. I felt rejuvenated and healthy.

I returned to the *estera* where my breakfast had been set out on a white plate next to an aluminum cup filled with water. A large spoon was the only utensil placed on the mat. Anticipating my question, Virginia informed me that for the next three months I would be eating on the floor seated on an *estera* with a similar place setting. She explained that, according to the tradition, I was a child and could not use a knife or fork. During the first three months, my head was to be covered, and in public I was to wear a shawl and stockings. Virginia explained that the first three months would probably be the most difficult, as I became accustomed to the rules and practices of the religion. Silently, I prepared mentally for the endless stares that I would attract in New York, dressing in white for a full year.

My godmothers began addressing me by the name that denoted my status as an *iyawo*. Zenaida again explained the importance of the year of cleansing that I would experience as an *iyawo*. "You will soon forget that you are dressed in white. It will become normal," she explained. In retrospect, I now realize that she was absolutely correct. My first year was a process of focusing on my spirituality and surroundings. I did lose sight of myself.

After breakfast, my godmothers dressed me in preparation for my public presentation to the Santería community in a ceremony called *El Dia del Medio*, which means the middle day; it is the ceremony after initiation and before the major divination session of initiation, the *itá*, that takes place on the third day. *El Dia del Medio* is the day the Santería community publicly acknowledges and celebrates the initiation of a new *iyawo*. The *iyawo* is dressed in the ritual colors of his or her *orisha*. The ceremonial clothing is especially designed for the *iyawo*, and will be worn twice in the life of the novice. The first time is for presentation to the public, then again for their burial ceremony, the *itutu*.

My regal white dress and crown were made of a Nigerian woven cloth I purchased in Ile Ife, and had been designed by Virginia and myself. The crown, sleeves, and hem were covered with pearl-like beads and silver strips of material that glittered subtly against the textured cloth of my dress. The style was a cross between Spanish colonial and West African fashion. The puffed sleeves and skirt were accented by a long shoulder scarf with appliqués of Obatalá symbols—a fly whisk, staff, and doves in flight.

Since I was considered a child, Zenaida and Virginia dressed me for my public presentation. The dress slipped smoothly over my body. My crown felt heavy on my newly shaved head. Bracelets identifying the *orishas* I had received were placed on my arms. The metal bracelets chimed gently as I moved around the room trying to adjust the layers of crinoline that held up the bell-like shirt of my dress. Zenaida and Virginia were my eyes since I was not allowed to look into a mirror. They fussed over me, making certain I looked perfect.

Zenaida called in Laura, who was waiting to see me. As she carefully pulled back the curtain and entered, I could see the sign of relief in her eyes. Laura had not seen me since her arrival in Cuba and had been unaware of the lengthy religious ceremonies I would undergo. She was understandably frightened and apprehensive as she watched the activities from afar. As she was the only member of my family able to attend my initiation, I was grateful for her courage in supporting my decision to initiate.

"You look absolutely beautiful," were her first words as she marveled in amazement at my appearance. "It is unfortunate that the rest of the family is not here to witness this important step in your life," Laura continued, as she walked around, admiring the dress.

"That is why it is so important that you are here," Zenaida remarked as she fussed with the crown on my head. "There is at least one who is the eyes for the whole family."

"How do you feel?" Laura asked.

Trying to find the right words, all I could say was, "Renewed."

When we were ready to leave the room, Zenaida placed a white *iroke* in one of my hands and a white lace fan in the other. Pleased with my appearance, they were ready to present me to the religious community.

They escorted me to the front room, where I saw an elaborately decorated altar in honor of Obatalá. Constructed in the corner of the room and draped in the ceremonial cloths lent by the elders, the throne was magnificent. Like a nineteenth-century parasol, it was covered with lace, intricately embroidered materials, and decorative doves, creating an environment of dignity and elegance. The artist who had constructed the throne had created roselike swirls from lace cloth, letting streamers of white satin ribbon erupt from the center. In place of the porcelain bowl with the sacred stones at the center of the altar, I would sit on a stool covered with white satin cloth, in my ritual dress, and the altar would become my throne. The throne radiated pride and pulsated with an energy that engulfed the room.

Zenaida and Virginia helped position me on the stool, spreading the skirt of my dress and placing my hands in a comfortable position to hold the *iroke* and fan for the long celebration. "Remember, my daughter, Obatalá is a king, and you are his daughter. You are royal and reflect his *aché*," Zenaida whispered as she arranged my dress. I felt magical.

The room was filled with well-wishers. The elders who had spent the night were the first to acknowledge my initiation. Family and godchildren of Zenaida, Elpidio, and Virginia had arrived, lending a festival atmosphere. I was reminded of my childhood Christmas celebrations in El Barrio when everyone assembled to enjoy one another's company; the rhythmic voices were the music, and their laughter the instruments. So it was with this gathering. Although there was no music, the chattering voices were like the flow of a dance beat. The saucy smell of hot food filled the air as the clatter of dishes joined in the escalating noise of the room.

Well-wishers graciously blessed me, as five *iyawos* sat on the

floor surrounding me. The others entertained themselves with the most recent gossip, while the *iyawos* and I talked about our initiation.

Sonia, a middle-aged mother of three who had initiated four months before, began the conversation, saying, "Electrical currents were running through my body as I sat on the throne. I was in a dream world. When my husband saw me on the throne, he cried with happiness, telling me I looked more beautiful than on our wedding day."

Then Tina, a small, perky teenager, joined in the conversation. Speaking with a nervous giggle, she said, "I initiated six months ago. When I sat on the throne dressed in the ritual dress of Yemayá, I felt like a queen. I didn't want to take off the dress at the end of the day."

Mario, a strong mulatto man in his thirties, smiled and thought carefully before he shared his experience. "I am a father of two children and have a wonderful, devoted wife. Before initiation I was always in nightclubs, had many women, and didn't attend to my family. Going home drunk one night, I was hit by a car and hospitalized with a broken leg. The doctors thought they might have to amputate my leg. I asked a *babalawo* friend of mine to divine for me to see if there was anything that the *orishas* could do. Oggun stood up for me in a divination session and said he would repair my leg, but I must initiate soon after leaving the hospital. He also said that I must change my life and take care of my family. Oggun has tested me this year. I avoided getting into fights. I've been faithful to the rules of the religion. I get home early, don't drink, and have not gone to nightclubs. My home life is wonderful, and it has been a very peaceful year," he said with a smile.

Virginia was right; I would never forget this moment. I felt spiritually engulfed by my ancestral lineage, family, and community. Like the others, I did not want the day to end. That evening, I was escorted back to my room by my godmothers.

Visitors came all during the week, sharing their memories of

initiation. The feeling of rebirth I was experiencing and the sense of being guided onto an enlightened path were reaffirmed in the stories they told. During my week's stay, Zenaida took every opportunity to share information with me, and she gathered material for me to study when I arrived home, including a series of mimeographed pamphlets developed by initiates.

Although I missed my family, it felt wonderful to have this glorious time to revel in my thoughts and surrender the responsibility of making decisions. My godmothers cared for me completely during this first week. I lived in a small space on the floor, sleeping, eating, and studying, and I was able to think and examine the meaning of my initiation and how my life would change. I did not worry about daily chores like selecting clothing, fixing my hair, preparing food, finding shoes, or looking in the mirror to check my appearance. During this week the responsibilities of taking my children to school, getting to work on time, writing proposals for funding deadlines, and cleaning the house were not a problem. My former life seemed to be eons away.

Emptied of the thoughts that generally filled my mind, I searched for new ideas. I gradually realized that my mind had been filled with thoughts of things I had to do, instead of the quality of being, or a contemplation of my family, my community, and myself. My life had been occupied with the doing of things, instead of the careful selection of priorities that would allow me time to find joy in daily occurrences.

The conversations with my godmothers were empowering; they told stories of miracles the *orishas* had performed, and of their faith in the powers of the divine gods and goddesses.

According to Zenaida, we live our lives between two worlds—one of the ancestors and *orishas*, and another in our secular existence. It is the successful intertwining of these realities that guide a healthy and prosperous life.

"The *orishas* are all-knowing and powerful, my daughter," Zenaida concluded. "You will witness this tomorrow, the day of *itá*, the special divination session of initiation." In preparation for the next day, she recommended that we rest and get to sleep

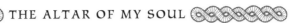

early. Virginia slept on a cot in my room, and Zenaida went to the front room to stay with Elpidio.

The darkness of the night quickly mellowed out the excitement of the day. Lying on the straw mat felt surprisingly comfortable that night. Virginia had opened the shutters, and the light of the moon filled the room with a pale yellow glow. As I silently recalled the details of the glorious celebration, the room suddenly became filled with the presence of my spirit mothers. The three were sitting on stools set on a throne similar to the one that had been built for me. Unable to move, I listened as they spoke to me.

Smiling in my direction, they assured me that I was on the right path. In the background, the overpowering beat of the *batá* drums grew louder, as Abuela stood up and danced to the rhythms of Obatalá. She raised her hand, swinging the *iroke* above her head, while her steps assumed the strength of a warrior. Then my mother and my great-grandmother joined her, following the powerful movements of my *abuela*.

My body, weighed down by an unseen force, remained immobile on the floor as the sound of the drums faded away and I fell into a deep sleep. When I shared the dream with my godmothers, they decided that my spiritual mothers wanted me to be presented to the sacred drums before returning home. Zenaida indicated that she would make the necessary arrangements immediately.

The next morning was similar to the previous one. After I showered, Virginia prepared breakfast and accompanied me, while Zenaida and Elpidio prepared for the divination session of initiation on the day of *itá, El Dia de Itá*. Virginia warned me that it would be a long session, but a rewarding one. Each of the *orishas* I received would reveal their names through the cowry shells of the *oriate*, the *santero* diviner, and my future would be determined by my *orishas* through the patterns of the shells.

We entered the room of initiation, where tureens containing the sacred stones of the *orishas* born on the day of my initiation lined the walls. The *oriate* sat on a straw mat on the floor. On a

low stool next to him sat Justina, who was to record in a book the names of each of my *orishas*, their prophesies, my new African name, and the names of the witnesses present.

Virginia explained that special care is always taken to make certain that these readings are conducted by expert *oriates*, because this reading would establish the foundation of special rules that would guide my life. Virginia cautioned that when I received the book, the *libreta*, it would be a detailed record of the way I must behave the rest of my life.

"It is your personal bible, your detailed horoscope," she added, trying to explain the profundity of my *itá*.

A tall, thin Asian man nicknamed El Chino welcomed me into the room. In a scene that reminded me of the photographs I had seen of the Afro-Asian visual artist Wilfredo Lam, El Chino was surrounded by the elder *santeros* and *santeras*. I sat on a low stool facing him, with my bare feet placed on the straw mat. When he began to move the sixteen cowry shells in his delicate hands, everyone stopped talking and focused their attention on him. El Chino began sprinkling drops of cool water on the ground, reciting the prayers calling the ancestors and then Ellegua to guide his hands.

Acknowledging all the *santeros* and *santeras* in the room, he then turned to me and asked, "Do you understand the significance of the *itá*?"

"Yes," I responded. "My *orishas* will talk to me through the cowries. I will be told how best to guide my life, things I should do and things I shouldn't do. What to eat for my health and which foods will be harmful to me."

Satisfied with my response, El Chino continued with the reading. Casting the *dilogun*, cowries, on the straw mat, he carefully studied the patterns. The patterns of the *dilogun* kept changing as he gathered them in his hands and gently let them fall again. The pleasant rustle of the cowries in his hands was the only sound in the room. With measured words he began to speak.

"Ellegua says to be cautious with your business negotiations. Read everything three times before signing any papers. Try to fi-

nalize your business negotiations during the day when the sun is bright. Ellegua says that when the time comes, he will bring many godchildren to your door. You will be very surprised at the large *orisha* house you will have." El Chino ended by saying, "Your Ellegua wants to be surrounded by toys, and he promises to care for you as long as you care for him.

"Oyá says to organize yourself totally. In your home, job, and social life, you must place everything where it belongs. She warns that your lack of organization will one day publicly embarrass you. Oyá says you should dress in white as much as possible. She wants you to place a tiger skin over your Shangó. Oyá tells you not to eat fried food. She says fried food is not good for your digestive system." With a shy smile that revealed his sparkling gold tooth, he said, "You enjoy fried food?"

"Yes." I nodded.

"Well, Oyá is telling you to stop immediately," he said gently. "Ochun is saying that many people talk about you. Whether it is good or bad do not worry. This is good for you; it means that people have to think about you. You are not invisible to the world. Ochun tells you that once you have made a decision, stick to it. She tells you to beware of where you eat. Your food must not be of the extremities of the animal. No tail, feet, or head. Do you understand?"

"Yes, I don't eat those parts anyway," I responded.

"Ochun is telling you not to start," El Chino murmured. "Yemayá tells you to honor your spirits; they will bring you health. When you have problems, go to the sea and tell Yemayá your problems. She will listen and help you to solve them. Yemayá tells you to make certain that you repair anything that is broken in your home. If it cannot be fixed, throw it out. Yemayá says to document everything you do; you will find out one day how important your notes will be.

"Shangó says that you must live your life without desperation. You must be calm in the face of adversity. Always leave with plenty of time to get to your location. He doesn't want you to rush anywhere; it is with calculated calm that things will come

your way." El Chino then added, "When you leave a place, never return immediately. Walk around the block, come back the next day. Avoid making hasty decisions.

"Obatalá wants you to be very respectful of children. Children will bring you joy and all that you desire. Embrace your children and yourself every day. Remember that Obatalá's domain is all that is white in the body. Go for checkups regularly, especially your eyes and teeth. Obatalá says that he wants you to give a *tambor* for the spirits of your mother and grandmother, because they are very close to you and are pleased with this important step you have taken."

Casting the shells, he determined that the road of my *orisha* was Obatalá. He said, "Obatalá Ayáguna, the young warrior, is your *orisha*. He is like Shangó, but younger and more daring. Ayáguna will protect you in times of crisis."

Without commenting, I realized that Yemayá's prophecy was already occurring; my dreams were predicting and confirming events before they happened. I had already known that Ayáguna would claim me.

"Do you have any questions?" El Chino asked tenderly as he looked from me to my godmothers. Then he asked Zenaida, "What name do you want to give your daughter?"

"Adufora," she said.

Casting the shells, he said, "Obatalá accepts."

As he gathered his divination objects, El Chino advised, "Make certain that you follow the instructions of your *orishas* for life; in helping yourself, you also protect your family. Having these sacred powers in your possession will radiate in everything you do. I wish you the very best," and then went to embrace Zenaida and Virginia.

"My daughter, the *orishas* have spoken clearly," said Zenaida. "It is your responsibility to follow what has been said."

Then she invited everyone to stay for dinner. The sacred bond among the initiates again filled me with joy. The gathering reminded me of the *terreiro* I had visited in Brazil, where everyone functioned as a loving family. Zenaida informed all that she had arranged to present me to the sacred *batá* drums at the end of the week. According to Zenaida, this public ceremony was a final reaffirmation of initiation before the *orisha* Añya, the *orisha* of the drum. These specially prepared drums had undergone a sacred ritual in which the *aché* of Orisha Añya is infused into the drum.

After dinner, Virginia and I returned to my room for the evening. Zenaida and the other *santeras* and *santeros* remained in the front room cleaning up. Virginia, arranging my sleeping area, said, "My daughter, I know this is all new to you and a little overwhelming. Don't be afraid to ask questions. Your *madrina* and I will do our best to answer all of them."

Enjoying the airy feeling of levitation, I didn't want to focus then; but I promised to have questions for her the next day. After making certain that I was comfortable, she left me alone to go help with the cleaning up. Lying on the straw mat, I couldn't help but wonder why I felt so comfortable and at peace in a small isolated room, far away from home. Somehow I felt as if I were in the sacred room of my *abuela*'s apartment in El Barrio.

The following day, I was prepared to question Zenaida and Virginia. Worried that it would not be easy to get them or my godfather on the telephone from New York, I said, "I have my personal book and the pamphlets, but are they enough to instruct and guide me?"

Laughing, Zenaida said, "The information you take back with you is valuable and it will assist you, but only if you study, study, study." Pausing a moment, she added with a mischievous smile, "I know what you're looking for: a Santería version of the Ten Commandments."

I thought it would be a great idea, and so teasingly I said, "Yes, tell me the ten commandments of Santería."

First jokingly and then with great seriousness, Zenaida and Virginia developed a list that has served me well over the eighteen years since my initiation.

Zenaida began, "Number one: Remember you are sacred. You carry the *aché* of your *orisha*. Respect your sacredness and

insist that others respect it as well. Remember we are all sacred, we have Orí, each of us has our own destiny.

"Number two: We are part of nature, and nature is part of us. We are one. Live a balanced life, taking care of both your spiritual and secular needs. Honor your spirits and your *orishas.* Yemayá teaches us that we must attend to both worlds, the spiritual and secular.

"Number three: We are social beings who live in a society. And we each have a contribution to make so that the society can function effectively. It is our responsibility to determine what our contribution will be. Like Ochosi and Oggun, we must cooperate, be trustworthy, and seek justice in all situations."

Then, Virginia joined in. "Number four: Everything begins and ends with Ellegua. Life presents us with constant choices, like coming to a crossroads, but we can travel only one road at a time. We must examine all possibilities in order to make informed decisions.

"Five: Don't be afraid of the unknown. Every day provides an opportunity to learn. Through the teachings of Orula, we can reveal the unknown."

Zenaida, invigorated by our discussion, again joined in. "Six: Power resides in a cool head. We must remember to use our heads at all times. Strive to develop good character and bring calmness into your life; let the *aché* of Obatalá flow into your life."

Virginia added, "Seven: Learn to shed those habits, behaviors, and things that no longer contribute to your life. Like Oyá, we must learn to sweep away unnecessary freight that weighs us down.

"Eight: Be a faithful friend, companion, and family member. Like Obba, trust in others, but at the same time remember to be vigilant against human failings, envy, jealousy, and treachery."

Then Zenaida added, "Nine: Learn to make war when necessary. There are many ways of waging war; learn them. Shangó reminds us that sometimes we need to enter into battle. Like a warrior, plan your attack."

With a sensuous smile she said, "Ten: Love makes the world go round. Like Ochun, always be prepared to pull out the honey, honey."

Ready to answer my most challenging questions, she said, "Do you have any more questions?"

"I want to know how to respond when people ask me about black cloth dolls pierced with needles and pins. What do I say when people tell me Santería is witchcraft, black magic, and evil? How do I respond?" I asked, with more emotion in my voice than I had intended.

Zenaida and Virginia glanced at each other and then hesitated. The room became silent, and I could hear the voices of people talking in the kitchen area, as they thought about a response.

Virginia, turning to Zenaida, said, "You speak first."

"My daughter, we know there is good because bad exists. We understand evil, because we have experienced goodness. Santería is a benevolent religion; it is about righteousness, about nature and living a blessed life. There are those who pollute the ocean, destroy the forest, and poison the air we breathe; they are evil. So it is with people who use their knowledge to hurt, destroy, and perpetuate jealousy, envy, and greed," she said with an unusual sadness in her voice. "It is unfortunate that some think they can use their knowledge incorrectly and go unpunished. But be absolutely clear, those who use their knowledge incorrectly are not following the teachings of Santería.

"When one doctor does not uphold the medical oath to heal, does that mean all doctors are unprofessional? We have heard of priests and nuns who have violated their vows, but should we assume that all the others have done the same? Of course not. Why then do people assume if one initiate functions against the laws of Santería, we are all bad?

"We believe that truth and good triumph over evil. Those who seek to do wrong are the outcast," concluded Zenaida emotionally.

Then Virginia said, "My daughter, do not allow anyone to put you in a defensive position because of your beliefs. Santería

practitioners have never oppressed others, nor have they imposed their religion on others. We have never forced baptism or the tenets of our beliefs on other groups in the name of Olodumare or the *orishas*. We have nothing to be ashamed of."

Our conversation left us fulfilled and at the same time opened avenues for further thought. However, we knew that we had concluded our discussion for the night. Virginia suggested that we rest in preparation for the *tambor* to be held on the following day.

In the morning, the house was alive with excitement. From my room, I could hear the banging of pots and pans as food was prepared for the drummers' early lunch. The high-pitched voices of the *santeras* rose above the clamor as they excitedly ran around the kitchen. The drummers' lunch would be served at eleven A.M., and the *tambor* would start at two P.M.

Virginia brought in my breakfast as usual and then began selecting the clothes I was to wear for the afternoon ceremony. She chose a long white gauze dress that I had purchased in an Indian shop in the West Village of New York, and an accompanying scarf to wrap around my head. Surprisingly, I was quickly getting accustomed to dressing without a mirror. It took little time to dress since my outfits required little coordination. Time moved quickly and suddenly I heard the drummers toning their drums in the distance. My godmothers and Laura entered the room, accompanied by an *arpon* who would lead me out into the courtyard.

From my room he led the procession ringing a bell that announced my arrival. I held my breath in anticipation, not knowing what to expect. The *arpon* started singing as we left the room. When we entered the yard, his voice filled the enclosure with Yoruba chants as he led us into a circle in a slow-moving dance. Soon we were joined by other initiates. The low, vibrating sounds of the drums slowly picked up momentum as the *arpon*'s voice reached to the sky, singing to Obatalá, "*Okuní Bamba* . . . That you live forever."

We kept moving in a circle, building an elusive invisible energy that touched us. I could feel the warm earth beneath my feet, and the heat within my body began to grow. I could feel a momentary breeze caress my face, and I followed the soft, swaying movements in honor of the *orishas*. The chants grew more intense with the initiates' call and response to elevate the energy and honor Obatalá. "*Okuní Bamba . . .* That you live forever." The heat in the yard intensified as the drummers' voices joined in the chants. *Santeras* pulled out their small hand fans and leisurely waved them back and forth, trying to lower the growing concentration of heat.

Then my godmothers led me from the circle and brought me before the drums. Crossing my hands on my chest, I bowed, placing my forehead on each of the three drums. The piercing sound of the thundering drumbeats penetrated my head and filled me with ecstasy.

That evening, I prepared my bags for an early departure the following day. Zenaida suggested that I wear a white T-shirt, blue jeans, and a colorful head scarf. "My daughter, if you dress in white, you will be stopped at the airport. Place your *elekes* in this white scarf and place them inside your bag, and put on a little makeup," she advised.

"Madrina, I understand your concern, but I would like to wear the T-shirt and white scarf and jeans. Let's forget the makeup. If I can't look into a mirror, I do not want to look like a clown," I said, poking fun at her suggestion.

"As soon as you get home, follow the rules," she said, hugging me as tears glistened in her eyes.

On the ride to the airport, I suddenly became anxious to see my sons and to be at home. Having wanted to go home almost as soon as she arrived, Laura was elated that we were leaving. "I want a nice, big, juicy steak with onions, a Coca-Cola, French fries, chocolate cake, a bottle of wine, a case of beer, all the fried plantains I can eat, and then some," she shouted as we rode to the airport. "When I get home, I'm going to play loud music, kiss my refrigerator, and give thanks for all I have," she said. "The people in Cuba are so strong and committed and I admire their courage,

their ability to withstand hunger and live with so little, but I could not continue to see so much pain in people's faces."

We arrived in the Bronx that night at ten. I went to Brooklyn to get the kids from Tom's house, and Laura went to pick up her children from her friend's home. The sight of the healthy faces of Sergio and Omar coming down the stairs swelled my heart with joy. Sergio was now thirteen and Omar was eight; though I felt they might understand why I initiated into Santería, it was too late that night to discuss my initiation with them.

The following day, when I told them about my trip, they were receptive and polite, which led me to believe they understood my explanations. Years later they told me that, while they respected my decision, they had been the targets of their friends' jokes and ridicule.

"Mom, how do you explain to teenagers why your mother looks like a snowman every day?" Sergio asked.

While Omar laughed hysterically, he said, "My friends called Mom a witch, and others would say, 'There goes the Pillsbury doughgirl.' I got into a lot of fights because of you, Mom."

Upon my arrival back in the States, my life quickly returned to the hectic schedule of balancing work, my home, and the children. The major difference was that I did these tasks dressed in white, and I attracted an incredible amount of attention wherever I went. Attending a meeting at city hall, a group of women approached and asked if I was Brazilian. In the pizza store, a Pentecostal woman shouted in front of my sons, "You are in the religion of the devil!" The winter was the worst. Dressed in a heavy white coat, in the dark subways of New York I stood out like a snowball in hell.

The planning of the First International Conference on Orisha Tradition and Culture occupied most of my time. Coordinating the program and the travel arrangements of international representatives of the *orisha* tradition to the conference placed me in contact with a wide range of practitioners interested in uniting the branches of the tradition.

In July 1981, the Caribbean Cultural Center was instrumental in planning, implementing, and supporting the participation of sixty initiates, scholars, and artists in this historic event. For the first time, representatives from Trinidad, Cuba, Venezuela, Puerto Rico, Haiti, and the United States came together as a community to the birthplace of their religion—the sacred city of Ile Ife, Nigeria. The overwhelming attention of the press placed the conference on the front pages. Headlines called me an "*orisha* woman" with a derogatory undertone, while others announced, "World Delegation of Orisha Worshipers Come Home."

In the emotionally charged public and sacred atmosphere, moments of pure magic occurred. The center sponsored the first trip of an eighty-year-old Brazilian priestess of Yemayá, Mâe Bida, to the conference. When we arrived in Abeoukuta, the city of Yemayá's birth, she was overwhelmed. We were greeted by high government officials who sponsored a lavish reception in our honor at the local palace. The reception did not impress Mâe Bida. She was concerned about communicating with a group of Yemayá priestesses who were discreetly sitting in a corner of the room. Mâe Bida, in a beautiful, lavish blue-and-white, shimmering and billowing brocade dress and head wrap, was a vision of Yemayá on Earth. She was a short, plump woman with smooth velvetlike chocolate skin, and her timid warm manner won us all.

I watched Mâe Bida as she tried to speak to the women in Portuguese, then tried the few words of English she learned for the trip. When their eyes clouded from a lack of understanding, she grew agitated and began nervously pacing the floor. Apprehensive, I dashed across the room to assist her. Suddenly, Mâe Bida, raising her hands toward the sky, started dancing in a wave-like movement as she began singing to Yemayá in Yoruba. The room stood still as everyone heard her beautiful voice rise above the reception chatter. The eyes of the Yoruba priestesses filled with recognition and tears as their voices joined in Mâe Bida's chant. Everyone in the room stood paralyzed as five hundred

years of stored tears trickled down their faces. This moment was an extraordinary revelation, but another incident was not to be as pleasant.

Chills shocked my body the first day of the conference when the entrance was blocked by Christians dressed in Western clothing and carrying large picket signs that read: DEVIL WORSHIPERS. I felt as if I were back in the pizza shop in the Bronx. Without warning, we were made aware of the depth of cultural devastation that had occurred in Nigeria, a situation that apparently was much like what we had experienced in the Americas.

I also realized the importance of having organized a world conference that would give birth to other similar events and would continue to establish a network of *orisha* worshipers and scholars expert in the history and culture of these traditions. Over time I organized two other international *orisha* conferences, one in 1983 in Bahia, Brazil, and the other in 1986 in New York City, in addition to many other African Diaspora events over the past eighteen years. Orula's prophecy had quickly become a reality. I traveled extensively, studying and developing programs on the branches of the *orisha* tradition, often taking my sons with me.

The prediction of the *orishas* foreseen in my *itá* also became realities. Initiation opened the sacred doors for the Orisha's *aché* to function on my behalf, allowing me to understand and fulfill my destiny. Each year new *pruebas* confirmed the prophecy of the *orishas*. Ellegua brought godchildren to my door unexpectedly. Yemayá listened to my problems and saved Laura from near death. Shangó and Oyá suggested that I continue my studies, and I received my doctorate in 1995.

The center had grown into an important cultural institution, promoting African Diaspora cultures throughout the world. My sons were now grown and brought tremendous joy and love into my life. Ayáguna gave me the courage to overcome the barriers that were placed in my path. How did all of this happen? By surrounding myself with positive people who had my best interests in mind—people who allow the *aché* of the *orishas* to work through them.

The lessons of Zenaida and Elpidio took on new meaning over the years. Santería was a way of life, a way of celebrating and guiding my life.

The advice of my *orishas* and godparents continued to be revealed in marvelous natural ways, as people flowed into my life, helping me fulfill my destiny. When I started thinking about completing my doctoral work, I received an unexpected call from Dr. Molefi Kete Asante, chairperson of the newly formed department of African American Studies at Temple University. Dr. Asante suggested that I consider returning to school; he felt that my work would be enhanced by enrolling in the department. As the idea of teaching at the college level took form, I received a call from Dr. Donald Smith, requesting that I teach one of his education classes at Baruch College while he was on sabbatical in 1994. The following year, in 1995, a position opened in the department of African and Hispanic Studies at Baruch College, which he recommended I apply for. In September 1995, I started teaching classes in Puerto Rican and Latin American history and culture.

The summer of 1996, I went to Puerto Rico twice to research my family tree. My recurring dreams of my mother, my *abuela*, and my great-grandmother had inspired my quest to learn more about them. I wanted the obscure silence of their lives to become known. My parents spoke little about their childhood experiences in Puerto Rico. It is as if they began to live when they arrived in New York as young adults. In the El Registro Demográfico of Hato Rey, the attendant assisted me in bringing down the dusty birth certificate books that were not yet computerized. Remembering that my father said he was born November 27, 1903, in San Juan, Puerto Rico, I began to look through the records that dated from 1900 to 1910. Turning the sepia-colored pages filled with beautiful script that seemed to dance on the page, I first came upon the birth certificate of my uncle Donato. When I turned the page, I found my father's.

In that early part of the twentieth century, children were often registered months and years after their birth. Often when families lived in distant rural areas, they did not have the means to travel to the city to register their children. My father's certificate indicated that he was born on January 28, 1904, and my *abuela* in 1884, but the birth date of my grandmother, María de la O, was not identified. My guess is that María de la O was probably born in the mid–eighteen hundreds, a period for which they did not have records.

The archivist suggested that I visit the churches and review the baptism records, which were generally more accurate. The churches in San Juan directed me to the archival records of Loíza Aldea, the place of birth. The attendants in Loíza informed me that most of their records had been destroyed in a fire and what was left was in the neighboring town. When I looked through the records in Canovanas, I found nothing. Then I returned to Loíza and started searching to see if there were any people left by the name of Moreno. I went to senior centers and walked through the town's oldest cemetery, looking at tombstones for the name María de la O. As I walked alongside the many unmarked graves, my soul wept, knowing that many of the stories of our ancestors will remain buried forever. A month later I returned and started looking through the records kept by the Spaniards, those who listed the names of their slaves. Again, I found nothing. I returned to Loíza four days before I was scheduled to leave Puerto Rico and went to the seashore to meditate. Listening to the soft rolling waves of Yemayá's ocean, I felt a soft breeze surround me as her gentle whispering voice assured me that I would find her story.

When I returned to the States, I received a telephone call from a long-lost cousin, Máximo Dueño Jr. from California, who had found my name on the Internet and wanted to reconnect. He began sharing his stories and then remarked that he had a photograph of my uncles, my father, and my grandmother. My cousin shared with me the only photograph I now own of my *abuela*.

Some will say this was just a coincidence; I know it was a sign

to continue my search. *Orishas* place angels in your path at the right moment. I know my ancestors and *orishas* are traveling with me, and I will continue to search until the stories of my parents and ancestors are unveiled.

The healing and empowering knowledge of our history and the understanding of our destiny are what define us; they let us know that we were on this Earth. As I see the growth in my godchildren and other members of my family, the power and the importance of our cultural legacy is affirmed. The changes I see in my godchildren confirm the power of *aché*. Mia is finding her spiritual path, and the spirit of her grandmother has spoken through her. Joe's unexplainable stomach pains disappeared when the *orisha* Oyá cleansed him. Carol, a young college student, is receiving messages through dreams. Three of my godchildren are preparing to fully initiate this coming summer.

Seeing my godchildren flourishing through my guidance and teachings lets me know that they will carry our cultural legacy. I see it in my granddaughter, Kiya, who started her altar with a collection of her favorite shells, rocks, photographs, and toys. When I visit, she makes certain that I look at the additional objects she has placed on the altar, recording the moments in her young life that she will remember growing into adulthood.

It is this uniting of *aye*, the visible world, and *orun*, the spirit world, that we must follow throughout our lives. Like the calabash of Olodumare, it keeps us intrinsically connected to the spirit realm.

From a distance, I heard the voice of Doña Rosa calling me. As I was lost in my thoughts, it took some time for me to remember where I was. Again, I felt the sticky heat of the kitchen against my moist forehead. Doña Rosa gently wiped my face with a cool washcloth, and she directed my attention to Pachuco, Zenaida's assistant, who was calling me into the initiation room. He had pulled the white curtain aside and was gesturing for me to enter.

I struggled to gain my balance as I tried to recover my consciousness. My nervous energy began to build as I felt Doña Rosa's fragile hands steadying me toward the curtain. The strong, intoxicating, pungent smell of the freshly prepared *omiero*, an herbal mixture, floated from the room as I entered. *Santeros* and *santeras* sat on low stools stripping the leaves from the plants, which they leisurely placed into a large round ceramic bowl filled with water.

When I walked into the room, Paco was kneeling on a straw mat with his head hanging over another large clay basin. Zenaida, standing in front of Paco, silently motioned for me to kneel down on a straw mat facing him. Once I was in position, she held a fistful of plants with a piece of castile soap toward the heavens and said, "Olodumare, I ask for your blessing as I prepare to initiate Paco Fuentes into my religious family.

"I ask that, as I wash his head with your sacred plants, you bring him the health, happiness, and prosperity that you have brought me."

Pachuco poured clear water over Paco's head as Zenaida silently and carefully washed his head.

She then placed the remaining sacred plants and castile soap in my hands and instructed me to repeat her actions. I could hear the sound of my heart beating against my chest as I tensely repeated what she did. Raising my right hand to the sky, I said, "Olodumare, I ask your blessings as I follow in the steps of my godmother and welcome Paco Fuentes into our family. Olodumare, please bring him the blessings that my godmother has shared with me because of your generosity."

A Message from My Godparents

Zenaida advises that everyone incorporate the ten commandments of Santería into their lives. By surrounding yourself with the energy and teachings of the *orishas*, you will be surrounded by positive energy. Suddenly, people will come into your life who will help you fulfill your destiny.

THE TEN COMMANDMENTS OF SANTERÍA

1. Spirit of Orí
We are all sacred. We each have the *orisha* Orí, our destiny.

2. Spirit of Olodumare
We are part of two worlds, the spirit world, *orun*, and the secular world, *aye*. We carry the sacred power, *aché*, of the Supreme Being because we are part of nature.

3. Spirit of Ochosí
We must be contributing members of society, working cooperatively, seeking justice, and being trustworthy.

4. Spirit of Ellegua
We must examine all our options and make informed decisions that adhere to our destiny.

5. Spirit of Yemayá
Don't be afraid of the unknown. Benefit from nurturing your abilities in order to reveal the unknown.

6. Spirit of Obatalá
Power resides in a cool head. Remember to use creative thought and logic in reaching a decision.

7. Spirit of Oyá
Bring positive energy into your life by eliminating negative thoughts and actions.

8. Spirit of Orishaoko
Be a faithful friend, companion, and family member.

9. Spirit of Shangó
Learn to resolve differences creatively, and select your battles with care.

10. Spirit of Ochun
Remember that more battles are won with sweetness than with offensive behavior.

Appendix

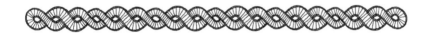

TABLE OF SELECT ORISHAS

RITUALS OF PROTECTION

RESOURCES

Table of Select Orishas

The *orishas* represent aspects of nature—they are the wind, ocean, trees, grass, whirlwind, thunder. The *orishas*, like nature's forces, reflect limitless possibilities, and this is why there are 401 *orishas*, with the "1" representing infinity.

In Santería, the *orishas* have roads, *caminos,* in which they represent different aspects of their power, *aché.* According to legend, Olodumare, the Supreme God, was the creator of *aché.* Lonely and tiring of his omnipotent power, Olodumare decided to create the *orishas*, endowing each with a particular portion of his power. Therefore, each *orisha* has domain over a portion of the Earth. Much like the varying roles we hold in life—parent, worker, lover, friend—the *orishas* also possess different roles in theirs.

Yemayá is the depth of the ocean when she manifests as Olokun, yet she remains Yemayá, the mother of all the *orishas*. So it is with Obatalá, the father of the *orishas* and emissary of Olodumare, who, as a mature adult, created human beings, but who also can manifest as the young warrior Ayáguna, a traveler of the world.

ORISHAS OF CREATION

	Olodumare	**Obatalá**	**Orí**	**Osun**
Spirit	Omnipresent creator	Father of all the *orishas*	Resides within each person	Messenger of Olodumare
Primary Form	Possesses both male and female energy	Male	Personal *orisha*	Male
Element	Air	Air	Air	Air
Nature	Heaven and Earth	Heaven and Earth	Earth	Heaven
Qualities	Omnipresence Purity Power	Creativity Truth Clarity	Intelligence Inner spirit Self-awareness	Strength Wisdom Understanding
Animals	Dove Goat White hen	Dove Goat White hen	Dove White hen Pigeon	All winged creatures
Day	Daily	September 24	Daily	Monday
Color	White	White	White	White
Symbols	Two halves of a calabash	White whisk White metals	Small cowry container	Silver staff One of the warrior *orishas*
Plants	All white flowers Coconut	Albaca	Coconut	Coconut
Number	1	8	1	1

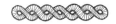 

ORISHAS OF WATER

	Yemayá	**Ochun**
Spirit	Mother of all *orishas*	Society and community
Primary Form	Female	Female
Element	Salt water	Fresh water
Nature	Ocean/river	Lake
Qualities	Maternal Strong Nurturing	Social Friendly Amorous
Animals	Duck Hen Calf	Bee Goat Hen
Day	September 7	September 8
Colors	Blue White crystal	Yellow
Symbols	Seashells Anchor Mermaid	Peacock feathers Coral A fan
Plants	Violets	Sunflower Honeycomb
Number	7	5

ORISHAS OF PROTECTION

	Ellegua	**Oggun**	**Shangó**
Spirit	Messenger	Blacksmith	Warrior
Primary Form	Male	Male	Male
Element	Earth	Fire	Fire
Nature	Crossroads	Iron	Thunder and lightning
Qualities	Playful Trickster Youthful	Strong Serious Muscular	Energetic Amorous Forceful
Animals	Smoked fish Black chicken	Red rooster Pig	Bull Red rooster
Day	January 6	Monday	December 4
Colors	Black and red	Green and black	Red and white
Symbols	Toys	Iron	Double-headed ax Thunder Stones
Plant	Pica Pica	Aroma	Okra
Number	3	7	4

ORISHAS OF THE EARTH

	Orishaoko	**Ochosi**	**Osain**
Spirit	Farmer	Hunter	Herbalist
Primary Form	Male	Male	Male
Elements	Earth	Earth	Earth
Nature	Agriculture	Forest	Medicinal plants
Qualities	Good friend Trustworthy Truthful	Just Ambitious Familial	Herbalist Healer Wise
Animals	Brown rooster Pigeon	Goat Pigeon	Turtle Goat
Day	Day and night	Tuesday	March 1
Colors	Brown	Prussian blue	Green Amber
Symbols	Bull pulling a plow	Three arrows Bow and arrow	Leaves
Plants	All plants	All plants	All plants
Number	7	7	3

ORISHAS OF THE AFTERLIFE

	Oyá	Obba
Spirit	Guardian of the gateway of the cemetery	Guardian of the tombs
Primary Form	Female	Female
Element	Wind	Water
Nature	Whirlwind	Cemetery
Qualities	Authoritative Devoted Powerful	Faithful Youthful Solemn
Animal	Goat Pigeon Black hen	Pigeon Goat Black hen
Day	February 2	Friday
Colors	Red, yellow, blue Blue, green, brown Purple, maroon, orange	Yellow and pink
Symbols	Brown whisk	Cemetery
Plants	Morirviví	Morirviví
Number	9	9

DIVINER

	Orula
Spirit Form	Palm nuts *(ikins)*
Primary Form	Male
Element	Air
Nature	Wisdom
Qualities	Intuitive Mindful Wise
Animals	Goat Deer
Day	October 4
Colors	Yellow and green
Symbols	*Opon* Ifá (Ifá board) *Oguele* (divining chain) *Ikin* (palm nut)
Plants	Palm trees
Number	16

Rituals of Protection

MY ALTARS

I have two different altars, one dedicated to the ancestor spirits, my *bóveda*, and the other dedicated to the *orishas*. On my *bóveda* I have placed seven glasses of cool water, each one serving as a dedication to the deceased who reside in the spirit realm in heaven. On *bóvedas* these glasses should be placed in two parallel lines of three glasses, with one glass in the center. Each glass should be held to the sky and offered to Olodumare for blessings. On Mondays, I change the water and dedicate each glass to my guardian angels. I ask Olodumare to accept my offering by saying, "With the blessings of the Almighty, I dedicate this glass of water to the spirits of my Yoruba ancestors." With the other glasses, I make the same prayer offering to my Native American spirits, Kongo spirits, spirits that need love, spirits that love me, and to the members of my family.

I then call the name of family members who have left the Earth. My prayer is designed to let the spirits know that I acknowledge and accept them in my life. "With the blessing of Olodumare and the benevolent spirits, I ask your blessings on this day for the protection and health of my family. I ask that the spirits of my mother, father, and sister bless me. I ask that the wisdom of my *abuela* and María de la O guide me. That my dear friends Gilberto and Jorge have found peace . . ." The prayer should come from your soul and intuition; it should not be scripted. Remember, you are speaking to loved ones, so speak freely and with admiration and respect.

My second altar is dedicated to the *orishas* that I received when I was initiated into the Santería religion. The sacred stones of my *orishas* reside in decorative bowls, in the colors of each one of the divinities, and these bowls are placed on display in a shelved cabinet. My sacred room for my *orishas* is similar to that of my *abuela*'s room, and it is filled with fresh flowers,

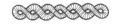 

scented candles, and the symbols of the gods and goddesses on the walls.

CREATE YOUR OWN ALTAR

For those who have not been initiated in the tradition and who therefore do not have patron *orishas*, an altar can be created by placing on a table or shelf objects that remind you of important people and events in your life. Collect beautiful glass vases, sculptures, or talismans, like shells and rocks, and place them on your altar. Make the altar a tribute to people, friends, and objects that have inspired you, and include their photographs for encouragement. Consider which is the color that brings you joy, peace, and tranquillity. Or think about the energy you enjoy being surrounded with, or the color that dominates in your wardrobe. Begin to decorate your altar with these colors, and your intuition will guide you. Take time from your day to quietly, prayerfully meditate before your altar on those aspects of your life that bring you comfort and happiness.

WORSHIPING OUR ANCESTORS

Each day, remember your loved ones who are no longer on this Earth; they need your prayers and candlelight to elevate in the spirit world. Always acknowledge the spirits and elders who have opened the roads for you, since they will help you accomplish your goals in life. Try to light a candle at least once a week, as it will bring spiritual light into your home.

DAILY MORNING PRAYER

Each day, I acknowledge the Supreme Being, Olodumare. I begin every morning by looking out the window toward the sky. I embrace myself and thank Olodumare for my blessings. Then I meditate in front of my *bóveda*, asking the spirits to accompany

me in my daily tasks, and to bring me wisdom and understanding. I then walk into my sacred room and, prostrating myself before my altar, ring the *agogó*, the bell of Obatalá, requesting that his calm yet warrior spirit inspire me. I give thanks for the blessings in my life, my family, my friends, and my community.

YOUR PERSONAL ORISHA

We all have our destiny, our Orí, and to thrive, we must honor and protect our sacredness. Orí requires that you honor yourself and others. Each day, care for the temple that houses your Orí, your head, the seat and power of your thought, wisdom, and creativity.

INITIATION

The process of initiation into the Santería religion is threefold, and as a *madrina*, I now lead my novices through each of these ceremonies, guiding them to understand the wisdom of the *orishas* and the empowering presence of their ancestor spirits.

In the first ceremony, the novice receives five sacred beaded necklaces, the *elekes*; each necklace is placed around the novice's neck in honor of an *orisha* that will protect the novice. Each *eleke* reflects the colors of one of the major *orishas*—white represents Obatalá; shades of blue reveal Yemayá; shades of yellow, Ochun; red and white, Shangó; and red and black, Ellegua.

In a second ceremony, the initiate receives symbols of the warrior *orishas*, the *guerreros*: Ellegua, Oggun, Ochosi, and Osun, which bring stability and additional protection to the apprentice. And with the final ceremony comes full initiation, *asiento*, during which the *orisha* who claims the novice as his or her own is ceremonially "crowned"—the *orisha* is mounted on the head of the novice, along with the *aché* of the *orisha*. The initiate then receives five primary *orishas*: Obatalá, Yemayá, Ochun, Shangó, and Oyá. Each of these *orishas* assumes the role of the initiate's

protector *orisha*, defending and empowering the young initiate. And throughout the life of the initiate, there are additional ceremonies and *orishas* that can be received, providing the blessings of health, happiness, and prosperity.

Through initiation into my religion, one is reborn. Our initiation is a conscious act of letting go of negative influences that weigh down the spirit, allowing it to soar and to embark on a new beginning. The energy that naturally flows from initiation opens up inner channels, granting the initiate the ability to see, feel, smell, taste, and hear more acutely, and to be more present in the world.

DIVINATION

SPIRITUAL CLEANSING BATHS

Obatalá: Calm

To attract positive energy, bathe with white flowers, cascarilla, milk, and your favorite perfume. Light a scented white candle, relax, and meditate. Think positive thoughts and let the water draw any negative energy that is surrounding you. Pray to Obatalá to calm and clear your thoughts.

Ochun: Energy

To lift your energy, bathe with sunflowers, a little honey, perfume, and cascarilla. Light a scented yellow candle and let the brightness of the sun bring you joy. Pray to Ochun to lift your spiritual energy.

Orí: Clarity

Wash your head with cooling products that include coconut, cocoa butter, white flowers, and cascarilla. Remember that your head is where your wisdom resides and should be kept clean and covered with light colors. After you wash your Orí with cooling products, light a scented white candle to enhance the spirituality of Orí.

 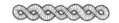

TO OPEN OPPORTUNITIES

When your life seems upside down, work at untangling the confusion by placing pieces of hard candy by your doorway or at a nearby crossroads. Remember that you can take only one path and that you must set priorities in your life. Appease the energy of Ellegua by offering him the candy and toys that bring joy.

SYMBOLS

To attract the positive energy of the divinities, decorate your home with the symbols and colors of the *orishas* with which you feel an affinity. Surrounding yourself with the colors of the *orishas* will assist in reminding you of the *aché* they bring to the world. Wear white to calm your energy field, blue to nurture your spirit, yellow to energize your aura, red to gather your force, and red and black when you need mischief in your life. Decorate your home with sunflowers to attract Ochun's sensual energy. Gather small rocks that attract you and develop a small rock garden in your home, reminding yourself that the *aché* of the *orishas* ultimately resides in sacred rocks.

Decorate with the bow and arrow of Ochosí or the double-headed ax of Shangó, recalling their warrior spirits. Beautiful peacock feathers bring the sensual energy of Ochun, while plants remind us of the healing powers of Osain, the *orisha* of medicine. Remember, your home is your temple, and you should create a nurturing, loving, balanced environment. As you decorate your home, remember to surround yourself with the symbols and colors of the *orishas*.

Initiates have sacred beaded necklaces, *elekes,* in the colors of the major *orishas*. These attractive necklaces are made by initiates and then blessed during rituals. Noninitiates can create necklaces using the colors of the *orisha* that they feel suit their personality. Bracelets made of silver and ivory can attract Obatalá energy, while Prussian blue and amber draw the power of the hunter spirit of Ochosí.

Increasingly, scientific studies are revealing the positive effects of color on our outlook. The importance of colors, symbols, and nature are central to the Santería religion. Having pleasant scents surround you also prevents negative energy from surrounding you. Florida water and the scents of tuberose, sandalwood, gardenia, and jasmine are most helpful in dispelling negative energy.

RESOURCES

Caribbean Cultural Center African Diaspora Institute
408 West 58th Street
New York, NY 10019
212-307-7420
www.caribectr.org
Melody Moreno Capote: Executive Director
Laura Moreno: Deputy Director
Marta Moreno Vega: Board President

The center's African Diaspora programs and bookstore are excellent sources of information. The public programs provide an opportunity to surround yourself with an international community of scholars, artists, and traditional leaders interested in African cultural traditions. The bookstore is well stocked with international recordings, jewelry, artwork, and books celebrating global African religions. There is also a resource library of videos and books, all for researchers.

College and university departments with African, Caribbean, and Latino Studies are also an important source of information.

LECTURES AND PRESENTATIONS

Contact the Caribbean Cultural Center to be notified of lectures, workshops, art exhibitions, and presentations by the author or check altarofmysoul.com.

Glossary

Aché   The invisible, elusive life force of Olodumare that was distributed to the *orishas*. *Aché* is the life force present in nature.

Aleyo   The term designating noninitiates.

Ancestors   Individuals who have entered the spirit realm. Friends and family members who have made their spiritual transformation.

Anya   *Orisha* of the sacred *batá* drums. A set of three drums used in ceremonies to call the *orishas* down to earth.

Arpon   A lead singer in rituals who has been trained and taught the myriad songs and chants to the *orishas* that entice them to possess an initiate.

Asiento   The mounting of the *orisha* on the head of the new initiate.

Aye   The world of the living. We live on *aye*.

Ayubona   A second godmother, central to an initiation ceremony.

Babalawo   A priest of the oracle *orisha*, Orula. Father of the secrets of the Ifá system of divination.

Batá   Doubled-headed hourglass-shaped sacred drums that are used in sacred ceremonies. They are blessed through a ritual with the *orisha* of the drum, Anya.

Cabildo   Society of African descendants instrumental in preserving the religion.

Camino   The roads on which *orishas* manifest variant aspects of their nature.

Cascarilla   Powdered eggshells.

Cuadro Espiritual   Guardian spirits who guide and protect the living.

Día del Medio   A ceremony on the second day of initiation, during which the new initiate is presented to the public.

Dilogun   A system of divination that uses sixteen cowry shells, and is performed by diviners known as *oriates*.

Ebó   A cleansing sacrifice that dispels the negative energy surrounding the initiate.

Ellegua   The *orisha* of the crossroads. A trickster and messenger of Olodumare and Orula, who travels between Earth and heaven.

Eleke   The sacred beaded necklaces that are made in the myriad colors of the *orishas*. Five basic elekes are generally given to the initiate—Obatalá, white; Yemayá, blue; Shangó, red and white; Ellegua, red and black; Ochun, shades of yellow.

Espiritismo   A system of worshiping the ancestors.

Espiritista   A medium, who has the skill to have the spirit of the ancestor speak through her or him.

Ifá   Identifies the system of divination and is another name for the oracle Orula. This complex system of divination is the domain of the *babalawo*, the father of secrets.

Iré   Positive energy that surrounds an individual.

Iroke   A fly whisk, symbol of the *orishas*; white for Obatalá or brown for Oyá.

Itá   The destiny of the new initiate is determined through this cowry divination session.

Iyalorisha   The mother of *orisha*, or *madrina*, godmother.

Iyawo   A new initiate, a stage of rebirth.

Lucumí   Yoruba name for Santería.

Madrina   A priestess of Santería, a godmother.

Moyuba   The praising of ancestors, and lineage of the *orisha* family.

Obatalá   The *orisha* that created humans; a direct emissary of Olodumare.

Obi   A system of divination that uses four pieces of coconut shell.

Oché   The double-headed ax sword of Shangó.

Ochosi   The hunter *orisha* of the forest.

Ochun   The *orisha* of fresh water and sensuality.

Odu A divination symbol that determines *pataki*, the parable and solution of the client's problem.

Oggun The warrior *orisha*, guardian of iron.

Oguele A divining chain used by *babalawos*.

Olodumare The Supreme God.

Oluwo The highest-ranking in the priesthood of the *babalawo*.

Omiero An herbal plant mixture used in ceremonies for cooling initiates and *orishas*.

Omo A child of an *orisha*.

Orí An inner-dwelling *orisha* who determines destiny. Each person possesses his or her own Orí.

Oriate A *santero*, diviner, who specializes in divining with cowry shells.

Orula The name for the oracle *orisha*, also called Orunmila and Ifá.

Orun The spirit realm, home to the ancestors and *orishas*.

Osain The *orisha* of herbal medicine, herbalist.

Osogbó Negative energy.

Oyá The *orisha* of the whirlwind, precedes Shangó in rituals.

Padrino A godfather, a priest of Santería.

Patakís Legends and stories in Santería that interpret the *odu* symbols in divination.

Regla de Ocha Rules of Santería.

Santería The popular name for the *orisha* tradition in Cuba and the Diaspora, which translates as: the way of the saints.

Santera A female initiate.

Santero A male initiate.

Yefa Pounded yam, used by the *babalawo* to cover the *opon* Ifá, the divining board.

Yemayá The mother of the *orishas*. Orisha of the sea.

Index

 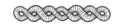

About the Author

MARTA MORENO VEGA, PH.D., is an assistant professor at the City University of New York's Baruch College. Professor Vega is founder of the Caribbean Cultural Center African Diasporo Institute and Amigos del Museo del Barrio. She has curated major visual arts exhibitions, including "Santería and Vodun in the Americas," and organized three international conferences on "*Orisha* Tradition and Culture."